I know of no one better qualified to provide wisdom and counsel on teamwork than Pat MacMillan. Pat is a 25-year friend whom I have been privileged to observe up-close. I personally, as well as my organization, have benefited from his insight and consultation. Pat has observed teams and leaders at the very highest levels in both the Christian and business world. He is a trusted and respected advisor at both the Fortune 500 level as well as with other significant leaders. I endorse this book without reservation.

Ronald W. Blue, Founder and CEO, Ronald Blue & Co., LLC

Teams and networks are the organizing forms of the future. Pat MacMillan and his associates have relentlessly focused on what it takes to build high performance teams—what works and what doesn't. At last, they have made their model available in clear, compelling, and memorable form.

Bob Buford, Founding Chairman, Leadership Network
Author, *Halftime: Changing Your Game Plan from Success to Significance*

The Performance Factor is not an ordinary book on teamwork and leadership. It is much more. From my experience, it deals frankly and effectively with the practical issues of performance and sustainable competitive advantage in today's marketplace.

J. Harold Chandler, Chairman, President and CEO
UnumProvident Corporation

This book is a penetrating and contemporary guide to leadership and team building for a business era of continuous change. The principles and practices espoused are conceptually sound, and the results in multiple, diverse settings are evident. I highly recommend it.

Max De Pree, Chairman Emeritus, Herman Miller, Inc.

This book provides an outstanding master plan for any organization that must improve its performance. I know. Team Resources has helped me supercharge performance at three different companies by building high performance teams. Best of all, this is not just theory. The techniques have been proven and refined through real world experience.

Richard W. Frank, Chairman and CEO, Evenflo Company, Inc

We have used the principles that Pat MacMillan shares in *The Performance Factor* at virtually every level of our organization to produce exceptional results. Whether it is functional or cross-functional teams internally, the senior executive team, or even the loosely structured teams between our leadership and the leadership of our key licensees, these principles work!

The Performance Factor is a must-read for everyone that is asked to deliver result through others.

Michael C. Howe, President and CEO, Arby's Restaurants

For those who need to build a strong and effective performance oriented team, *The Performance Factor* is a MUST read. It is not just theory, his ideas WORK.

JoelManby, CEO, Greenlight.com

The future vitality of any organization will be dependent upon effective cross-functional teamwork. Teamwork that encourages cooperation and participation across traditional lines of title, position, job description, and business unit. But how does it all add up for a combined result and superior performance? In this book, Pat MacMillan brings to us ways to organize and lead this creative function which is so essential to the future or our organizations.

C. William Pollard, Chairman and CEO, ServiceMaster

Not only does Pat make a compelling case for the need to build an effective team, he carefully walks you through an entertaining and challenging process. Few companies today can succeed without effective teams, and there has never been a more difficult time to master the art of high performance teamwork. This book can help your team to peak performance.

Steven S. Reinemund, President and COO, PepsiCo, Inc.

The practical issues of high performance teamwork that have made such a difference in our business are detailed in *The Performance Factor*. I highly recommend this book for any individual serious about gaining a competitive advantage.

Horst Schulze, President and CEO, The Ritz-Carlton Hotel Company, LLC

As a creative company, we live at the intersection of art, commerce—and most recently—technology. Creativity is no longer an individual sport. This book is about increasing organizational creativity in very common-sense ways. Pat MacMillan redefines leadership based on what it's like to motivate a high performance team at today's e-commerce pace. It works. Read it, and you'll agree that leading high performance teams is a critical skill everybody can improve on.

Fred M. Senn; Partner/Group Director, Fallon McElligott

THE
PERFORMANCE
FACTOR

THE PERFORMANCE FACTOR

❧

*Unlocking the Secrets
of Teamwork*

Pat MacMillan

B&H
PUBLISHING GROUP

Nashville, Tennessee

ISBN: 978-0-8054-2375-4

Published by B&H Publishing Group,
Nashville, Tennessee

Dewey Decimal Classification: 658
Subject Heading: BUSINESS

Library of Congress Cataloging-in-Publication Data

MacMillan, Pat, 1944–
  The performance factor : unlocking the secrets of teamwork / Pat
MacMillan.
    p. cm.
  Includes bibliographical references and index.
  ISBN 0–8054–2375–3
  1. Teams in the workplace. 2. Management. I. Title.

HD66.M333 2001
658.3'128—dc21

                                                00–066746

6 7 8 9 10 11   10 09 08 07

TO

The Team at Team Resources

Although my name appears on the cover, I am merely the scribe for the insights and lessons outlined in this book. The real authors are a team of committed coworkers who have collected and practiced these truths about teams and teamwork for nearly 20 years.

My partners Jim Webb and Don DeMichele have been, in the very truest sense, my mentors in the principles of team. The support team at Team Resources has demonstrated these principles day in and day out, showing us the power of high performance teamwork in practice. Like any team, we have our bad days, but in most instances a few hours in our offices would convince even the toughest skeptic of the power found in a group of people pursuing a clear, common, compelling purpose.

Captain Al Haynes first modeled and then took the time to share many of the team insights in this book.

My children, Becki, Jennifer, and Matthew, have provided so many anecdotes that bring these principles alive.

And, to my wife, Jill, who, for over 35 years, has shown me the power of these principles in the context of our marriage team and encouraged me to share them with others.

Contents

Preface

T his book is about leadership, teams, and life in 21st century organizations. Its origins were planted nearly 20 years ago when I first began to explore the power of teams and the principles necessary to implement them successfully in client organizations. Over the years, we learned what worked and what didn't. The faint outlines of a book about teams and teamwork began to emerge with the hope that it would reinforce what we were attempting to achieve within the context of our consulting practice.

In large measure, this book is built around a model that describes high performance teams. The six team characteristics described in this model have proven to be exceptionally effective in designing and training teams that consistently deliver exceptional business results. It is a straightforward, easy-to-remember model that will allow you to navigate the world of teams and teamwork with confidence.

In many places in New England, when approaching a small town in rural areas, a sign reading "Thickly Settled" forewarns motorists. I have always found the phrase to be delightfully quaint on one hand and a creatively clear message on the other. It has become a metaphor in our home to alert family members that a book, idea, or discussion is filled of relevant and interesting information. My intention is that you will find this book to be thickly settled with ideas, how-tos, and practical real-life examples of how to build a high performing team. It is certainly thicker than most books written for the typical business reader, for I have "stuffed" it with all manner of tools, diagnostics, and case studies. It is my hope that this book, once read, might become much like a textbook that would be an ongoing source of reference as you lead your team to exceptional levels of performance.

THE CHALLENGE OF CHANGE

Leadership in today's world has never been so important and at the same time so difficult. As you will see in the first few chapters, change has challenged the way we do things in the world of organizations. Strategies and structures that worked so well in periods of stability have floundered in this era of rapid, discontinuous change. During the late 1940's through the early 1960's the winds of change were calm. But then a faint breeze began to stir.

By the mid 1980's the Western economies were in the midst of gale force winds of change. The tall, thin hierarchies that had dominated the organizational landscape could not withstand the velocity and impact of this change. They began to reshape themselves much as the trees along a wind-driven mountain ridge or ocean shore adapt to the consistent and forceful influence of prevailing winds. It was becoming apparent that organizations in the new century must be fast, flexible, and focused, and that such organizations will be team-based, if not always in structure (teams) then in spirit (teamwork). In the 1970's it was not unusual to find large, complex organizations with as many as 12 to 15 levels separating the top from the bottom. By the early 1990's companies as large and complex as FedEx and General Electric could boast of no more than five levels. These flatter, broader structures were better able to endure the turbulent climate.

As business strategies and structures changed, the processes that supported them needed to be rethought as well. The horizontal dimension of organizational life took on new meaning as functional fiefdoms and departmental boundaries fell victim to hoards of reengineering consultants and new thinking. Technology allowed information and decision making to be pushed down in the organization and out to the edges—close to the customers.

In such a world of change, an organization will need to engender levels of leadership and cooperation from its work force seldom experienced in industry. Only by releasing leadership at every level in the organization and fostering the development of high performance work teams can organizations create the "empowered-involvement" necessary to achieve the quality, service, and value required to succeed, if not merely survive, in this world of tough, unrelenting global competition. Those organizations that can blend the power of team and leadership will experience exceptional results in a world that will allow nothing less.

INTRODUCING THE PERFORMANCE FACTOR

New strategies, structures, and systems demand new styles of leadership. In the 1960's and 1970's the role of the typical manager was to direct, control, audit, and decide.

Leadership today requires leaders who are able to tap into the resources of the group—leaders who can release the initiative and leadership in everyone. The higher the levels of cooperation within the group, the lighter the leadership load on the formal team leader. This is critically important because the horizontal dimension in both the structure and systems of today's organization places new, externally focused responsibilities on the leader as well. Networking, negotiating, and boundary management are as important to the modern manager as are the skills of coaching and facilitation. The mindset and the skills of traditional managers need to be brought into alignment with new organizational realities.

Managers today may feel as though they are working on an organizational version of a waterbed. Everything is in constant motion. In many contemporary organizations we find managerial spans as wide as 15 to 25 people. With this many people, the term *span of control* challenges common sense. Such a relationship might be described as a span of communication or coordination, but clearly not control. As the number of direct reports has grown, traditional-minded managers feel like sheep dogs running madly from one part of the flock to another, nipping on the heels of a large number of unruly sheep. By the time they get the front of the flock headed in the right direction, those in the back have headed into the underbrush.

In today's world, team leaders often lead teams whose members report formally to someone else. Not only that, but everyone seems to be on multiple teams, often with different roles and conflicting demands. Matrix organizations have been resurrected; there is a proliferation of dotted lines on what used to be fairly simple and easy-to-understand organization charts. Team leaders are caught up in the complexity of attempting to maintain a sense of authority on one hand and to be colleagues and team members on the other. They are challenged with having to deliver extraordinary results with fewer people and less time. Yet the time needed to meet, communicate, make decisions, and resolve conflict within the team adds another layer of challenge to an already time-challenged schedule. Welcome to team leadership in the 21st Century!

In a world of discontinuous change, organizational survival and success rests on the organization's ability to develop and deploy two essential elements: exceptional leadership and high performance teamwork. One without the other does not provide enough organizational muscle to compete in a world of formidable and mean-spirited global competitors. When organizations are able to successfully blend the power of leadership and team they will experience what we call the *Performance Factor*. Salaried employees become *volunteers* and exchange compliance for commitment. Acceptable results become unacceptable and are replaced with new standards many would call "exceptional." Most books about teamwork call this phenomenon synergism, a term that describes results that exceed the effort or input that produced them. However, for most organizations, synergy is a theory, a pipe dream that is beyond the pragmatic realities of day-to-day experience. The principles and practices in this book will help you turn theory into an everyday reality.

Unlocking the Secrets of High Performance Teamwork

This book will give you the principles and practical how-to's you need to be an effective team leader. I don't know about you, but I am at a loss when I look under the hood of my car. Unlike the more straightforward V-8's I grew up with in the 1960's, I am now confronted with an indecipherable tangle of wires and tubes, pieces and parts. It's all crammed into an unbelievably small space and controlled by microchips that defy understanding. In some respects, the changes in the way my car engine is put together parallel the changes organizations have experienced over the past 20 years. The function is the same, but the processes and principles of operation have changed.

As leaders in today's organizations you must be able to build effective teams, start stalled ones, and fix broken ones. If you want to become a master mechanic of team effectiveness, you must understand what lies under the hood of a high performance team. That is what this book is about. Its purpose is to help you understand the context that makes teams a critical ingredient in every organization's business model, the characteristics of high performance teams, and a set of practical applications for increased team performance.

Part One—New Century, New Rules, No New Rulebook!

Why the business environment of today makes teaming-up so important for organizational success and survival, and what makes a team different from any other type of group.

Part Two—Characteristics of a High Performance Team.

The six characteristics of a high performance team are described in detail, explaining the importance of each characteristic to team effectiveness and how you can apply these insights to your particular team situations.

Part Three—Turning Principle into Practice: Building the Team

Team development is explored both from the perspective of an individual entity, as well as within the context of the larger organization.

Throughout the book I speak to you as the current or future team leader, clearly identifying your role in every dimension of team life as well as providing the trail markers you will need as you lead your team into the white area of the map of team performance.

The principles and how-tos outlined in this book are not theory and they weren't designed in a lab. They were developed in the caldron of day-to-day realities in real organizations striving for real and important goals. They have been successfully tested under fire with firms like Procter & Gamble, Helene Curtis, Bayer Corporation, Campbell Soup Company, Kentucky Fried Chicken, Evenflo Company, Inc., McNeil Consumer Healthcare, and many smaller organizations in both the profit and nonprofit sectors. The insights in this book do not require organizational experts for implementation but rather study, practice, and a liberal dose of common sense as you adapt them to the needs of your specific team. Consider this book your operator's manual for team design and development.

ACKNOWLEDGMENTS

This book is, in every sense, a collective endeavor. The discussion, deliberation, and debate among the Team Resources partners both here in the U.S. and in our Latin American offices played a significant role in the recognition and refining of insightful principles of teams and teamwork. The ideas and insights contained in these pages are as much theirs as mine. Team Resources' clients who read this book will recognize their fingerprints as well. Many will remember the numerous times when, in the midst of a workshop, I would call time out to write notes of new observations about teams that surfaced during our dialogue.

The support team at Team Resources again worked a miracle, turning a rough-hewn manuscript into an acceptable offering to our publisher. Many thanks to Pam McFee who led the team, spending endless evenings and weekends typing and retyping. Most importantly for applying her discriminating mind to catch places where important passages were lost between one version and another or where the author's logic and/or English grammar failed him. Donna Rohm, whose tenacious detective work pulled together message fragments of footnotes and references which, in many cases, were hopelessly confused and years old. Beverly Swofford, whose sharp eye never missed the dot of an "i" or the cross of a "t. " Dr. Beverly Langford, a longtime consultant to and associate of Team Resources was a great partner as well. She invested many, many hours working with us on the basic structure of the book and then helping me to communicate these key principles. Nicola Hollis, our very competent Curriculum Director, who has a book in her future but loaned a bit of it to this effort. And, Isa Williams, our very talented graphic designer, who not only turned her calendar upside down to meet our deadlines, but also helped us communicate important concepts in creative, easy-to-understand ways.

PART ONE

New Century
New Rules
No New Rulebook!

CHAPTER ONE

"What's the Standard Operating Procedure in This Situation?"

ENGINE FAILURE AT 37,000 FEET

To survive the next few minutes, Captain Haynes and his crew were going to need every bit of wisdom, luck, and creativity they could muster. Their wide-body jet, carrying 295 passengers to Chicago, had just experienced a catastrophic failure of all three hydraulic systems. All flight controls were totally inoperable. The odds of this happening were over a billion to one—the odds of surviving considerably less. Like so many cataclysmic events, its origins were small, obscure, and in the distant past.

A series of discrete occurrences had led to this awful moment.

February 23, 1971: a high-quality titanium ingot, number K8283, is cast by Titanium Metals Corporation in Henderson, Nevada.

The ingot contains one minor imperfection, a microscopically small amount of nitrogen that had not completely dissolved into the molten titanium.

Titanium Metals Corporation ships a 6,000-pound block of titanium to Aluminum Company of America, which cuts it into eight sections, each weighing about 700 pounds.

ALCOA crafts these sections into high-precision fan disks that will be used by General Electric Aircraft Engine Division to manufacture its powerful CF6-6 turbofan aircraft engines.

One of those engines, with its tiny imperfection, is bought and installed by McDonnell Douglas in its 118th DC-10 manufactured.

United Airlines buys this jet in 1971.

July 19, 1989, nearly 18 years later, this plane, designated United Flight 232, takes off from Denver and heads for a stopover in Chicago en route to Philadelphia.

At 3:16 P.M. the fault in the fan disk manifests itself in a most extraordinary way.

In the cockpit, Bill Records had just finished leveling the aircraft from a course change when the crew heard a bang. Captain Haynes later recounted that the sound could better be described as a "kaboom," and at first no one knew what it was. Then Captain Haynes saw on his flight panel that the No. 2 engine, the one that sits high in the tail, had failed.

Since a DC-10 is designed to fly adequately on two engines and everything else appeared reasonably normal, the pilots were not overly concerned. Records kept the controls, freeing Haynes to work on the problem with flight engineer Dudley Dvorak. This arrangement also enabled Haynes to double-check everything that was done visually since he could see all the flight panels. He asked Dvorak for the procedure to begin shutting down engine No. 2, and the two men began working through the checklist.

Not far into the checklist, they discovered that the problem was much bigger than expected, "because the things that were supposed to move didn't." Dvorak reported they were losing hydraulics. Yet when Captain Haynes looked back to the flight engineer's panel, he saw conflicting information. All the gauges read "no fluid" and "no pressure," but the warning lights didn't support that.

As they attempted to define the scope of the problem, Haynes heard his copilot behind him say, "Al, I can't control the plane."

The DC-10, like any jumbo jet, is too massive to be flown manually. Hydraulic systems power the movable parts that maneuver the airplane—rudder, elevators, ailerons, and wings.

A catastrophic failure of this type was considered impossible because each engine powers a totally separate hydraulic system, and all three are redundantly connected to each control surface. There is only *one place* in the plane where all three systems even run close to one another. That section is at the base of the tail—just where the imperfection in titanium ingot K8283 made its presence known.

Over the years, the minute nitrogen impurity had caused a small crack that evaded stringent inspection procedures. During the course of 15,503 take-offs and landings, the crack had lengthened, weakening the fan to the breaking point. When the fan disk broke first into two sections and then disintegrated, the impossible happened. The spinning, flying engine parts severed all three hydraulic lines and tore through the skin of the plane like a hot knife through butter.

As it became clear that they were totally without hydraulics, Captain Haynes asked Dvorak, "What's the procedure for total hydraulic failure?" The engineer already had the book out to deal with engine failure. It didn't take him long to check and respond, "I can't find anything. *There's nothing in here.*"

At 3:27 P.M., the crew advised SAM (United Airlines' San Francisco maintenance facility) of the loss of all hydraulic systems and requested assistance.

At first, the staff at SAM didn't believe the crew's report because the built-in redundancies make it almost impossible to lose all three hydraulic systems. When they finally did believe it, they realized it was just as impossible for the plane to continue flying. SAM concluded they could provide no assistance or any additional instructions.

For the second time in a few short minutes, Al Haynes was told there was no book of procedures on how to fly a DC-10 without hydraulics. Complete hydraulic failure was such an unprecedented event that procedures for dealing with such a situation didn't exist in the training manuals.

ORGANIZATIONAL FAILURE AT 37,000 FEET

Like Captain Haynes, over the past few years, the captains of many organizations have faced inconsistent, even inconceivable, information when they examined their organizational dashboards to review the economic and key result indicators. Economists, business leaders, and government bureaucrats peer into their studies and data banks attempting to discern the signs of the times. As with the instruments on Flight 232, it's clear that something's amiss, but the causes and implications of this trouble are murky and difficult to determine. The question arises: are current difficulties the result of temporary correction, a passing economic storm, or the siren of fundamental economic change?

Many organizations fail to meet these external challenges because they fail to recognize or respond to change. They become victims of tradition and past successes. They are trapped by conventional paradigms.

The term *paradigm* was first popularized during the 1960's by Thomas S. Kuhn, a philosopher who studied how scientists discovered or failed to discover new ideas. Kuhn defined a paradigm as an accepted model or pattern.[1] In broader terms, a paradigm is a theory or assumption about how things are and will continue to be. Paradigms are mental frameworks that allow us to filter efficiently and organize complex ideas. Without such filters we'd quickly be overwhelmed with raw data.

One author notes, "The problem with paradigms is that we tend to see *through* them, and so the degree to which they filter our perception goes unrecognized."[2] Kuhn wrote that people tend to fit information, no matter how contrary, into their previously constructed frameworks. That is, they'd literally *make* the data fit their expectations.[3]

Thus, when reality changes and our paradigms don't, we lose the ability to see and respond appropriately to change.

At times, some landmark event catches us by surprise—a major tax act, the fall of a government, or a scientific breakthrough. However, most changes creep up on us so slowly that we are often unaware of their existence until years later.

For example, in 1962 Japanese automobiles accounted for only four percent of U.S. car sales. Their sales increases were slow but steady. But it wasn't until the early 1970's, when they had captured nearly 15 percent of the market, that U.S. manufacturers became alarmed. Finally, in 1984, General Motors took the threat seriously and initiated its first reorganization since the early 1920's.[4]

A better term for such changes might be paradigm *drift* rather than *shift*. Most often, the tiny, cumulative changes creep up and capture us. The landscape is littered with organizational carcasses which, like the dinosaurs, got caught by surprise in the vise of change. In the mid 1990's, in discussing the tribulations of several large and historically successful companies, *Fortune* magazine observed, "What swept over these companies was profound change in their markets, to which they were required to adapt. None did, neither fast enough nor fully enough, in part because the erosion of their positions was so gradual as to leave them unaware that they were descending into a state of crisis."[5] Indeed, between 1985 and 1990, 143 *Fortune* 500 companies disappeared from the list. And today's headlines give every indication the trend will continue, even accelerate.[6]

In 1982, Tom Peters and Bob Waterman published their landmark book *In Search of Excellence*. This book was based on a study of 43 companies whose performance over a 20-year period accorded them the accolade "excellent." Today fewer than 10 of the original 43 could meet the stringent criteria for excellence.

The specific reasons for their fall are varied. But an underlying theme was the inability to see and respond effectively to change. Business sections of newspapers across the country daily tell of troubled companies and remind us that, in spite of loud warnings in the market place, old paradigms dull our hearing. And when the rules no longer apply, we can't keep our organizational plane in the air.

NEW RULES BUT NO NEW RULE BOOK

Like the casting imperfection in ingot K8283, the seeds of many problems facing American business were planted many years ago. After World War II, the world experienced an unprecedented era of stability. The United States supplied the bulk of the manufactured goods while the rest of the world licked their wounds and began to rebuild. Older Americans still express nostalgia over the world they remember in the late 1940's and 1950's—a world often described best by well-known television shows like *Leave It to Beaver* and *Father Knows Best.*

Not far into the 1960's a more normal world, from a historical perspective, began to assert itself. Over the past several decades, a number of subtle but fundamental changes began and continue today at an ever-increasing rate. Each decade represented a significant change in specific areas.

1960's: Era of Reexamination—The *values* changed

During the 1960's a number of core cultural values came under siege. The social consequences are just now being grasped as we watch with concern the transformation of key institutions, including family structures, religious institutions, and educational programs. With these changes comes erosion of the values these institutions propagate: values such as honesty, commitment, self-discipline, loyalty, and compassion.

This social trend has a significant impact on the corporate community. Much of my time as a consultant in organizational and team development is spent helping businesses cope with the lack of such values in their workforce. It's virtually impossible to build a team-based organization without the necessary levels of trust, acceptance, and respect among co-workers that will allow them to be open to interdependent relationships.

1970's: Era of Deregulation—The *rules* changed.

In the 1970's many industries experienced the freedom of deregulation for the first time, as well as the brutal competition that came with it. Although the rules changed in the 1970's, the implications, occured during a different watch. The effects of deregulation in one industry weren't felt until the next decade, when 20 airlines with nearly $30 billion in assets declared bankruptcy.[7]

1980's: Era of Realignment—The *players* changed.

The 1980's brought a realignment of focus for many organizations. Greyhound sold its buses to devote its energies to consumer products. General Electric sold $11 billion worth of businesses, including coal mines, semiconductors, and TV sets, while buying $26 billion in new businesses, including investment banking and network television empires.[8] Such transactions among powerful corporations changed their characters and identities, thereby changing the marketplace.

1990's: Era of Globalization—The *boundaries* changed.

The 1990's were largely characterized by a trend that has been gaining momentum for a number of years—globalization. Trade walls came down, and big new markets were formed. But with them came increased, bigger, and even better competition. On January 1, 1993, the European Market Accords went into effect. In early 1993, the U.S., Canadian, and Mexican Free Trade Act was signed. The markets of Eastern Europe and the Russian Commonwealth have opened up. The falling trade barriers, coupled with significant technological advances in transportation and communication, make for a much smaller world, a world of increasing competitive intensity. The typical U.S.

businessperson faces foreign competition in his or her own backyard, many times competing against better products and better, faster service. In today's marketplace nearly 80 percent of American products face stiff foreign competition, and the percentage is still climbing.[9] And, as we look to the future, we see change continuing.

Early 2000's: Era of Leadership—The nature of organizations will change.

The coming decades will be characterized even more by change than their predecessors. Whether we call this discontinuity, inflection points, or paradigm shifts, change will come hurtling at us faster than ever before. Information drives the amount of change; communication drives the speed of change. Information of every type is proliferating at rates never imagined and is available to virtually everyone because of technology (computers, Internet, etc.). Because of the same factors, communication is ubiquitous and almost free. The convergence of communication and information doesn't bode well for those who are waiting for things to "get back to normal."

The first few decades of the 21st century might well become known as the *Era of Leadership*—an era in which we normalize what seemed so exceptional and unusual in the previous one. The 1980's and 1990's were populated with generations whose roots were in times of stability and for whom the concept of "future shock" was a believable possibility. The majority of adults in the new century were raised in the chaos of change. To them, change is the norm. They will not stand to the side marveling at change as did my generation, but they will experience it much like dolphins, which thrill in surfing the bow wave of a fast moving boat.

This era will be defined by a new breed of leadership. Whereas management is sufficient in times of rest and stability, in a world of white-water change, leadership is a non-negotiable essential. A world of constant change is a new game and it will be a new game every day. In this kind of climate, we need men and women who can provide direction and boundaries in the midst of constant shift.

It will be an era where many of the emerging trends of today are present and in full bloom. It will be a world of networks of independent individuals and entities separate but connected on a moment's notice to pursue mutual but most often temporary goals. Distributed workforces of both permanent and contract personnel will be connected through broadband, digital technology that transmits video, voice, and data at real-time speeds. Organizations will have to truly institutionalize learning and the ability to adapt to the point where it's almost instinctive. They will have to please customers who will demand degrees of customization, speed, and prices that would seem unimaginable today.

As we enter a new century, we are confronted with new values, new rules, new players, new boundary lines. The game is changing—not *changed*, but *changing*. In today's fast-paced, competitive marketplace, the rules change every day. Just when you think you've got it, just as you pause to rest a bit, you are confronted with another fluctuation.

It's a tough game! And as the barriers—geographic, regulatory, and technological, for instance—that once protected many businesses disappear, the basis of competition shifts back to "Who's better at it?"[10] Unfortunately, it's not always the home team!

In reality, we are experiencing major fundamental changes that will dramatically and permanently change the way we work and do business in any type of organization.

During the past few years, I have had many business leaders ask me when I thought things were going to get back to normal. My response invariably is that, if you are hanging on by your fingernails waiting for things to get back to normal, you're in for a very long wait. This *is* normal! It was the 1950's, 1960's, and part of the 1970's that weren't normal. Waiting until things blow over isn't going to cut it in today's turbulent business environment.

Like Captain Haynes, the crew, and the passengers of United Flight 232, many organizations find themselves in a dangerous predicament where nothing is "in the book." At this point, Captain Haynes had to begin writing his own book. In such unusual circumstances, standard operating procedures no longer apply.

We too must become accomplished authors of a new way of doing things. And, like the crew of Flight 232, we'd better write fast! Too many years have been wasted on one effort after another, attempting to adapt old procedures to new realities. The evolving marketplace calls for new strategies and structures. Investing more effort and resources behind old strategies wastes valuable time in circumstances where time is at a premium.

Effective leaders must be pragmatic realists. They ensure that their organizations constantly scan the horizon for emerging trends that can challenge, the way they, or their customers, do business. When such trends become visible they don't deny the change or defend the old way of doing things. Rather, they take the initiative to confront the implications of this change for their business strategies.

To win in this new game we must stop trying to cram old ways of doing things into new business realities. We must craft new paradigms. Those business leaders who rewrite the book about "doing business" will write about quality, speed, responsiveness, breakthrough, innovation, exceptional value, and brilliant execution. The successful organizational forms in the early part of the 21st century will be *fast, flexible,* and *focused.* And, if they want to keep their customers and staff, they must add the words *fun* and *friendly* to the list as well.

Increasing competition forces the typical organization to operate with leaner, more agile structures. Many corporations have found themselves woefully overweight and out of shape for this level of world-class competition. They have been forced into crash diets, cutting entire layers of management from their structures.[11] These leaner organizations have neither the time nor the resources to do the job twice. Their focus must be on doing it right the first time and doing it better than anyone else. They must, therefore, squeeze every ounce of synergy out of the few people who remain. The typical company must accomplish its work better, faster, and with fewer resources than was done in years past. The task is as challenging as it is straightforward.

What Will a Successful 21st Century Organization Look Like?

Business in the early part of the 21st century will be played on a new field with new rules and world-class competitors. Every day the world gets smaller, the pace and scope of change increases, and the level of competition intensifies. Global-level competition demands new standards of excellence. Organizations must offer the highest levels of quality, service, and value or perish like the dinosaurs. These are demanding criteria. It was much easier to compete on the basis of price, creative advertising, and style.

Quality

We know we need it, but we aren't sure exactly what it is. Not even the quality experts can agree on a definition of quality, nor do they agree on how it is to be achieved or measured. Definitions run the gamut of possibility. Is quality doing something better than anyone else? Is it whatever the buyer says it is? Is it conformance to stringent requirements? Is it continual improvement? Is it all of these?

Quality might be hard to define, but most of us, as consumers, know it when we see it. It's not merely a technical term or even something that's precisely measurable. Rather, quality is in the eyes of the "*buy-holder.*" The only acceptable judge of quality is the customer, not the engineers or product managers. Japanese automakers recognize this and attempt to go beyond merely eliminating zero defects and build cars that also "fascinate, bewitch, and delight." IBM also considers "delight factors" as an essential part of quality.[12]

Service

Service has been and will continue to be another battleground as we move into a new century. Service might be defined as living up to our commitments and meeting customer expectations with unparalleled levels of consistency and predictability. Tom Peters, one of the most articulate spokespersons for customers everywhere, stresses that success will come with "shockingly high levels" of customer service and extraordinary responsiveness. He reports the results of a major customer service survey conducted of "former" customers of 14 major companies in which two-thirds indicated their defection was a result of how they felt about dealing with the company (that is, its people) in contrast to price or product quality issues.[13] The bottom line is that *quality* decides who gets to play in the game, but *service* and *value* will determine who wins.

Value

Value is the third dimension of excellence. Jack Welch, the renowned CEO of General Electric, is often described as an executive known for breakthrough ideas and the will to apply them. General Electric could have suffered the same malaise experienced by other corporate giants formed around the turn of this century if it had not been for the foresighted leadership of Welch since 1981. While many large and formerly prosperous firms foundered, he helped transform GE from an unwieldy, bureaucratic structure into an agile, powerful competitor. Based on stock valuation, GE became one of the most valuable companies in the world.

In their book *Control Your Destiny or Someone Else Will*, Noel Tichy and Stratford Sherman summarize over 100 hours of interviews with Welch. They reveal a man who understands the realities of business in the 21st century. "Our standards are tougher than ever," says Welch. "They have to be. The Value Decade has already begun, with global competition like you've never seen. It's going to be brutal. When I said the 1980's was going to be a white-knuckle decade and the 1990's would be even tougher, I may have understated how hard it's going to get . . . Everywhere you go, people are saying, 'Don't tell me about your technology, tell me about your price' . . . there's an enormous drive to get value, value, value . . . Only the most productive companies are going to win. If you can't sell a top-quality product at the world's lowest price, you're going to be out of the game."[14]

As the CEO of my own company, albeit a small one, I find myself more challenged by his comments than comforted. I see the same response with many of our clients. The latest management books and articles often raise more questions than provide feasible solutions. We must ask, "What's it going to take to play in this new game and win? How can my organization deliver top quality, service, and value? How can my organization find the necessary resources to confront today's challenges?"

The solution depends not on resources but on resourcefulness. The organizations that survive and succeed in the current business environment will not be defined by assets but by other qualities such as:

- *Flexibility, speed, agility, and responsiveness.* Organizations must be able to turn on a dime and respond to change and opportunity quickly.

- *Fast, high quality decisions.* Companies must learn how to tap into the "collective brilliance" of the organization quickly, effectively, and efficiently. They must learn how to mobilize diverse groups of people with different skills, experiences, and knowledge to attack a problem, decision, or opportunity, and then disperse.

- *Ongoing learning and exceptional creativity and innovation.* The IQ of the team is considerably greater than that of the individual team members. Put another way, "all of us" are smarter than "one of us." In a world characterized by speed and constant change, the ability of an organization to learn and adapt is crucial to its survival. High performance teams are not only good at learning, but they quickly spread the lessons well.

- *Quick, precise, consistent execution.* Many analysts believe that time will be the currency of the new century and that companies that can continue to cut their product development cycles will gain significant advantage over their more lethargic rivals. In this new game of business, speed coupled with nimble execution creates almost insurmountable barriers to one's adversaries. This level of execution will deliver the levels of quality and service demanded by the marketplace.

EMPOWERED STAFF, HIGH PERFORMANCE TEAMS, SUPERIOR LEADERSHIP

These qualities are not the products of capital expenditure, economies of scale, or massive R&D efforts. Rather, they are the result of an empowered and involved workforce. Although the quality experts don't agree about much, they do agree that people, particularly the ones most closely associated with the work, are the key to organizational excellence. In their book *Quality or Else*, Lloyd Dobyns and Clare Crawford-Mason observe, "Natural resources mattered most under the old rules and matter least under the new ones. What matters now is the production of quality with the only natural resource that counts—people."[15]

A business organization will need to engender levels of participation, ownership, and cooperation from its workforce seldom experienced in industry. If I had to summarize the most appropriate corporate strategy and structure to best achieve such qualities, one word would suffice: *team*. Only through the development of high performance work teams can organizations create the "empowered involvement" necessary to achieve the quality, service, and value required to succeed in this world of formidable global competition.

All of us have seen or been a part of groups that were extraordinarily effective. They achieved exceptional results—results that cannot be accounted for by either the size of the group or their resources. This group has an intangible dynamic that isn't often found in other groups.

It has a special spirit or sense of confidence, belonging, and commitment. Such a group shares common goals and achieves results well beyond their individual abilities. Their relationships are characterized by high levels of acceptance, respect, and trust. Ideas and communications move like quicksilver. These people make the hard seem easy as they sweep past the rest of us straining under the load. It is upon *this* group that we bestow the accolade "team."

We find such a team on United Flight 232, responding with extraordinary resourcefulness and collaboration when faced with the loss of all their normal resources.

Finally, organizations that aspire to excellence in times of constant change must embrace the need for leadership—great leadership and lots of it. Successful 21st century organizations will do everything in their power to release the leader in everyone, at every level of the organization. But few places within the typical company will benefit more from strong, capable leaders than the team. Teams will continue to be the load-bearing beams of organizational structure as we move into a new century. As we will see throughout this book, the power of teams, in the right setting, is compelling. However, effective team leadership is critical to unleash that power.

The problem is that, in spite of the potential of teams, too few organizations have been able to turn this potential into performance. After nearly 20 years of helping client organizations build all types of teams from temporary task forces to top management teams and everything in between, I believe that building effective teams appears deceptively easy. Within minutes after being formed, the typical team (and, at this point, I use this term loosely) experiences all sorts of barriers—some corporate, others team specific. Looking only at the team itself, it's not unusual to be confronted with an unclear task, ill-defined roles, inadequate processes, failing relationships, or awful communication. However, as real and challenging as these problems are, a capable, committed team leader can generally navigate his or her team successfully through them. This book will give you the practical insights to help you do just that.

THE BOTTOM LINE

Teams and teamwork are not passing fads but a fundamental shift in how organizations approach work. However, unthinking implementation of teams without a clear understanding of the underlying principles, careful design, and adaptation to organizational needs can create cynical attitudes among the participants and render teams useless in the pursuit of organizational objectives.

- Business in the 21st century will be played on a new field, with new rules and world-class competition.

- We live and will continue to live in an era of new rules but no new playbook. The game has not only changed but is changing and will continue to do so.

- Competitive advantage will be determined by an organization's ability to consistently deliver quality, service, and value.

- In this new game, the typical corporation must do what it does better, faster, cheaper, and with fewer resources.

- These qualities are not the product of resources only but also the result of "empowered involvement" on the part of the workforce.

- Everyone, and I mean everyone, must be involved in getting the organizational plane to its destination and safely on the ground.

- Team-based strategies introduce a solution that spreads the stress of change, and creates a structure with speed, flexibility, and collective competence. Team-based organizations will be the survivors and winners in today's tough environment.

MESSAGE TO TEAM LEADERS

Metaphorically, leaders in many organizations face the same challenges that confronted Captain Haynes and his crew. The rules have changed, and what has always worked before is no longer effective. The hydraulics have failed, and people in our organizations depend on us to figure out the problem, establish new rules, and bring us in for a safe landing. During a meeting several years ago, the chairman of a Big Six accounting firm summarized the problem: "In today's business environment," he said, "I feel like we are flying a 747 from New York to Los Angeles, and trying to rebuild it en route."

A world of turbulent change is chaotic and unpredictable. In such a world, leadership is at a premium and takes precedence over management. Leadership is all about change. It is most needed when organizations must change direction or style, when they must shift, adapt, or move to respond to changing circumstances. Management, on the other hand, is concerned about production, consistency, and flow. It is needed in times of stability and predictability.

In times of change, organizations need more leaders and more capable leaders. They need leadership at every level of the organization. Experience has proven that team-based organizations fare better in fluid situations than the more typical hierarchical organizations. One reason is that teams spread the stress of change, not only because they are stronger and more resilient but because they introduce an added element of leadership into the equation as well. There is a leader in every person, and a team structure provides a medium for this leadership to be released as individual team members are encouraged to express their functional expertise. One key role of a team leader is to find and facilitate the collective element of leadership within the team.

CHAPTER TWO

Business in the 21st Century
Is a Team Sport

TEAMWORK AT 37,000 FEET

United Flight 232 had suffered what the airline industry calls a "catastrophic uncontained failure." At 37,000 feet, one hour and seven minutes out of Denver, the No. 2 engine literally broke apart. Over 70 pieces of shrapnel ripped through the skin of the aircraft at high velocity. The heavy plane was virtually unflyable. Captain Al Haynes later described the scope of the damage: "With no hydraulics we had no ailerons to bank the airplane. We had no rudders to turn it. We had no elevators to control the pitch (that is, nose of the plane up or down) of the aircraft. We had no spoilers that come up on top of the wing to help us descend or to slow down on the ground. And, once on the ground, we would have no way to steer the plane to keep it on the runway, and we had no brakes to stop."

The engine failure was so unique that there was no standard operating procedure for this type of event. After the accident, a United vice president was asked by the press why no procedure had been developed for such an event. "Well," he said, "we don't have a procedure for how to fly the plane if a wing falls off either." The bottom line was clear. The plane was not designed to fly without hydraulics.

During the next 41 minutes, Captain Haynes led an extraordinary effort that proved to be unique in the annals of aircraft emergencies. The cockpit crew and ultimately an entire network of other teams formed a larger "232 organization." Flight attendants, air traffic controllers, SAM, and several dozen different ground rescue and emergency agencies worked together to achieve unprecedented results. Subsequent to the event, McDonnell Douglas and United simulated 45 flights attempting to re-create the same conditions, but were unable to simulate a successful landing. Other studies confirmed that there were so many unknown variables that the maneuvers accomplished by the 232 organization were "not trainable."[1]

Captain Haynes attributes their success to five special factors—luck, communications, preparation, execution, and cooperation. He doesn't mind if I, and a good number of his passengers, choose to include the possibility of *divine* intervention.

As I have studied this effort, I find almost all of the organizational qualities that I listed in the previous chapter (agility and responsiveness; fast, high-quality decision making; constant learning; the ability to tap into the collective IQ of the group; and exceptional creativity and innovation) are reflected in this team. The crew demonstrated the ability to build the team en route, taking advantage of every possible resource, skill, and experience in the most expedient manner.

Today's organizations must have both exceptional teamwork and excellent leadership. Although the ride may not be as immediately life-threatening as that of Flight 232, the corporate cockpit faces uncharted territory and catastrophic upheaval even when things seem to be going according to plan.

Such a remarkable human effort deserves a happy ending. But unfortunately, when the plane approached the end of the runway, the autopilot, locked in the "on" position as a result of the incident, attempted to reassert its influence. As the crew increased power to attempt to level the aircraft, the left engine responded with too much power, and the right wing dipped down into the dirt just short of the runway. The plane smashed into the concrete, breaking apart in a cloud of fire, smoke, and debris. One hundred and twelve people died in the crash.

However, 184 people miraculously survived due to exceptional team effort. Certainly the teamwork of the flight crew was key. They were able to keep the disabled jet aloft for over 41 minutes as they figured out how to maneuver it through a series of wide 360-degree turns for nearly 60 miles to Sioux City. But other teams were also at work that day. Emergency rescue and medical teams from the surrounding area had planned and practiced for such an event. That afternoon it paid off since 162 of the 184 survivors were injured, many seriously.

Captain Haynes may not be a management expert on the theoretical aspects of teamwork, but he demonstrated one of the best practical illustrations of how to build and lead a high performance team I've ever seen. Haynes himself provides the best summary of their efforts. In his first press conference, while still in the hospital in Sioux City, he was asked how it felt to be a hero.

"There is no hero," he said. "There was just a group of four people who did their job. It was an unusual circumstance, but we put our best resources and mileage together and did what we thought was best. Everyone either helped in running the airplane, flying the airplane, or doing the many, many radio reports that were required, dealing with flight attendants, dealing with passengers, dealing with the Flight Center. Everybody kicked in, everybody offered their own assistance without being told, and everyone acted as a group. We agreed among ourselves before any particular thing was done and that, of course, was a very important part of our survival."[2]

TEAMS ARE A KEY VARIABLE IN THE FORMULA FOR ORGANIZATIONAL SUCCESS

The crew of Flight 232 experienced luck, but didn't "luck out." They didn't just discover how to work together as a team. Each of the four pilots had been through extensive team training in United's Denver training facility in a program called Command Leadership Resource Management. Captain Haynes believes it was this training that allowed the crew to creatively mobilize the skills, instincts, and experiences of nearly 103 years of accumulated flight time among four men. It was this training that taught them how to take initiative, communicate clearly, and work together effectively in a crisis. And these principles of team-work that seized some success from what could have been total disaster can also be applied in the business world.

Organizations can create corporate cultures that tap into the collective brilliance of everyone from the top to the bottom. But let me be clear. Teams and teamwork are not *the* answer, but rather an essential ingredient in the total answer as organizations reposition themselves for success in the 21st century. For the most part, if we examine today's high-performance organizations, we'll find teams inextricably woven into their structures and strategies.

The list of companies which have successfully implemented team-based structures continues to grow:

- Contrasting its new team-based pet food manufacturing plant to one of its more traditional plants, General Foods found the team approach 30 percent more productive.[3]

- By reorganizing a large group of clerical workers into five-to-10-person teams and giving them the training and authority to manage themselves, FedEx cut service glitches such as incorrect bills and lost packages by 13 percent over two years.[4]

- After organizing home office operations into teams, Aetna Life and Casualty Company reduced the ratio of middle managers from one in seven employees to one in 30, while at the same time improving customer service.[5]

- GE's Salisbury Plant, which uses a team approach to produce lighting panels, has increased productivity 250 percent compared to traditional GE plants producing the same product.[6]

- In the early 1970's, Motorola claimed that a team approach reduced turnover by 25 percent and increased productivity by 30 percent.[7]

- Since introducing a team strategy to their cereal plant in Lodi, California, General Mills has seen productivity rise 40 percent.[8]

- Boeing Aircraft reports that in the period between 1994 and 1998, it cut the time to build a C-17 by 80 percent, built it better, and increased overall employee productivity of the C-17 workers 63 percent, as a result of successfully implementing teams against the project.[9]

The results described above have been mirrored in the teams our firm has worked with through the years. Some of our most interesting assignments have involved temporary task forces assigned to design and make recommendations, as well as sales teams deployed in environments typically hostile to team strategies.

The principles for team development and effectiveness are the same for temporary task forces as for permanent operational teams. Short time frames coupled with the fact that often team members don't know one another or haven't worked together provide added dimensions of difficulty for task forces. Due to short life spans and the urgency of the task, task forces often discard the possibility for team development because they don't have time and they won't be in business long enough to reap the benefits. Nothing could be farther from the truth.

For example, a bureau of the U.S. Department of the Interior initiated a major organizational redesign. It formed a series of teams to tackle various aspects of the project. One team was assigned the task of dissolving two separate divisions and reforming them into a single, smaller entity that would support the operating divisions. The team consisted of 11 members, most of whom had never met and who lived in different cities, making communication that much more difficult. Fully half of the team members were from the departments that were under redesign and had a vested interest in the outcome. The team needed to create a design that would maximize cost effectiveness and service quality on one hand and minimize emotional loss and service disruption on the other. To make the task even more challenging, the team had only six months to finish the work.

In spite of the short time frame, the team leader retained Team Resources to spend several days with the team. We reviewed their task, worked through the characteristics of high performance teams, and facilitated the development of the operating principles by which the team would govern itself. Over the course of the project, we spent time with the team leader coaching him in the application of team processes. Their recommendations were heartily received, and the closing comments of the bureau director after reviewing the recommendations were: "You just set the standard by which we will judge all other design teams."

We experienced a similar result in a division of Procter & Gamble. An organizational team was to design a strategy to integrate ten different sales organizations into a single entity that would represent the entire product line to all customers. The objective was to enhance customer focus and value. The design task was assigned to a nine-person, multi-functional team formed specifically for this purpose. Although the project timeline was 15 months, a short time for such a complex restructuring, the team decided to invest considerable time in team development during the first month. We helped the team get rapidly up to speed with the principles of high performance teamwork. We also spent time helping the team understand how to best leverage the different temperaments, skills, and experiences of strong-minded team members coming out of multi-functional backgrounds. Again, we were available to the team facilitator throughout the project to help him implement various team principles as well as problem-solve when the team got stuck.

The design was successfully implemented, and business results at the end of the first full year of operation were up 7 percent in a situation where most organizations experiencing such major restructuring would have taken a loss. At the end of the second year, the growth was in double digits and described by the team as "breakthrough" results.

When it comes to working with permanent team structures, some of the most challenging development tasks we have undertaken have been helping clients develop cross-functional sales teams. Sales organizations are invariably comprised of highly independent people who don't typically like to ride in posses. These are the gunslingers of the corporate world, rugged individualists who ride off into the sunset and bring 'em back dead or alive. We have worked with Procter & Gamble, Campbell Soup Company, Helene Curtis, and a number of other firms to help design and implement successful customer business teams. Most of these teams, often led by a "reformed" gunslinger, experienced significant results as they learned to leverage the collective IQ of the cross-functional resources on the team (for example, logistics, customer service, finance, etc.). Customers received significant value-added services as well, as the teams deployed multi-functional resources against the mutual goals of both parties.

TEAMS AND TEAMWORK

Many organizations seem confused about the difference between teamwork and teams. Teamwork is an organizational philosophy or value system, an occurrence, whereas teams are specific and discrete organizational units. Many companies have attempted to form team structures merely because they felt there was intrinsic merit in teams, or because it seemed like the thing to do in the 1990's. Such efforts are doomed to failure.

The confusion stems from seeing teams as the *end* versus the *means* to the end. Teams are a *means* of achieving goals too big and complex to reach through individual efforts. Don't misinterpret what I am saying. I strongly advocate that every company does whatever is necessary to engender a spirit of teamwork and cooperation throughout the organization. The decision to form teams, however, should be made in response to particular objectives and strategies in which teams represent the most appropriate organizational response. Opportunities to leverage teams are found in situations that demand high levels of integration between highly interdependent people or functions, in fast-changing environments in which the rule book is constantly out of date, and in work environments which must quickly and effectively integrate a broad array of expertise (Figure 2-1). Basically, teams work best in and bring a lot of value to fast-moving, uncertain, non-routine environments in which interdependent people must perform at exceptional levels.

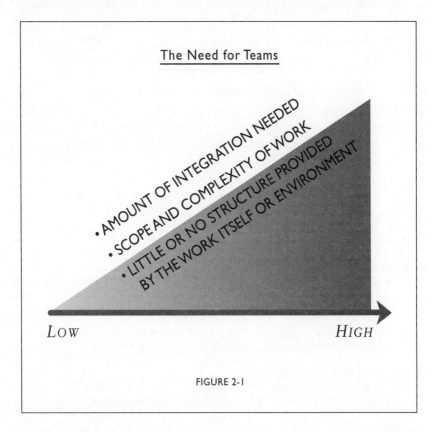

The Need for Teams

• AMOUNT OF INTEGRATION NEEDED
• SCOPE AND COMPLEXITY OF WORK
• LITTLE OR NO STRUCTURE PROVIDED BY THE WORK ITSELF OR ENVIRONMENT

LOW   *HIGH*

FIGURE 2-1

If we are to master the art of team building, then we must not only know when to build a team; we must also know exactly what we are attempting to build. What distinguishes a team from any other type of group?

CALLING THEM A TEAM DOESN'T MAKE THEM ONE

I'm often invited by executives to meet their leadership teams. Most of the time, however, I don't see any evidence of a team at all. Confused crowds, warring factions, unruly mobs, maybe, but not teams in the truest sense. Most managers intuitively sense that their teams aren't really teams at all, but they have little understanding about how to get their arms around this vague, somewhat nebulous concept of team. Using the term *team* to describe their particular posse is, in many cases, one way they believe they might motivate their staff to act like one—if they think they are a team, maybe they will act like one.

The problem is that they really don't know what a team is. For all the richness and variety of the English language, many of us live on a bland and often very meager diet of what it has to offer. An unabridged dictionary might contain over a half million words. A typical collegiate dictionary averages 200,000 words. But the average American uses only about 1,200 words with consistency. Thus, many of us use words somewhat indiscriminately, applying a large variety of meaning to a small number of words, thereby stretching their original intent well beyond the point of usefulness. *Team* is such a word.

In today's culture, the word *team* has come to mean many different things. In athletics, a team is an entity merely because it exists, regardless of how well it performs. In a business setting, the use of the word *team* implies some level of exemplary performance. If we are going to invest a significant amount of energy and effort into building a high performance team, we'd better be clear about what we are building. A key question arises: what is the difference between a team and any other type of work group?

When I ask participants to define a team in our team workshops, I get all kinds of answers. The most frequent response is that a team is a group of people with a common purpose. Unity of purpose is certainly a necessary ingredient to teamwork, but it's not sufficient. Many groups that are clearly not teams display commitment to the same purpose.

Another frequent response is that a team is a group of people who must coordinate their activities to accomplish a common goal. Mutual accountability, complementary skills, and communication are also frequently pressed into the definition of a team. All of these elements are important; however, many of them are found in non-teams as well. Ultimately, *performance* will be the unique, distinguishing characteristic that sets a team apart from any other type of group.

The purpose of any team is to accomplish an objective and to do so at *exceptionally* high levels of performance. Teamwork is not an end in itself but rather a means to an end. Therefore, a team must ultimately be judged by its results. By *exceptional* I mean synergistic. Synergy is the state in which the output is greater than the sum of the inputs. One plus one equals three, four, even five! The roots of this word are found with the classical Greek word *synergos*, which means "working together." It combines two Greek words: *syn-*, together + *ergon*, work. The Romans weren't far behind in seeing the benefits of joint effort. Cooperation finds its origin in the combination of two Latin words: *co-* with + *operari*, to work. The Latin word *cooperari* means to work together. Synergy is a product of cooperation but, as we shall see in a moment, only very high levels of cooperation.

SHOW ME THE SYNERGY!

A few years ago a client firm was in the process of reorganizing its sales force into customer business teams. Prior to this, each division sent its own salesperson to call on the customers, most of whom carried all of this manufacturer's products. Although they were market leaders in virtually every product category, competition was intensifying. Company leaders felt that a unified presentation of their products and services would give them significant competitive advantage, not only through increased sales and better service but through greater efficiencies as well. In staffing these customer business teams, they not only combined the individual product salespeople, but they added technical support staff as well.

In a major planning session, the newly formed teams excitedly presented their sales and revenue projections. Listening from the back of the room, the national sales director wasn't so excited. It didn't take him long to see that their projections were nothing more than the sum of the sales each team member would have achieved individually. These were new teams, and they had not actually worked together. It was clear they had no understanding of the concept of synergism. How could they? They had never experienced it. The national sales director sent them back to the planning tables with this message: *"There is no way that this company is going to invest the time, expense, and effort to train and staff these sales teams for the same results that we would have had with all of you working individually. Where's the synergy?"*

The sales director was on to something. He knew, even if only intuitively, that properly structured and trained teams should be able to outperform any other type of staffing structure. Teams accomplish *more* than can be accounted for by numbers alone. It's this *more* that I attribute to the synergistic effects found in true teamwork. It's the difference between *acceptable* and *exceptional* results.

This primary difference between a team and any other type of group is synergism. Many groups have a common purpose; most even see some level of cooperation. But in a true team the combination of factors and the intensity and consistency with which they are applied allows a team to experience results on a regular basis.

One interesting example is found in the 1885 world series of mule team competition was held in Chicago. The winning team pulled 9,000 pounds, the second place team a little less. Someone suggested that they see what the two teams could do together. The result was 30,000 pounds, much more than the sum of their separate loads.

Not long after the competition in Chicago, a young foreman working in a mine in Death Valley, California noticed that 12 mules could pull twice as much as eight. After some experimentation he determined that 20 mules was the most efficient combination. He was experimenting with synergism. Some readers have already guessed that the mine's product was Borax. And those 20-mule teams became the symbol and brand name of this product—Twenty Mule Team Borax.[10]

In the flight pattern of geese we see another example of synergy. When geese fly, the wing movement of each bird creates an uplift for the others that follow. The design of their classic V formation is such that the whole flock gains 71 percent greater flying range than if each bird flew alone. When a goose falls out of formation, it quickly feels the drag and scrambles back into its position to take advantage of the bird immediately in front of it. The author of this example points out that people who share a common direction and sense of community can get where they are going quicker and easier because they are traveling on the thrust of one another. If they have as much sense as a goose, they will stay in formation with those headed where they want to go, accepting the help of others and willingly giving it in return.[11]

COOPERATION IS A CHOICE

Teamwork is cooperation at its highest level, and the level of cooperation drives the level of the results. It's important not to see cooperation as an on-off concept, but a matter of degree. Think of cooperation

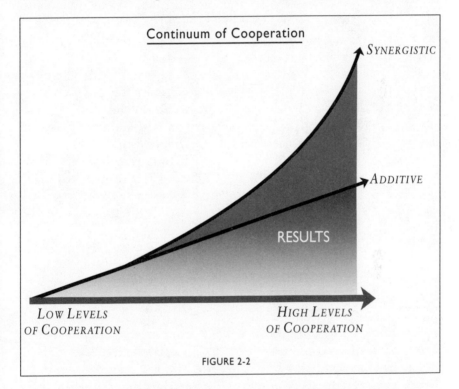

Continuum of Cooperation

SYNERGISTIC

ADDITIVE

RESULTS

*LOW LEVELS
OF COOPERATION*

*HIGH LEVELS
OF COOPERATION*

FIGURE 2-2

as a continuum (Figure 2-2). At one end we have little or no cooperation and a commensurate level of results. On the other end of the continuum, cooperation is very high, as are the results. At some point in our efforts, we begin to see signs of synergy. That is, the results are greater than the sum of the parts. It is at this point, the group becomes a team.

Seeing cooperation as a *relative* concept allows us to appreciate the dynamic between individual team members and the larger team itself. Team leaders must balance the tensions between the *task*, the *team*, and *individual members* on the team. Too much emphasis on one element at the expense of the others throws the team dynamic out of balance.

Where each member stands on the continuum is a matter of choice—individual choice. A team is a collection of individuals, and those individuals are "all over the landscape" or, in this case, "all over

Levels of Cooperation

LOW LEVELS   HIGH LEVELS

FIGURE 2-3

the continuum" (Figure 2-3). A goal of every team leader is to motivate individual members to "move right" on the continuum to higher levels of cooperation. Because cooperation is a choice, a choice made on an individual basis, you are, in reality, leading the team one person at a time. Every time an individual team member moves evan a little to the right, the entire team moves right.

EXODUS 18

However, the choice to cooperate and to enlist the aid of others is generally not our first choice. I have always been infatuated with the insights into human nature presented in the Bible. We see roots of the basic problem nearly 3,500 years ago in the life and leadership of Moses. The people's progress through the wilderness had bogged down as more and more time was spent working through the bureaucratic tangles and resolving disputes. (This particular group had a lot of them!) Moses was starting to burn out under the load of leadership when his father-in-law, Jethro, arrived for a short visit. Jethro provided some much-needed counsel to his overly tired son-in-law: "You cannot do it alone."[12]

This message, echoed throughout both the Old and New Testaments, challenges the individualism that lays at the very core of Western culture. In *Habits of the Heart,* Robert Bellah observes that Americans believe in the dignity, even the sacredness of the individual. Anything that would violate our right to think for ourselves, judge for ourselves, make our own decisions, live our lives as we see fit, is not only morally wrong; it is sacrilegious. It is America that invented the most mythic individual hero, the cowboy and his more modern version, the hard-boiled detective.[13] However, God did not create people to be self-sufficient and to move through life alone. He didn't intend his work to be done by gunslingers, who ride alone into the sunset, but rather by posses. Creation itself was not complete until there was a community. However, as all of us have discovered, the presence of community is not a guarantee of cooperation.

TEAMS ARE VOLUNTEER ORGANIZATIONS

Adding the concepts of results and choice to the more traditional ideas of team allows us to see that a team is *a group of people committed to a common purpose who choose to cooperate in order to achieve exceptional results.*

Don't miss the word *choose* in our definition of a team. That's the volunteer part. Teams are, in the very truest sense, volunteer organizations. You cannot force someone to cooperate, you cannot mandate teamwork, you cannot declare a group to be a team. Cooperation at high levels is a product of choice—choices made one person at a time for reasons that are often unique to that individual.

THE BOTTOM LINE

- When done right, teams work. Companies have discovered and documented startling gains in productivity in the 30- to 60-percent range, increased levels of quality, reduced costs, and faster time to market.

- Although every organization should do whatever it can to foster a team spirit throughout its culture, formal teams should only be deployed against tasks that demand a team approach.

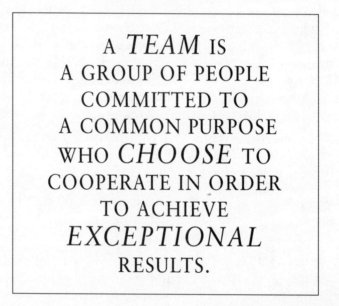

A *TEAM* IS
A GROUP OF PEOPLE
COMMITTED TO
A COMMON PURPOSE
WHO *CHOOSE* TO
COOPERATE IN ORDER
TO ACHIEVE
EXCEPTIONAL
RESULTS.

- The primary distinction between a team and any other type of group is the results. Teams achieve exceptional, synergistic results on a consistent basis. Without evidence of synergy on a regular basis, you probably have merely a group or a team in a slump.

- Synergism is a phenomenon in which the output is greater than the sum of the inputs and occurs at the highest levels of cooperation.

- Cooperation is not an on-off concept but a matter of degree. The goal of any team is to maximize the level of cooperation of each team member.

- Cooperation is a choice made by each individual team member. This decision is based on his or her perception of whether or not cooperation is the best way to achieve a desired goal. Therefore, teams are "volunteer" organizations.

MESSAGE TO TEAM LEADERS

- Many new or young teams have never experienced the synergy that comes from high levels of competent cooperation. They need help calibrating their expectations, setting goals, and establishing a vision. Team leaders must help them come to grips with what they can realistically accomplish if they get their *collective* act together. In helping them define what synergism looks like for this team, team leaders must, like any coach, take the maturity of the team into account. A young team won't achieve the level of results that can be accomplished by a more mature, seasoned team.

- Where every team member stands on the continuum is a matter of individual choice. This means leaders must work with each individual team member to find out where they are and what it will take to get them to move to the right. Such motivation is accomplished one person at a time.

- Because "moving to the right" is an individual decision, we can see that teams, in the very truest sense, consist of volunteers. Volunteers need leadership, not management. In many cases, whether an individual is on the team or merely on the payroll is a product of effective team leadership.

PART TWO

Characteristics of a High Performance Team

CHAPTER THREE

The Characteristics of a High Performance Team

W hat the cockpit team of United Flight 232 accomplished has never been replicated. The National Transportation Safety Board performed a number of simulations and was not able to get the plane on the ground safely.[1] McDonnell Douglas, which manufactured the DC-10, and United Airlines simulated 45 flights under the same conditions of Flight 232 and did not have one successful landing.[2] To be certain, the number of random events that insert themselves into such a situation are too numerous to calculate, but in spite of them, this one team achieved something extraordinary—something no one else has been able to do. What made this particular team so unusually successful?

WE WERE DOING GREAT AND THEN . . .

For most of us, positive team experiences are rare. If you have been part of an extraordinary team in the past, you will probably long for that experience again. People often drift into and then out of extraordinary team situations, wondering what made that group "click" and how to replicate it. A key first step to more predictable and enhanced team performance is understanding the common characteristics of teams that consistently achieve exceptional results.

A team is like an automobile. Many of us don't understand the inner workings of a modern automobile. Should we ever look under the hood, we see an indecipherable tangle of wires, tubes, pieces, and parts. And if anything breaks down, we very often don't know how to get it running again. As with cars, if we are going to build effective teams, start stalled ones, or fix broken ones, then we must become master mechanics of team dynamics.

As we have studied and researched teams and teamwork over the years, we have found consistently similar qualities and characteristics in teams that achieve exceptional results. This list of characteristics has proven to be of immeasurable value as we have worked with clients to establish new teams or to intervene when team effort was less than effective. It's a short list; in fact, it contains only six characteristics. But each characteristic plays a specific and vital role in making the team effective, and therefore it is worth a closer look. If one of these six characteristics is missing or inadequate, the team is, at best, limping. If two or three are lacking, this group is probably not a team at all.

The following model shows the six characteristics in abbreviated form. In the next few chapters, we are going to examine a high performance team and explore each characteristic in some detail.

COMMON PURPOSE

The single most important ingredient in team success is a clear, common, compelling task. The power of a team flows out of each team member's alignment to its purpose. The task of any team is to accomplish an objective and to do so at exceptional levels of performance. Teams are not ends in themselves but rather means to an end. Therefore, high performance teams will be purpose directed, ultimately judged by their results.

CRYSTAL CLEAR ROLES

High performance teams are characterized by crystal clear roles. Every team member is clear about his or her particular role, as well as those of the other team members. Roles are about how we design, divide, and deploy the work of the team. While the concept is compellingly logical, many teams find it very challenging to implement in practice. There is often a tendency to take role definition to extremes or

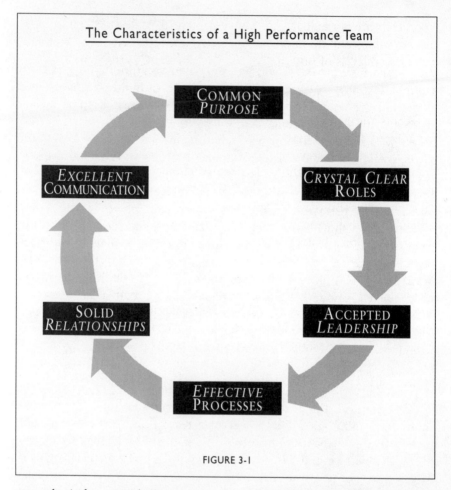

The Characteristics of a High Performance Team

COMMON PURPOSE

CRYSTAL CLEAR ROLES

EXCELLENT COMMUNICATION

ACCEPTED LEADERSHIP

SOLID RELATIONSHIPS

EFFECTIVE PROCESSES

FIGURE 3-1

not take it far enough. However, when they get it right, team members discover that making their combination more effective and leveraging their collective efforts is an important key to synergistic results.

ACCEPTED LEADERSHIP

High performance teams need clear, competent leadership. When such leadership is lacking, groups lose their way. Whereas a common, compelling task might be the biggest contributor to team effectiveness, inadequate team leadership may be the single biggest reason for team ineffectiveness. Teams are, in the very truest sense, volunteers.

Volunteers are not managed, but they demand *accepted* leadership capable of calling out the levels of initiative and creativity that motivate exceptional levels of both individual and collective performance.

EFFECTIVE PROCESSES

Teams and processes go together. Many professions take processes for granted. It would never occur to a surgical team, construction crew, string quartet, film crew, or the team on the flight deck of Flight 232 to approach their tasks without clearly defined processes. The playbook of a football team or the score sheet of a string quartet clearly outlines their processes. Business teams have processes as well. Instead of a run off tackle, or executing the scene in Act II, such processes might include making decisions, managing a meeting, processing insurance claims, or any other activities we undertake in pursuit of our mission. Hopefully, in each of these group processes each team member has a clear, specific role based on their function, skills, and expertise. In many business settings, however, such processes are often ill-defined or missing entirely. High performance teams identify, map, and then master their key team processes. They constantly evaluate the effectiveness of key processes, asking: How are we doing? What are we learning? How can we do it better?

SOLID RELATIONSHIPS

One of the biggest misperceptions I find in the world of teams and teamwork is the belief that to work and communicate effectively, team members must be close comrades. Not true. In fact, the diversity of skill, experience, and knowledge needed effectively and creatively to divide the task almost precludes high levels of friendship, which is most often based on common interests.

Speaking of diversity, we find that the more different a team is, the smarter it can be. A team whose members look at the world through the different lenses of function, gender, ethnicity, personality, experience, and perspective has a decided advantage over a more homogenous group. The diverse group will be able to surround problems, decisions, and other team issues with a brighter collective IQ. They will see more solutions and more creative solutions if they can channel their differences into synergy rather than strife.

Because diversity provides plenty of opportunity for discord, conflict, and communication breakdowns, especially among teams that must accomplish their tasks in complex, high velocity, dynamic environments, their differences must be offset by trust, acceptance, respect, courtesy, and a liberal dose of understanding.

EXCELLENT COMMUNICATION

Communication is the very means of cooperation. One of the primary motives for companies to implement teams is that team-based organizations are more responsive and move faster. A team, or the organization in which it resides, cannot move faster than it communicates. Fast, clear, accurate communication is a hallmark of high levels of team performance. Effective teams have mastered the art of straight talk; there is little wasted motion from misunderstanding and confusion. Ideas move like quicksilver. The team understands that effective communication is key to thinking collectively and finding synergy in team solutions. As a result they approach communication with a determined intentionality. They talk about it a lot and put a lot of effort into keeping it good and getting better.

When it comes to teams, these six characteristics are the lightning in the bottle. If a team gets these few things right, they will realize exceptional results. By effectively applying the principles and practices I will explain in the next several chapters, teams will avoid many of the pitfalls and problems that derail many team initiatives.

However, the major focus of this book will be on ensuring that you, the team leader, have a clear grasp on the qualities that describe a high performance team. When I was a young U.S. Army finance officer serving in Europe in the late 1960's, the Army sent me to a course where I would learn how to recognize counterfeit currency. America has some of its biggest problems with counterfeit currency overseas because foreign nationals have a strong desire for U.S. dollars and are so unfamiliar with them. I went to the course anxious to see actual counterfeit money; but I was sorely disappointed when we went through almost the entire day without a peek at the stuff. We spent the day studying authentic U.S. currency, learning about the paper quality, the engraving, ink, and printing. Late in the afternoon, one of my classmates could contain his frustration no longer. "How will we ever be able to recognize counterfeit money if we never see any?" he asked. The instructor explained that the very best way to be able to recognize a fake is to be intimately familiar with the "real McCoy." And that's my strategy in this book as well. My objective is to introduce you to the real McCoy when it comes to building high performance teams.

In the next six chapters we will look under the hood of a team. Each chapter will address a specific team characteristic in detail. We will explore what each characteristic brings to team performance, and we will also provide practical exercises that will help you make this quality an integral part of your own team experience.

THE BOTTOM LINE

High performance teams have six characteristics that allow them to consistently achieve exceptional levels of results:

- Common Purpose
- Crystal Clear Roles
- Accepted Leadership
- Effective Processes
- Solid Relationships
- Excellent Communication

MESSAGE TO TEAM LEADERS

If these few characteristics are critical to team success, you, the team leader, are critical to these characteristics.

- The team leader helps the team clarify the task and align behind it.

- The team leader has the power to call the time out needed to allow the team members to clarify roles and the authority to resolve conflict when they can't agree about who does what.

- The team leader must earn the acceptance of team members. The only boss of a team is the task; if you want your team members to serve the task, you must learn how to serve them. Volunteers, and that's what every team member is, will only respond to leaders they accept.

- High performance teams have high performance processes. Again, it is generally the team leader who can create the time and space for the team to identify and design its processes as well as evaluate its effectiveness on a regular basis.

- Team leaders model the qualities of effective team relationships and create opportunities for the team to develop the needed levels of trust, respect, and acceptance.

- Team leaders must create an environment that fosters open, clear, accurate communication—communication that clears the way for exceptional levels of creativity and that allows the team to efficiently implement its processes and move quickly against problems and decisions.

CHAPTER FOUR

Clear, Common Purpose

I t was only 41 minutes from the time of the explosion until impact in Sioux City for United Flight 232. During these few minutes, the clarity, focus, and unity of purpose was unquestioned: find out what's wrong, figure out how to fly the plane, and get the plane and its 296 passengers safely on the ground. The scope of the crisis, the lack of time, and the consequences of failure fostered unusual levels of motivation, eliminating any possibility of wasted motion or idle chatter. Every thought, action, and interaction was devoted to the accomplishment of that purpose. History is clear that, in most endeavors, success is a product of uncompromising attention to purpose. The team of Flight 232 could certainly be described along those lines.

Clearly, the circumstances of Flight 232 were unique. No organization would want to pay the price needed to achieve that level of focus. However, if the typical business team could achieve just a small portion of the unity of purpose held by Captain Haynes and his team, they would move a long way toward exceptional performance.

THE TASK FORCE WITHOUT A TASK

Too many team leaders are complacent about a foggy, uninspiring, ill-defined purpose. They wrongly assume that because the purpose is

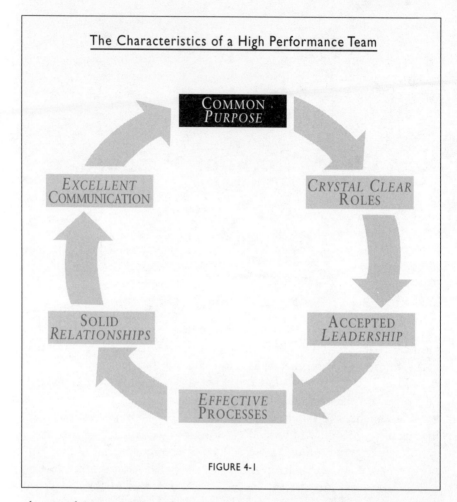

The Characteristics of a High Performance Team

COMMON PURPOSE

CRYSTAL CLEAR ROLES

EXCELLENT COMMUNICATION

ACCEPTED LEADERSHIP

SOLID RELATIONSHIPS

EFFECTIVE PROCESSES

FIGURE 4-1

clear and important to them, it must appear that way to their team members as well.

We recently consulted with a project development team in the pharmaceutical industry that was victim to just such thinking. The team had been in existence for nearly ten years with the mandate to develop and bring to market a certain type of medication. The current team did not consist of the original members, who had long since moved on. This team was merely the latest set of members in a long line of rotating team members and leaders who had passed through this team over the years. However, with team membership came the stigma that "they" hadn't been able to deliver for nearly ten years. It is probably clear that there weren't many volunteers looking for assignment to this team.

For years, management and a series of team leaders had lived with a vague, ill-defined mission statement and little sense of urgency. In one recent meeting with the new team leader, the president of the firm asked in frustration, "What's it going to take for this team to bring a product to market?" To him, the task was clear but, in spite of its importance, no one had ever drawn a line in the sand as to when the product needed to be on the shelf. Because of the complexity of the task, there had always been a hesitancy to spell out specific dates or even product formulation. Other important but more urgent tasks stole the time and energy of team members.

A few months later, we facilitated a session with the team to discuss their purpose. After several hours of intense discussion, the team had successfully created a sense of edge and urgency about their purpose that had not been evident before. They got clear about time frames and took the risk of being explicit about what they were attempting to accomplish. Success measures were spelled out, and milestones were identified. It's ironic that the fear of failure, which motivated their predecessors to be very general and murky in defining their mission, ultimately caused their failure. This team realized that the tensions and stimulation of a clear purpose would be motivational and foster the energy and focus needed to succeed.

Later when they reviewed this with their management sponsors, the level of excitement continued to grow. The project began to take on a life and energy of its own. The pace quickened as the project took on a higher priority for the time, attention, and resources of the team members as well as the firm.

The basic intent of the project had not changed. However, the verbal underbrush in the form of vague meaning, cliches, and jargon had been cleared away. The team boldly decided to eliminate any hiding places for nonperformance and to make the project benefits and their commitments very clear. The risks went up—what if they were wrong or didn't deliver on their promises? But with the risks came higher returns as well. They decided the risk was well worth it.

TASKS AND TEAMS

Many organizations seem confused about the difference between teamwork and teams. Teamwork is an organizational philosophy or value system, whereas teams are specific and discrete organizational units. Often companies attempted to form team structures merely because they feel there is intrinsic merit in teams, or because it seemed like the thing to do in the 1990's. Such efforts are doomed to failure.

The confusion stems from seeing teams as the *end* versus the *means* to the end. Teams are a *means* of achieving goals too big to reach through that of individual efforts. Although I strongly advocate that every company do whatever is necessary to engender a spirit of teamwork and cooperation throughout the organization, the decision to form teams should be made in response to particular objectives and strategies for which teams represent the most appropriate organizational response.

A team is defined by its task or purpose.[1] The purpose of every team is to accomplish an objective and to do so at exceptional levels of performance. It is a clear task that gives birth to a team in the first place. Like the grain of sand in a Japanese pearl oyster, the task of the team is the critical ingredient around which the team will form. Regardless of whether the life of the team is temporary or long lasting, its purpose is the motivation for its existence. Because high performance teams are invariably mission-directed, ultimately team effectiveness must be judged by the results.

ALIGNMENT TAPS THE POWER OF PURPOSE

A clear, common, compelling task that is important to the individual team members is the single biggest factor in team success. All the team workshops in the world pale to insignificance in comparison to a clear and challenging task or goal.

It is the task or purpose of the team that provides the reason for cooperation. One of the biggest reasons for team failure is an inadequate answer to the question: "Why should we?" The correct answer to this question is to achieve more than any of us could do alone. The outcome is what each team member wants but can't achieve on his or her own. To get the job done, we must *team up*.

The diversity of specialties within the modern team makes unity of purpose critical. Purpose not only *calls* the team together but, like glue, *holds* the team together during the inevitable turbulence the team will experience on its journey. Without such a bond, the centrifugal force of individual interests would pull the team apart. Ill-defined team purpose sows the seeds of confusion and conflict. Team members assigned from different functions or departments become confused between their departmental priorities and those of the team.

I recall one instance in which a firm was forming cross-functional teams, and as one assigned team member was getting his instructions from his department manager he was told, *"Don't forget which side your bread is buttered on."* Obviously, this department head wasn't clear about the team purpose or its benefits for either the firm or his individual department. With that kind of send-off, what are the odds that this team member will define team success in terms of the values and interests of his department rather than those of the team?

It takes more than a well-crafted purpose statement to generate the levels of commitment required for high performance teamwork. Individual team members must truly want to achieve that goal, and this introduces the concept of alignment into the equation.

Alignment is the link between the individual team member's goals and the team purpose. Individual team members agree that the task of the team is important. It is important because it *lines up* with their individual goals and interests. They want the team to succeed because if it

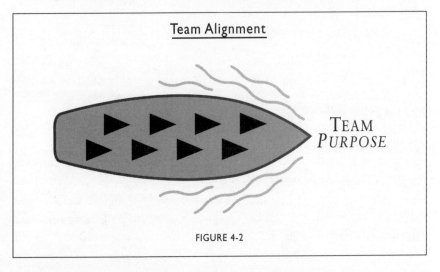

Team Alignment

TEAM
PURPOSE

FIGURE 4-2

succeeds, they succeed. When a team is in alignment every member is highly committed to the team purpose. They are in the same boat, heading in the same direction, pulling together. Alignment provides the focus that unleashes the potential power of the team. An old Ethiopian proverb observes that when the spiderwebs unite, they can tie up a lion. When team members are in alignment, they are unified in their intentions. And because they are pulling together in the same direction, there is less wasted energy (Figure 4-2). The efforts of one combine and build on the efforts of another and the output often exceeds the sum of the individual inputs. Without alignment around the team purpose, synergy becomes impossible.

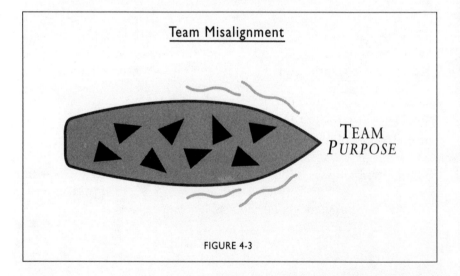

Team Misalignment

TEAM
PURPOSE

FIGURE 4-3

In Figure 4-3 we find a team out of alignment. Instead of pulling together, some members are putting their creative energies and efforts behind a different direction or strategy. If such misalignment is allowed to continue, it's unlikely that the team will accomplish its purpose (Figure 4-4). Although they are in the same boat, everyone is doing "his or her own thing."

Such a situation is more common than you might think. On many teams we find a lot of activity but little accomplishment because team members are at cross-purposes, wasting energy by pulling against one another rather than together. It's not long before these tired, frustrated

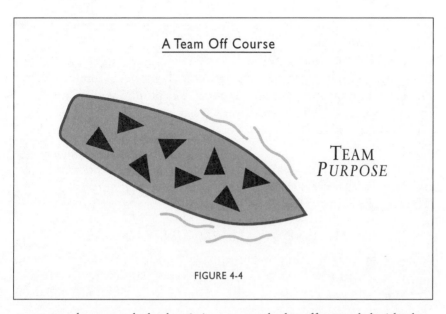

A Team Off Course

TEAM
PURPOSE

FIGURE 4-4

team members conclude that it is not worth the effort and decide they would rather do the job alone.

Alignment is about direction and destination. I grew up in Seattle, a city surrounded by the waters of Puget Sound. The waterfront has a large central ferry pier from which you can catch ferries to several destinations among the surrounding islands and peninsulas. Clearly, you would expect everyone on a specific ferry to be "aligned" in their desire to get to a specific place. However, I can remember once getting to the pier late and, in my rush to catch the boat, I didn't listen as attentively as I should have to which boat number was going to my destination. It was only minutes into the journey when I realized that I was on the wrong boat. This mistake would cause me to miss an important lunch meeting; and the closer we got to the wrong place, the higher my frustration and blood pressure levels rose. I wanted to shout to the crew to turn the boat around.

As I looked around me, my fellow passengers seemed so content as they enjoyed the journey and the beautiful scenery. My panic and preoccupation didn't allow me much enjoyment at all. I suspect this is what many team members feel when they are on a team but not aligned with its purpose—frustration, anger, apathy, and preoccupation. Certainly none of these emotions will provide the motivation and commitment of team members to volunteer their best efforts to help the team get to its intended destination.

Why would anyone get on a boat that's not going to his or her destination? As I demonstrated on that ferry dock, people naïvely climb on board teams with unclear or undefined purposes (either because they just aren't listening carefully, or because they are "assigned" by a higher authority), then discover that the team is not going where they thought it was.

Invariably, a lack of alignment is discovered in the middle of the bay, often when the seas turn stormy. The time to gain alignment is at the dock, not in the middle of a storm!

THE ESSENTIALS FOR ALIGNMENT

Creating alignment is one of the most important roles of leadership. It often falls to the team leader to ensure the purpose of the team is defined, clear, and communicated. He or she must make sure the team mission meets five criteria:

1. *Clear* (I see it). The benefits of team effort must be clear and understandable to every team member. Countless team leaders have shared their frustrations with me about the apparent indifference of team members to the benefits of higher levels of cooperation. *"Don't they understand that if they cooperated we could . . . ?"* The problem is that often they don't understand. Don't assume that the benefits are as clear to others as they are to you. Don't gloss over the pragmatic elements of the team purpose and related goals with eloquent generalities.

2. *Relevant* (I want it). The end results to be achieved by the team must be closely tied not only to the purpose of the overall organization but also to the needs, interests, and goals of the individual members. The degree to which the mission of the team is desirable and wanted by the members will greatly influence the energy and effort they employ to attain it. In this respect, team purpose is a motivational force, a source of power that fuels the energy needs of the team.

3. *Significant* (It's worth it). The objectives of the team must not only be relevant, but also of sufficient magnitude to make it worth the effort. Teamwork is *hard* work (TeamWORK!) and team members

won't pour out their energies for small ends. They must see the objective as "exceptional."

The results of team effort must be significant not only to individual team members, but also to the parent organization. Because teams are an expensive structure to support, the sponsoring organization must realize a meaningful return on investment.

4. *Achievable* (I believe it). Individual team members, as well as the team as a whole, must really believe that this task or mission is achievable. If it is perceived as unrealistic or unattainable, they will not invest the emotional energy needed to achieve exceptional results. This is where the art and tension of goal-setting reside. I've already made the point that teams need to go after big goals and exceptional results. However, it's important not to go to the extreme. Exceptional does not mean exaggerated or excessive. In a team environment, unbelievable goals sometimes go unchallenged. Not wanting to rock the boat or appear lacking in commitment, an unbelieving team member might quietly go along with a goal he or she does not feel the team can achieve; however, it's unlikely this team member will throw his or her body over the cliff for this goal.

We also need to take the specific team into account when setting the goals. A new or young team won't achieve the level of performance of a more mature team that's been working together for a while. In fact, a new team may even accomplish less than the sum of their individual efforts as they work through some of the basic skills of cooperation. The first few attempts at accomplishing a complex task in an interdependent setting can be awkward and cumbersome. Effective teamwork takes time and practice. The size of the goals must reflect the skill of the team, walking that fine line between exceptional and believable.

5. *Urgent* (I want it, . . . now!). When we share the sense of urgency of Flight 232, team leaders are quick to respond that they had unfair advantage. Crisis is a tough way to press urgency into the team task. I agree. But the point remains: a sense of urgency and timeliness is an important ingredient in achieving the alignment and motivation needed to drive high performance teamWORK. Effective leaders understand this and invest effort and creativity into identifying and communicating the benefits of *now* versus *later*. Often it's not the

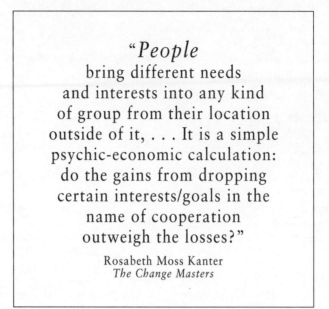

> ## "*People*
> bring different needs
> and interests into any kind
> of group from their location
> outside of it, . . . It is a simple
> psychic-economic calculation:
> do the gains from dropping
> certain interests/goals in the
> name of cooperation
> outweigh the losses?"
>
> Rosabeth Moss Kanter
> *The Change Masters*

circumstances they change, but rather the "optics" by which team members see the goal. You won't have the urgency that confronted Captain Haynes, but every bit of time value you can attach to the team goal will help. On a high performance team urgency translates into energy. It pushes individuals beyond themselves.

Alignment is achieved one person at a time. It cannot be attained through mandate or a passionate plea from the podium. Each team member must work through his or her issues of alignment that motivate their willingness to cooperate. Revisiting the earlier metaphor of the boat, even though we are all heading in the same direction, we can appreciate that each member has his or her own reasons for wanting to go there. Growth, recognition, challenge, compensation, and achievement might be a few typical reasons. As each team member considers joining the crew, he invariably weighs the costs and benefits. An alert team leader ensures that the benefits are not only clear, but are "positioned" in a manner that is most relevant and meaningful to each individual team member.

TURNING PRINCIPLE INTO PRACTICE— HOW TO ACHIEVE ALIGNMENT

The above sounds so straightforward and logical—make the team's mission statement clear, relevant, significant, believable, and urgent to each team member. However, most experienced leaders know that actually doing this is much harder than it sounds. Over the years we have discovered a few practical steps team leaders can take to increase the odds of gaining team member ownership of the team mission. When team members have the opportunity to put their fingerprints on the mission statement, even if it involves only minor changes to the initial mission (if there is one), the level of ownership goes up dramatically.

New Teams or First-Time Mission Statements. With new teams or teams that have never developed a formal written purpose statement (e.g., management teams), the following process has proven effective:

Team Purpose Statements

Below are several purpose statements that illustrate the qualities of good team statements.

•

Develop and implement a strategy to increase gross margins on our copper line of products by 2 percent no later than 6/30 of this next fiscal year.

•

Design a product development process that will reduce idea time to market from 28 to 9 months with no erosion of current quality standards.

•

Design and implement a team-based compensation strategy for the Customer Business Teams by 9/30.

FIGURE 4-5

---

1. Schedule several (2-3) hours for uninterrupted discussion.

2. Explain the role and components of the team mission, that is, a short statement (1-3 sentences) that explains why the group is in existence and generally identifies the team's stakeholders, the product, outcome, or service the team will provide, and the anticipated benefits of this outcome to the stakeholders.

3. Using a flip chart or overhead projector, capture the bullet points or descriptive phrases used by team members when discussing the various mission components. Do not attempt to wordsmith, but rather capture the main thoughts as you would in any brainstorming session.

4. If time allows, break the team down into several subgroups of two to four members, and let each group take a first pass at integrating the above phrases and ideas into an integrated mission statement.

5. Have each group present their draft and get feedback from the others, particularly ideas or phrasing they feel really capture the essence of the team's mission. If time and energy allow, attempt to integrate the best ideas from each group into a single draft. It's important to note that this will most likely still be rough from a grammatical perspective (you will wordsmith it later), but it will be together enough for the team to evaluate it against design criteria.

Most team mission statements start with "outcome verbs" like *provide, achieve, implement, design, complete, decide, demonstrate, and develop.* Effective team mission statements are short—three or four short sentences at most. They clearly spell out what needs to be done and what it will look like when it's finished. Although we typically use the words *mission* or *purpose* to describe the task of a team, as we can see in Figure 4-5, the architecture of such a statement meets all of the criteria we typically ascribe to well-written goals—specific, measurable, attainable, realistic, and time based.

It takes time and plenty of revisions to find the wording and tone that captures the qualities I've described above. If the mission statement is wrong, everything that follows will be wrong too.

6. Give the team the opportunity to evaluate and discuss the mission statement using the criteria we described above. You may want to provide an evaluation form like the following:

Evaluation of Our Mission Statement

	VERY LOW	LOW	AVERAGE	HIGH	VERY HIGH
CLEAR — *Characterized by single-minded direction*	☐	☐	☐	☐	☐
RELEVANT — *Characterized by deep-seated desire*	☐	☐	☐	☐	☐
SIGNIFICANT — *The results to the company if achieved as well as the benefits to me are such that the possibility of success creates enthusiasm, initiative, and energy*	☐	☐	☐	☐	☐
BELIEVABLE — *I believe this task/goal is achievable and will pursue it with bulldog tenacity*	☐	☐	☐	☐	☐
URGENT — *There is a clear time-value attached to the achievement of this mission*	☐	☐	☐	☐	☐
OVERALL MOTIVATION — *Inspires my dedication and commitment*	☐	☐	☐	☐	☐

FIGURE 4-6

How Do We Unaverage This? This past year we worked with the top management team of a consumer products company. The team members decided that they needed to develop a team mission as it related to a new long-term strategic initiative they were leading. After some discussion and following the process described above, they sat back and examined their work. I then asked them to evaluate their new mission, using the six criteria shown in Figure 4-6. After we tabulated the scores from the individual team members, I asked them what they thought. One team member, noting that the rating was in the middle or average observed, "It seems very average to me and not very motivational."

I asked them what changes would have to be made in the statement to make it "unaverage," and they began the discussion anew. Within thirty minutes they had cut out some of the verbal underbrush, tightened their wording, and were expressing an obvious excitement over the task they were now describing. Within two months the mission statement had spread throughout the organization and had become the cornerstone for the new strategy.

Established Teams with Developed or Assigned Mission Statements. For teams that have previously developed a team mission statement, you would move directly to the evaluation and discussion. We often find that when teams have time to discuss, clarify, and even fine-tune the mission statement, the level of team alignment increases tremendously.

Recently, we spent several days working with the global strategy team of a large, international over-the-counter pharmaceutical products company. Although the team had been in existence for several months, this was the first time the entire group had come together. The team leader is one of the brightest young leaders with whom I have worked. The company obviously thought so as well when they made her the youngest vice president in the company. Our objective over the two-day session was to work through a long list of team issues. However, we ran aground on the first topic: team purpose. It was clear that this was a topic of intense interest to the team members. They wanted to explore every nook and cranny, discuss every word and nuance.

The team leader was fit to be tied. In large measure, the team mission had been part of the original charter given by top management when the team was first formed. She had worked hard to clarify and negotiate various elements of the mission before the team was even formed. In her mind, the mission was crystal clear. It was beyond her comprehension that they could "waste" this much time on this issue. Didn't they understand they had eight more issues to resolve? By the end of the day, the team agreed they had wrestled the mission statement into submission. Although the team leader was relieved that, in spite of so much energetic discussion, they had changed only a few words, she was stressed that they were so far behind in their agenda. However, the next day she grasped one of the most important lessons a team leader can master. The team arrived with a tremendous amount of energy and enthusiasm. They charged through the rest of the agenda with a ferocity that surprised all of us. As we debriefed with the team leader after the session (which had finished almost two hours early!), it was clear that she was beginning to realize the power of alignment and the importance of not moving on until it was achieved.

When the mission is mandated from above. Teams tend to believe that when the team purpose is mandated from above or from outside the team, the team has little input into its scope and how it's framed. As a result, members don't always take ownership of the purpose. My experience is that, in many of these situations, teams generally have a fair amount of latitude to deepen and enrich their purposes. As we have seen in the case described above, although the team must meet the intentions and objectives of its larger organization, they can often recast it into their own terms.

DEALING WITH UNALIGNED TEAM MEMBERS

When team leaders take the time to work through the issues of team purpose, most often people of like minds will "join" the team (i.e., volunteer commitment, creativity, and energy). Those who are not will have to find the boat that's going to their destination. This is a critical point, because too often in a team setting we have people who are in the boat but not on the team. They are not going to pull their oar with a lot of energy when they realize that the team goal is not their goal.

Like many team concepts, alignment is a relative concept. As we see in Figure 4-6, one team member is a little out of alignment (#2); others are way off. Which ones are going to hurt the team the most? Often our first reaction is to name those who are most out of alignment (#4 or #7), but my experience doesn't support this observation. Those who are very much out of line with the objectives of the team tend to be outspoken about their displeasure. Their lack of alignment is clear to everyone.

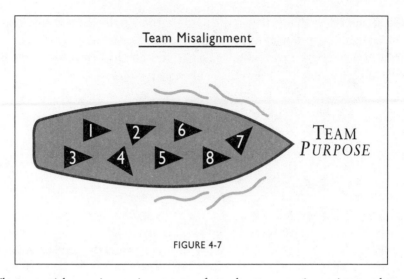

Team Misalignment

TEAM
PURPOSE

FIGURE 4-7

They are either going to jump out of our boat, or we're going to throw them out. It's the individuals who are just a little off in alignment (#2) who tend to blunt the effectiveness of the team. Their lack of alignment is hard to discern, for them as well as the other team members. In this case, the signals aren't strong enough to point to the problem—just a lot of little things. Discussions get drawn out; meetings run longer; arguments are more heated; and responsiveness is slower and less crisp. The cause of degradation of performance is difficult to determine. The team assumes it just needs a little more time, training, or effort.

What do you do with a #2? When we talk about someone who is out of alignment, it's important that we distinguish between those who are sincerely wrestling with an issue and those who are firmly committed to another direction. In the case of the former, it is important that the team and particularly the team leader make sure the unaligned team member is heard and that he, in turn, hears the team's rationale as well. It is possible that this team member has an insight that will influence the team's strategy, and you don't want to miss their input. Also, it's important that team members feel they have been listened to and understood. We don't want to railroad people into compliance and a false appearance of alignment because the team doesn't tolerate contrary opinions. We are looking for creativity and commitment, not compliance; and as we'll see in a later chapter, the collective IQ is not found in "groupthink."

On the other hand, if it is clear that people have been truly heard and understood and a team member still feels that he or she can't enthusiastically support the mission, then the team leader must move to replace him or her.

ALIGNMENT IS A PREREQUISITE FOR EMPOWERMENT

Alignment is not only the source of team *power,* but it is also a prerequisite for team *empowerment.* In today's business environment

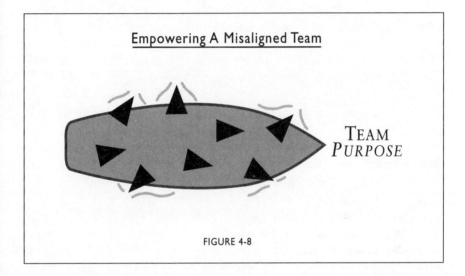

Empowering A Misaligned Team

TEAM
PURPOSE

FIGURE 4-8

teams and empowerment go hand in hand. As shown in Figure 4-8, empowering individuals when there is a low level of alignment can create havoc and will likely tear the team apart.[2] When top management is confident that the team and its individual members are aligned with organizational objectives and strategies, they will be much more amenable to empowering the team to set its own agenda for accomplishing its task.

A clear purpose brings additional benefits to the team as well. It serves as a gyroscope, providing stability and allowing the team to maintain its footing and sense of direction in turbulent, fast-changing environments. It provides the boundary lines in which the team can set clear, realistic, but exceptional goals. It enables the team to monitor and evaluate progress.

MUSHY MISSIONS IN THE CORNER OFFICE

Developing a clear, compelling purpose comes easier to some teams than others. Katzenbach and Smith write about three different types of teams: teams that recommend things, teams that make or do things, and teams that run or manage things.[3] Developing a specific purpose comes easier for the first two types of teams, for their work generally has somewhat tangible results and clear end dates. However, teams that run things have a challenge in the area of specificity, for their work never ends. For example, our experience is that top management teams tend to embrace the organizational mission for their specific team task. Such a mission, critical for decision making and navigation at the enterprise level, doesn't generally provide the urgency and edge that would motivate an individual team. Our most difficult creative challenge in working with top management teams is to convince them to identify and attack a clear, important goal that has a sense of immediacy embedded in it. We strongly believe that the best way to build any team, including those at the top, is to work with them as they chase a clear, common, and important goal. This goal not only provides the relevancy to team development initiatives, it becomes the measure of team effectiveness as well.

Recently, I worked with the leadership team of a large broker-dealer that sold a broad array of financial products through independent salespeople. We spent several hours discussing possible goals or tasks that would require a high level of teamwork between all members of the team (the CEO and vice presidents) and which were important to the success of the firm. They were under tremendous competitive pressure from other broker-dealers who wanted to recruit the sales force of my client. As a result of the competitive structure of the industry, a broker-dealer recruited and retained a sales force by offering higher commissions. The result was that margins were razor thin. This team decided that their team task for the coming year would be to review the primary processes throughout the firm with the objective of streamlining them and finding cost savings that would increase their margins from 1.7 percent to nearly 4 percent. The energy level of the team was perceptively higher as the team left the room, and they hadn't even begun!

THE BOTTOM LINE

I can summarize the key idea in this chapter in four words: *no task, no team.* So often we misconstrue the concept of teams, stressing the need of good interpersonal relationships. While such relationships are an important ingredient of effective teams, it is the wrong emphasis. *The most critical component in building a high performance team is a clear, common, compelling task.* The goal of a high performance team is not merely to get *along,* but rather to get *aligned,* and, through that, to get results!

The power of teamwork flows out of alignment between the interests of individual team members and the mission of the team. To achieve such alignment, team members must see the team task as:

- Clear—*I see it.* Every team member must have a crystal clear understanding of the team task. Without such understanding the needed alignment cannot be achieved. Don't assume such understanding exists. Both the team members and team leader should keep talking until the light goes on.

- Relevant—*I want it.* The degree to which the mission of the team is desirable and wanted by the members of the team will greatly influence the energy, creativity, and effort they exert to achieve it.

- Significant—*It's worth it.* Team objectives must be of sufficient magnitude to make it worth the effort.

- Urgent—*I want it, . . . now!* There is a clear time-value attached to the achievement of this mission.

- Achievable—*I believe it.* The team must really believe this task is achievable. This is where the art of goal-setting resides. On one hand, the goal must be big enough to motivate the needed effort; on the other, it must be realistically achievable.

MESSAGE TO TEAM LEADERS

Defining direction is a key role for leaders in any setting. John Kotter explains that effective leaders master three key skills:[4]

- *Establish direction.*

- *Align people.* Communicate the direction to those whose cooperation is needed so that they understand the vision and are committed to its achievement.

- *Inspire.* Keep people moving in the right direction despite the inevitable barriers.

No less is required from a team leader. The team task is the cornerstone on which the team will be built. Get this wrong, and the whole structure will forever be at risk. Clarifying the task and gaining alignment of each team member requires communication collectively and individually. Remember that alignment is an individual issue. It's achieved one person at a time.

Too many team leaders make the mistake of thinking they can lead their team from the podium, that they can get their team heading in the same direction with an inspirational message and some good graphics. The team leader must ensure that every team member understands on an *individual* basis what the team is attempting to accomplish, why this is important to the organization, why they are important to achieving the goal, and why it is important to them as an individual. If you are successful, everyone *will be* going in the same direction, even if for different individual reasons.

One last point. Don't push your boat away from the dock until you have alignment. Gaining alignment is not something you want to be doing in the middle of the inevitable storm.

CHAPTER FIVE

Crystal Clear Roles

N o one in the cockpit of United Flight 232 was confused about his role. In the left seat was Al Haynes, captain, team leader, and primary pilot. Bill Records, in the right seat, was first officer and co-pilot. Second officer Dudley Dvorak, in the aft seat, served as flight engineer, monitoring various panels and assisting in communication. Later, Denny Fitch, after coming forward from first class to assist, was assigned to help work the throttles. At the time of the incident, Records was flying the plane, which was on autopilot at the time. Al Haynes was drinking a cup of coffee and discussing a change in direction just assigned by air traffic control that would delay their arrival in Chicago. As soon as they felt the explosion, Records grabbed the steering column. When there's a problem, standard operating procedures call for one person to fly the plane while the other two work on solving it. Captain Haynes let Records continue flying, because from his seat he, unlike the co-pilot, can see the instrument panel of the flight engineer (Dvorak) and could double-check everything.

Crystal clear roles characterize high performance teams. Every team member is clear about his or her particular role as well as those of the other team members. While the concept of roles—how we design and divide the task—is compellingly logical, many organizations find it very challenging to implement in practice. Role issues are invariably one of

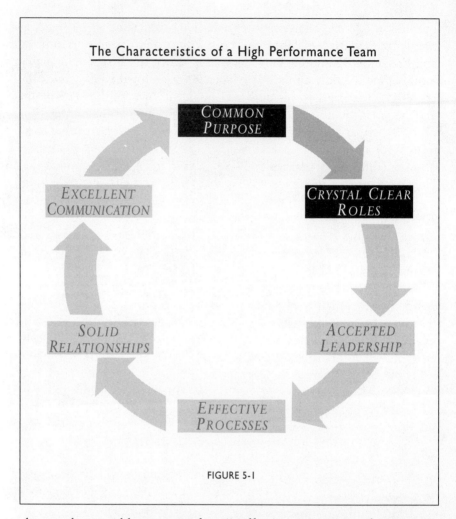

The Characteristics of a High Performance Team

COMMON PURPOSE

CRYSTAL CLEAR ROLES

EXCELLENT COMMUNICATION

ACCEPTED LEADERSHIP

SOLID RELATIONSHIPS

EFFECTIVE PROCESSES

FIGURE 5-1

the top three problems teams face (ineffective processes and communication represent the other two major team problems). Achieving role clarity is challenged both by old paradigms and new business practices.

"ONCE A GOOD IDEA, ALWAYS A GOOD IDEA," IS A BAD IDEA

In March 1776 Adam Smith, in his book *The Wealth of Nations*, introduced the concept of division of labor to the Western world. Smith was the Tom Peters of his day, traveling the countryside, observing how business was done, analyzing the underlying principles, and spreading the word.[1] Division of labor had been a part of work in one form or another since Og and his brothers chased down the first woolly mammoth. Some would wait in hiding, spears poised for the kill, while others chased the beast to his destruction. But it was Smith's description and explanation of its underlying principles that caught the imagination of 18th century business people. Many historians believe his observations were a key factor in the spread of the Industrial Revolution.

In one illustration, Smith used the process for making straight pins. He explained that making a pin involved approximately 18 steps. The best anyone not highly trained in the process could hope to make was 20 straight pins a day and "perhaps not one." By breaking the task down into simple parts, ten untrained men could make about 48,000 pins a day, an increase in productivity of 240 times over the efforts of an individual worker![2]

In the early 1900's, Frederick Taylor, the father of scientific management, turned many of Smith's insights into practice, demonstrating that many jobs could be broken down into their smallest components, analyzed, and designed so that the workers' efforts would be extremely efficient.[3] Henry Ford proved to be a worthy disciple, applying Taylor's principles to production lines for his Model T, dividing the original 18 operations needed to produce a car into 7,882 simple, discrete tasks.[4]

This approach to work made good sense in Taylor's time. Low educational levels and lack of a common language among immigrant workers made the idea of breaking a task down to its most basic components an effective way to increase productivity. However, this strategy introduced other changes as well. The interdependency introduced by divided tasks created the need for coordination of various parts of a job, and thus the managerial role began to change significantly. Management was charged with the responsibility to coordinate, plan, and make decisions. As organizations grew in size and complexity, the management structure needed to coordinate them grew as well. The design of management structures was governed by principles that defined clear *lines of authority* and *chains of command, channels of communication,* and *spans of control.* These principles, fervently applied, led to our modern hierarchy.

But, like so many good ideas, the fit between strategy, structure, and the situation degenerated over time. The notion that a good idea is always a good idea is a bad idea. Breaking the task down into its smallest parts (horizontal division of labor) led to increased functional specialization. Over time these functions developed their own processes, terminology, and ways of doing things. Invisible but very real walls began to develop between functions and then thickened, becoming "functional chimneys" or silos. Communication and coordination between one department and another, blocked by these thick walls, was forced up the vertical chain of command, which felt compelled to check and control everything, bringing decision making to a near halt. Key processes transcending several departments were chopped into small segments—segments that made perfect sense to an individual department but that were totally illogical for the organization as a whole. As a result, organizations became slow, stiff, unresponsive, and unbelievably inefficient.

The principles designed for a workforce and stable business environment of a hundred years ago have proven woefully inadequate for today's unstable, changing world. Intense competition and demanding customers put a premium on speed, flexibility, and responsiveness. The challenge today is to rethink the underlying principles of organization and adopt ones more in keeping with the demands of our contemporary work environment. In many respects, that's what reengineering is all about. Michael Hammer notes: "Companies that reengineer are, in effect, putting back together the work that Adam Smith and Henry Ford broke into tiny pieces so many years ago."[5] The principles of reengineering stress ideas such as:

- organizing around processes rather than functions,
- using teams as basic organizational building blocks,
- tapping into the power of technology,
- pushing decision making to the lowest level, and
- reducing checks and controls.

Change comes hard, because we find nothing more traditional than traditions. We put so much effort into designing and building these hierarchies that we are tremendously resistant to rethinking them in spite of the pressure to do so.

It's not the concept of hierarchies that's wrong but rather the implementation of the concept. Too many levels, too much complexity, too many rules, excessive bureaucracy, and narrowly focused control are but a few of the evils attributed to the hierarchical organizational forms of the corporate community. Such design issues can be remedied. What are the needed number of levels, given the organizational mission and strategy? What is the role for each level? What value does each level bring to the customers? What is the role of management? What is the best way to distribute authority? What is the best way to maintain appropriate levels of accountability? All of these questions and others, if answered properly, would lead to a healthier hierarchy, but a hierarchy just the same. In fact, there is no such thing as a non-hierarchical organization. Virtually any organization can be described as a series of interlocking work groups (potential teams) through which the work of the organization gets done (Figure 5-2).

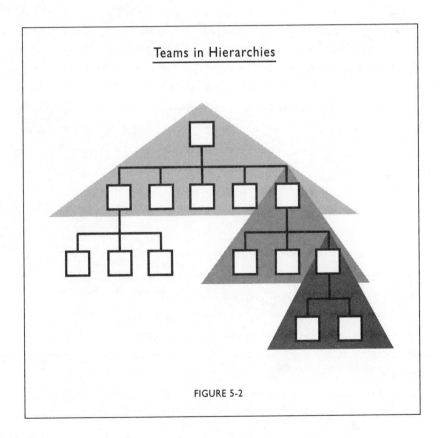

Teams in Hierarchies

FIGURE 5-2

TEAMWORK IS THE HORIZONTAL EXPRESSION OF A VERTICAL ORGANIZATION

All organizations have both a vertical (functional) and a horizontal (across functions) dimension. In most instances it is the vertical dimension that is accountable for results and the horizontal dimension that produces results (Figure 5-3). These two dimensions make up the warp and woof of the organization. The difference between the "old" hierarchy and the new one is that the old version stressed the vertical dimension and the new one stresses the horizontal. The vertical dimension of structure shows how we are organized; the horizontal dimension is about how we work together to produce results.

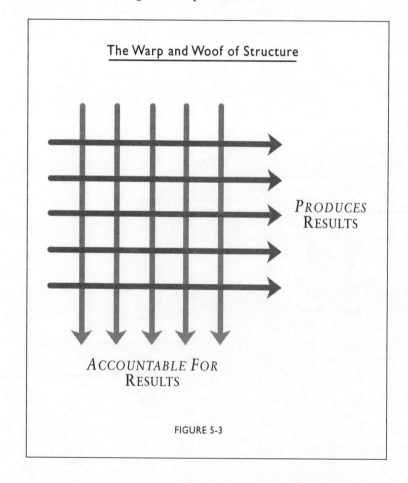

The Warp and Woof of Structure

PRODUCES RESULTS

ACCOUNTABLE FOR RESULTS

FIGURE 5-3

I believe that teams are the basic building blocks of a well-designed organization. This means that teams *do* work within hierarchies. The types of teams you develop depend on your organization structure and the work goals or mission of each team. Many types of teams are possible in an organizational setting—functional teams, cross-functional teams, temporary task forces, process teams, integrating teams, and customer teams, just to name a few. Any of these teams can bring value to the appropriate task within a healthy hierarchy.

A second dimension of the new ways of work is that we must often manage membership on multiple teams. It's not atypical for an employee to spend more time working with groups outside of his or her functional assignment than within it. Several years ago we tracked the time of one mid-level accounting manager in a client organization only to find that he was actively engaged with seven teams outside of the accounting unit for which he was responsible. Some of these teams were permanent, like a customer business team that was assigned to service two of the firm's largest clients; others were temporary like the Compensation Review Task Force that would disband after it made its recommendations to division leadership.

On many of these teams, even the temporary ones, some members were fully dedicated, having 100 percent of their time assigned to the service of that team. Other members, like this accounting manager, were part-time, spending anywhere from 10 percent to 30 percent of their time serving a particular team. Traditionally, employees found their sense or organizational identity within their primary function (for example, Marketing, Finance, Quality Assurance, etc.). However, in organizations that make extensive use of cross-functional teams, the functional department from which individual team members come serves more like a "home room"—a place to which they can go for technical training in their specialty, performance reviews (if not done in the team), compensation, and expertise when they need help.

Effective leaders understand the challenge of maintaining role clarity in such a dynamic environment and do all they can to help team members manage ambiguity. One way to do this is regularly to revisit team member roles, particularly as the team moves from one phase of its task to another or as goals or project milestones are established.

The organization itself can increase team effectiveness and help manage potential role and process confusion by using the same team model, training, processes, and terminology throughout the organization. This allows team members to move quickly between one team assignment and another and get to work, rather than spending inordinate amounts of time figuring out *how* to get to work. Uniformity also allows different teams to interface effectively and efficiently.

In today's work environment, at almost every level in the organization, reengineered jobs are both enlarged (widened) and enriched (deepened). Team member roles are not only more complex but also more dynamic, evolving as the team continually improves its processes. From a vertical perspective, a department leader might be the *team leader* for his or her departmental team while at the same time being a *member* of the team of his or her manager. Horizontally, this same individual might serve on several other teams—one or two permanent teams (for example, the Compensation Review Committee and the Quality Process Award Team) and a few temporary task force teams (for example, the Customer Service Survey Team and the Inventory Process Design Team). This person is juggling six different team roles. It's not difficult to understand why he or she may be a little confused about who does what on what team. This is why it is so important for team leaders to remember that many team members are juggling multiple roles and provide constant reminder to the team regarding individual assignments.

DIFFERENT KINDS OF TEAM ROLES

Broadly speaking, there are three types of team roles. The first is the role of bringing *functional (technical) expertise* to the team. We recently worked with a large consumer products manufacturing company in the food industry to design and deploy customer business teams for their larger, more complex customers. These customers (food retailers) defined the product as much more than the can or box of food product. They were also interested in total system costs which put emphasis on better and constantly improving inventory, shipping, computer, and accounting systems. They wanted more sophisticated marketing strategies that allowed them to better meet differing consumer preferences in various locations. Finally, these retailers demanded comprehensive approaches that would allow them to develop effective strategies for entire categories of products to better meet increasing competitive pressures. To address these multiple needs, the manufacturer's customer teams needed to bring

---

North Star Enterprises

MEMO

TO: Project Team
FROM: Bill Smith
RE: Project Team Resource Needs

As I have discussed with each of you, we have accomplished a great deal this year and we should all be very proud of what we have done. Now it is time to concentrate on the coming year and what we are being asked to deliver this year to improve the effectiveness of the Project.
- Significantly improve the financials of the existing Project stores
- Install another 137 stores
- Build an alternative Project structure for the small stores in the system.

One key element is a clear understanding of the accountabilities each of us face. The purpose of this memo is to recap for each of you the accountabilities that I have asked you to assume as part of the Project Team.

Sarah Williams:
Your key contribution to the team will come from your analysis of our financial results.
1. You need to tell us what our results are and why we are producing them.
2. You need to help us develop the appropriate benchmarks and cost targets for the field.
3. Once these are developed we need a system to track and report individual operator's results against these benchmarks.
4. You need to help us manage the necessary capital to deliver the needed installations the next year. We will handle the capital in three phases. The phases will coincide with the first three quarters of the year.
5. Finally, you need to serve as the financial watch-dog of the team. We need you to evaluate each of our decisions to insure they make financial sense in the long run.

George Marshall:
Your key contribution to the team will come from your ability to provide tactical operations management.
1. You need to manage the quality aspects of our effort:
   - Work with Marie Benson to detemine how we track these results for the Project stores.
   - Based on analysis to these results how do we improve our results.
2. You need to lead our efforts to integrate the Project initiatives into the ASPC program.
3. You need to manage the tactical execution of Project once it is installed:
   - Work with finance and the field to develop the required management systems and the data-based depletion targets to help us improve the financial results of each Project store.
4. You need to review each of our decisions to insure they are operationally sound and appropriately reflect the needs of the field operators.

FIGURE 5-4

---

together people with different technical expertise—Sales, Marketing, Accounting, Information Systems, Logistics, and Customer Service.

An effective team leader will go to great ends to ensure that team members are quite clear about their functional roles. In Figure 5-4 (North Star Enterprises), a portion of a memo from a task force leader in a large consumer beauty care company provides a good example of helping team members understand their roles. Notice how he spells out their contributions in detail. Including every team member's role in a single memo helps each individual see the bigger picture and how all of the roles fit together.

Team members must not only understand the roles of other team members; they must also appreciate the unique contribution of those roles. They not only know what other members do for the team, but also have a clear understanding of why they are vitally important for accomplishing its mission.

Second, there are specific *formal team roles* that are needed to help the team to function effectively. Using the customer team described above, we needed a team leader, a facilitator, and a team administrator. With the exception of the team leader, the individuals chosen for these roles were selected not because of their functional expertise but rather because they possessed the skills needed to perform these roles well. Because this was a customer business team, the team leader functionally represented the Sales Division. However, in assigning team leaders, the company first identified the qualities needed to be an effective team leader and then assigned positions accordingly. Remember, every team is a volunteer organization, often made up of "part-timers" who come from different levels (that is, pay grade, titles, or authority). Therefore, it is critically important that roles are not only spelled out but agreed upon by the team members.

Several years ago I helped a company put together an important team assigned to meet regularly to manage a rolling calendar that determined the key marketing initiative for the firm for the next six months. The team consisted of the CEO, two vice presidents and several of their direct reports. Everyone agreed that the best facilitator was one of the direct reports of the vice president of Marketing. This woman had the skill and chutzpah to do the job. However, the team wisely agreed to some critical meeting ground rules, one of which was that they would actively support the facilitator when she had to enforce the ground rules, even if it was telling the vice president of Marketing that his time was up: something she had to do on a regular basis.

Finally, there are *general team member roles*—the expectations we place on any member of the team if we are to achieve our objectives at exceptional levels of performance. These general role assumptions may be as basic as specifying expectations about attendance and behavior at team meetings to the more complex issues of conflict resolution and communication.

APPROPRIATE DIVISION OF LABOR REQUIRES EXCELLENCE IN THREE AREAS

How we divide the task will in large measure determine the synergy we will experience as a team. No amount of team spirit can overcome the wasted motion and energy of poorly designed tasks or survive the frustrations of unclear roles. The first step always starts with design: who will do what? Secondly, there is a need to manage attitudes that can shape how individuals approach their roles and those of others, no matter how well designed. Finally, we must learn how to blend and leverage the different roles on the team against the

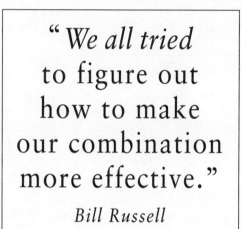

> " *We all tried to figure out how to make our combination more effective.* "
>
> *Bill Russell*

collective work product. It is only in this way that we can hope to achieve the synergies embedded in the concept of a team strategy.

DESIGN—WE STILL NEED TO DIVIDE THE TASK

If a clear, common, compelling mission is our *reason* for cooperation, appropriate division of labor, and clear roles is our *strategy* for cooperation. If everybody did the same task, we wouldn't need a team, just a lot of people. On a team we do, in fact, have division of labor. In today's world of the "knowledge worker," we might better call it "division of knowledge." The key is dividing it appropriately because synergy comes from leveraging the gifts and skills of individual members as they exercise their specialty. Few say it better than Bill Russell as he describes his experience with the Boston Celtics in their glory years: "By design and by talent we were a team of specialists, and like any team of specialists in any field, our performance depended both on individual excellence and on how we worked together. None of us had to strain to understand we had to complement one another's specialties; it was simply a fact, and we all tried to figure out ways to make our combination more effective."[6]

When an architect begins to design a structure, he or she will first identify the design criteria (that is, the objectives the structure must meet). As with the case of any structure, the use of criteria is needed if you want to design roles effectively. Over the years we have found the following five qualities valuable in role design:

1. *Clear.* With complex jobs you must have role clarity or you will have role confusion. If left unfixed, role confusion soon becomes role conflict. As a team member, I must not only be clear about my role but those of other team members as well.

2. *Complete.* Cover the whole task—no gaps. Synergism is found in the white space on the organizational chart, or, in this case, in the crevasses between roles. If the baton is going to be dropped, you will generally find it in the undiscussed and undiscovered gap between roles. Make sure everyone is clear about the handoffs. We can all picture tennis doubles partners in such a situation . . . "I thought you had it!"

3. *Compatible.* Match tasks to individual strengths and skills. Educator George H. Reavis, makes this point with a great story about animals in an unusual school:

   > Once upon a time, the animals decided they should do something meaningful to meet the problems of the new world. So they organized a school.
   >
   > They adopted an activity curriculum of running, climbing, swimming, and flying. To make it easier to administer the curriculum, all the animals took all of the subjects. The duck was excellent in swimming, in fact, better than his instructor. But he made only passing grades in flying and was very poor in running. Since he was a slow runner, he

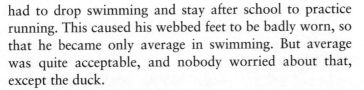

had to drop swimming and stay after school to practice running. This caused his webbed feet to be badly worn, so that he became only average in swimming. But average was quite acceptable, and nobody worried about that, except the duck.

The rabbit started at the top of his class in running, but developed a nervous twitch in his leg muscles because of so much make-up work in swimming.

The squirrel was excellent in climbing, but constantly frustrated in flying class, because his teacher made him start from the ground instead of the treetop. He developed "charlie horses" from overexertion and so only got a "C" in climbing and a "D" in running . . .[7]

Well, you get the point. The moral of this tale is that the animals were failing to leverage each other's strengths and specialties. Remember, a team is really a collection of specialists.

The need to leverage one another's technical specialties is generally obvious. But few teams take gifts, skills, and experiences into account when assigning the tasks that come into existence with the formation of the team. For example, who should be assigned the task of meeting facilitator? Often the first suggestion I hear is the team leader, but the correct answer is the best facilitator on the team. The same would be said for the team administrator, minute keeper, and other roles that provide the administrative infrastructure for the team. High performance teams take time to get to know one another and inventory not only the functional skills of each member but also past experiences, gifts, skills, interests, and other dimensions that define compatibility with one task or another.

4. *Complementary.* When designing a role, it is important to configure it in such a way as to make sure that in the process of executing it, the incumbent isn't hindering or blocking someone else attempting to perform their role. If I can't perform my role while you're performing yours, we will not experience much synergism as a team.

5. *Consensual.* I have seen teams with roles that meet all the above criteria but are still experiencing role frustration. They are clear

about one another's roles; the role map is complete, not leaving gaps in the team's perimeter; roles are compatible to individual team members; and they have been designed to be complementary. Sounds perfect, and it would be, if all of the team members agreed with who was to do what and how. But they don't. Mary thinks she should be the facilitator instead of Bob. And George feels that Mike has a portion of a task that he could perform better. Hardly the feelings on which to build high levels of collaboration. Team leaders should facilitate discussions until the team reaches consensus regarding the roles of its individual members. It is amazing what a few well-worded, straightforward questions will surface. Some time during the last 30 minutes of a team meeting try a few of these:

- Are we leveraging our team roles to the extent that we could? How could we make our combination of roles, skills, experience, and knowledge more effective?

- Is everyone doing the things best suited for their role (skills, knowledge)? Would any adjustments make the team more effective overall?

- Are there things each of us could do to help others in their roles—things we are doing that we shouldn't, things we are not doing that we should?

MANAGING ROLE ATTITUDES

Remember those functional chimneys? Sometimes people bring the mind-set they had in the old role paradigm to their new role paradigm. *"Okay,"* they think, *"I'm the finance expert—it says so right on this memo about my role. It's a good thing too, because it's clear that none of these other bozos knows anything about finance."* This person approaches the job as though he or she were still back in the finance department acting as a policeman to enforce rules and protect the finance department's interests. His or her basic attitude is, "This is my job. Stay out!"

Others might be more laid back about role responsibilities. They are busy, and they are more than willing to let everyone do "his or her own thing." They seldom demonstrate any initiative to help colleagues who

are stretched with their assigned responsibilities. Their basic attitude is, "That's your job."

No one is finished until everyone is finished. Many years ago when our now grown daughters were approaching their pre-teen years, my

wife decided it was time for them to learn what every child must experience—how to do the supper dishes. She reminded me that I, being the management consultant in the family, should be the one to spell out the

> # THIS IS
> # *MY* PART
> # OF *OUR* JOB
> # AND NO ONE IS
> # DONE UNTIL
> # EVERYONE
> # IS DONE.

role and individual responsibilities. Becki was about 11, Jennifer about 8. Wanting to use the dishes again after washing, I assigned Becki the task of rinsing and loading the dishes into the dishwasher. Her younger sister merely had to clear the table and sweep the floor. I, in the meantime, retired to the downstairs rec room to watch the news. Minutes later, Jennifer was at my elbow. "What are you doing?" I asked. She explained that she was watching the news with me (at 8 years old!). "No way," I responded." You're to stay in the kitchen until Becki's finished."

"Oh Dad!" she exclaimed, as she stomped back up the stairs. The next few nights we replayed the same scenario. But then, it began to dawn in Jennifer's mind that the sooner Becki finished, the sooner she, Jennifer, could get out of the kitchen. She soon figured out that by clearing the clean dishes out of the dishwasher while Becki pre-rinsed the new load, both she and Becki could finish faster.

Nothing speaks to me louder about the team spirit at Team Resources than when employees ask others what they can do to help

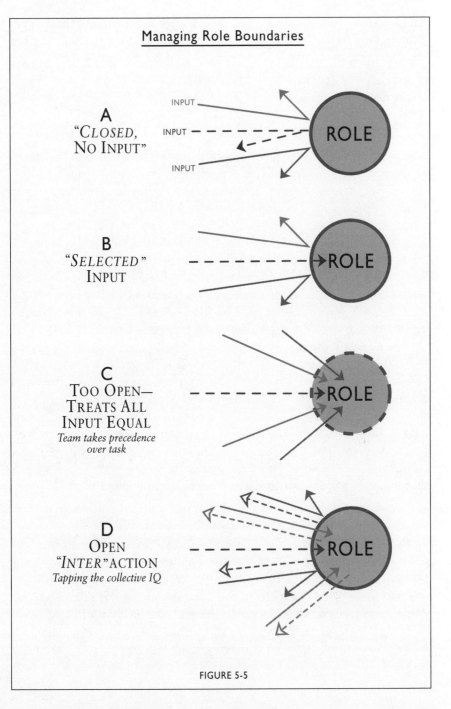

Managing Role Boundaries

A
"CLOSED,
NO INPUT"

INPUT
INPUT
INPUT

ROLE

B
"SELECTED"
INPUT

ROLE

C
TOO OPEN—
TREATS ALL
INPUT EQUAL
*Team takes precedence
over task*

ROLE

D
OPEN
*"INTER"*ACTION
Tapping the collective IQ

ROLE

FIGURE 5-5

when one team member is bogged down or working late. Often, there is nothing the other can do (other than make copies or coffee) but the gesture doesn't go unnoticed. Everyone understands that his or her job is just the "my" part of "our" job and that no one is done until everyone is done.

MANAGING ROLE BOUNDARIES

Every organizational entity has boundaries, be it a division, department, team, or even an individual role. Boundaries are needed and necessary, but if mismanaged can block and hinder team effectiveness. When it comes to the boundaries of an individual role, it's a matter of which and how much input I allow to influence my decisions, actions, and attitudes. If I have the attitude that I am the expert and no one has anything to offer, I become closed to any input (Figure 5-5-A). Sometimes the role incumbent accepts selected input, possibly from only the functional head or team leader, and although that's better than no input, it's not much better (5-5-B). The input is too one-sided or agenda-driven to be of real value to the team objectives.

Then, there's the team member who puts team above all else (even the task), accepting and responding to input from everyone (5-5-C). Not wanting to leave anyone out or hurt anyone's feelings, they find themselves buried with data, suggestions, and feedback. It's unlikely these people will be able to dig themselves out from under piles of raw data to bring an expert and objective perspective to the issues that confront the team. Finally, we find the open but balanced role manager who evaluates the value of each input with an open mind and accepts that which is helpful but provides feedback to all contributors (5-5-D).

LEVERAGING TEAM MEMBER ROLES

Bill Russell's observation, *"We all tried to figure out ways to make our combination more effective,"* sums up the issue. How do we multiply the impact and effectiveness of our combined roles? How do we produce synergistic results from this diverse soup of skills, experiences, perspectives, knowledge, personalities, and responsibilities? Creatively dividing the larger task, assigning its various pieces to individuals best suited to do them, and then managing implementation in a cooperative fashion is our *strategy* for achieving something more than we could do alone and doing so at exceptional levels of performance.

Blending and leveraging roles in a team setting doesn't happen naturally. You have to work at it with serious intentionality. Below I list four ideas that might help you, as a team leader, tap into the collective IQ of your team by making the combination more effective:

1. *Look to the edge.* Here I mean the edge of expertise and experience. For example, on a cross-functional team with all varieties of experience and functional expertise, don't assume that the marketing person is the only one with a contribution to marketing issues.

   It breaks my heart to see the wasted intellectual capital in many customer business teams on which the finance, logistics, and information services people are sidelined for most of the discussions and decisions because they revolve around sales and marketing issues. Frequently the most helpful insights come from people not held captive to the prevailing paradigm of a particular function. In our firm, everyone from the CEO to the receptionist is involved in our strategic planning sessions because we don't want to miss any idea and we believe that no one has the inside track on insight. If the team is mutually accountable for the final results and every individual is working on a part of the total job (that is, their part of our job) then every team member ought to have a say in every aspect of the task if such a say can add value.

2. *Read the book on everyone.* One of my favorite scenes in the movie *Patton* is set in the North African desert, where Patton is confronting his adversary, Rommel. Patton is standing on a high bluff looking into a broad, wide valley below in which he has laid his trap. We see Rommel's Panzer tanks coming down the valley and then, suddenly, the American and English tanks attack from the sides in a surprise maneuver. Patton, realizing his ambush will be successful, raises his fist and shouts, *"Rommel, you old fox, I read your book!"* Patton had studied his foe. He knew his strengths and weaknesses and was able to anticipate his moves.

   We need to read the book on the people on our teams. Where do they come from? What do they know? What are their interests and skills? Often, some of the biggest contributions of team members don't come from their functional contribution but from an insight gained in a previous job, their personality, interests, and perspectives.

A few years ago we lost our CFO and administrative officer who had been with us for many years. This was an important role on our management team, and we were aggressively pursuing a replacement. Our Chief Operating Officer had interviewed about three promising candidates and was feeling hopeful. That week, one of our administrative assistants, a woman who had worked for us about six months, asked for an appointment. "I understand you are looking for a new finance and administrative person," she said. "Do you know much of my background?" As she gave a brief overview of her previous work experience, which included extensive administration and financial responsibilities, our COO realized that we hadn't done a very good job of reading the book on this woman. We had been blinded by our assumptions that her skill set was primarily secretarial. Luckily for us, our new administrative officer took the initiative to point out a few chapters that we had missed.

3. *Proactively seek input.* Often, those who do not understand the technical nature of an issue or are not familiar with the more complex issues of a certain function tend to become quiet and uninvolved during a lively debate. They are not confident in the subject matter and might feel, *This is none of my business, I'm here to represent customer service issues.* Team facilitators should consistently poll these quieter members about any input they might have on any issue. After a while they may begin to get the picture that everyone's input is always welcome on any topic. Team leaders should work diligently to create an open, safe environment that encourages a willingness to express one's opinion.

4. *Ensure you have enough difference and the right difference on the team.* The more different a team is, the smarter it is. Team leaders need to ensure their team has the diversity needed to attack problems, decisions, and strategy with a broad inventory of perspective, skill, and knowledge. Don't "dumb down" the team by collecting a group of very similar people with the same

backgrounds. Such a group may get along, but they won't necessarily get results. In a later chapter we will discuss how to ensure that such difference leads to synergy rather than to strife. For now, accept the possibility that the risks of conflict are far less important than the returns gained from a diverse and talented group of people who choose to work together.

A Practical Tool for Clarifying Roles in a Team Setting

In discussing team problems with team members, the lack of role clarity frequently receives top billing. When we ask why they haven't resolved role issues, the answer is invariably lack of time. However, when we ask team leaders why the team hasn't addressed these issues, a common response is not time but rather the need for a simple, straightforward process. We have found that when team leaders have a framework that will help them facilitate role discussions, they will find the time for the team to have those discussions. The role worksheet and process shown below is an effective means of organizing a session regarding team roles.

Roles can be defined from either a *positional* or *process* perspective. When we take the *positional* approach, the focus is on a single primary role, even though the roles of supporting players might be reflected for activities in which roles intersect or overlap. When *process* is the organizing theme for role definition, all of the steps or activities of the process are identified and listed and the roles of everyone involved in the process are spelled out. On the following pages we will look at an example from both perspectives, but first let me outline the process:

1. Identify the major elements of work for either the process or position, listing them in the first column of the Roles Worksheet.

2. List the "cast of characters" (those who have a relationship to the role) across the top of the worksheet.

3. Identify the role of each player for each work element using the following descriptors:

   - R = person ultimately responsible for this work element (there is only one R per work element),

- S = person responsible to support the issue, decision, work, etc.,
- C = person to be consulted,
- I = person to be informed.

Using a positional approach, let's look at the primary work elements of an account executive for **DDD**, an ad agency serving small business accounts. Notice that because we are outlining the account exec's position, he or she will have the **R** for each line item.

Account Executive, DDD Advertising

Work Elements	Position Titles				
	Account Exec	Creative	Media	Planning	Account Mgmt. Director
Establish a knowlegeable, high-trust relationship with assigned clients	R				C
Identify client business objectives	R				I
Work with client to develop overall client advertising plan incorporating both media and PR objectives	R	C	C	S	I
Coordinate development of DDD's strategy (Approach, budget, schedule)	R	C	C	C	C
Present DDD recommendations to client	R	S	S	I	C
Coordinate implementation of strategy	R	C	C		I

Next, look at how a team might outline the roles of various team members for a specific work process. Again we will use the ad agency **DDD**, and process the development, approval, and implementation of a print ad series for clients.

Development and Implementation of Print Ads, DDD Advertising

Work Elements	Position Titles				
	Account Exec	Creative	Media	Planning	Account Mgmt. Director
Review and confirm client objectives, budget (Client Plan)	R	C	C	I	C
Develop alternative creative approaches to achieve client objectives	C	R		C	I
Develop team consensus on approaches presented to client and primary recommendation of the team	R	C	C	C	C
Develop budget for media implementation	C	I	R	I	I
Develop presentation outline for client meeting	R	C	I	I	I
Develop actual presentation (PowerPoint and boards)	C	R	S	I	C
Facilitate team presentation of recommended strategy to client	R	C	C		

As you can see, because the focus of this approach is on the process rather than the position, the R moves from player to player as the team moves through the process.

We find that working through roles in this fashion is a fruitful exercise for any team. We recommend the use of a flip chart or overhead when developing the role work sheet so that everyone can see the big picture. Depending on the nature of the work you can take this process to any needed level of detail, but be careful not to dig too deep. Roles in today's work environment are very dynamic and need to be reviewed on a fairly regular basis. If the process is too detailed or burdensome, the team will hesitate to engage in the process.

Stop, start, and continue. When roles are somewhat defined, as with the roles worksheet above, we often find that a review of each role with the entire team is extremely important. Every team member must be familiar not only with his or her own role, but also with those of their teammates. It's more than just familiarity; roles must be integrated. To facilitate such a review we have found the *Stop, Start, Continue* exercise to be a simple but powerful communication exercise.

Each team member presents his or her role, using the roles worksheet format. The other team members then give feedback, explaining the things the role owner should start, stop, and continue doing to become more effective. This discussion helps to integrate roles better and ensure that members can communicate not only what they need from the other roles but also what they think other roles need from them. Gaps, overlaps, and points of confusion can be quickly surfaced and dealt with.

WHAT ABOUT STAR PLAYERS?

Can you have stars on a team? Some of the most memorable stories about teams are those in which a group of ordinary people, through teamwork, accomplished extraordinary things. However, there is plenty of room for star players on teams of any kind. In fact, the more stars we can recruit, the greater the potential of the team. Peters and Waterman in *In Search for Excellence* noted: "Man needs at one and the same time to be a conforming member of a winning team and to be a star in his own right."[8]

I would push this concept even further and suggest we attempt to staff teams with "super-heroes." Star players, although extremely proficient in skill, may or may not have a collaborative spirit that allows them to subordinate personal interests to those of the overall mission. I define a superhero as one who possesses both exceptional ability and a cooperative attitude. The first violinist in a symphony orchestra is, by definition, a star. However, to deliver a truly great symphony, he or she must successfully blend his or her exceptional skill into the entire output of the orchestra. Teams are egalitarian in nature. Everyone is needed and brings a vital contribution to the group. We're looking for people who play like stars yet don't demand to be treated like one.

While serving as coach of the U.S. Olympic Basketball Team, Bobby Knight observed that there is no *I* in the word team. It's a catchy quote, but if applied without thought, can lead down the wrong path. A team incorporates a whole bunch of *I*'s—one for each member. Sometimes we forget that and overemphasize interdependence at the expense of individuality. A strong team consists of strong, capable individuals who *choose* to subordinate a number of their personal interests and aspirations for the larger team goals. They make this choice because those goals are important to them individually.

If you are going to build a strong team, you will want to recruit the strongest individual players you possibly can. You want people who have demonstrated they are capable individually before you chain them together in an interdependent strategy. High performance teams balance individual responsibility and mutual accountability. Effective team leaders attempt to staff their teams with superheroes who are highly motivated to cooperate. As we all know, not all talented people are willing to work in a cooperative fashion.

DIVIDING THE TASK INTRODUCES A SIDE EFFECT

So far teamwork seems pretty straightforward. Purpose provides the *reason* for cooperation; appropriate division of labor and clear roles is our *strategy* for cooperation. However, as soon as we divide the task into different roles, a problem surfaces for the team. I have become inextricably linked to you and your portion of the task. If either you or I don't do our part because of attitude, ability, or any other reason, we won't get the job done. Together we can do more; apart we can do less or nothing. When we divided the task, we introduced a side effect: interdependence (Figure 5-6). Division of labor allows us to tap into the potential of synergism, but with this promise of increased productivity, we also run the risk of little or no productivity if we don't properly manage interdependence.

Interdependence is an investment (and a risk); synergism is the return on investment. If we are to reap the rewards of interdependence, we must cooperate. But remember, cooperation is a choice, and despite the obvious logic, we often see interdependent people acting independently.

Trust is the biggest factor in my choosing to cooperate. If I don't trust you (both your character or competence), it's highly unlikely that I will *choose* to be "dependent" on you to achieve my goals and interests. Trust glues a team together.

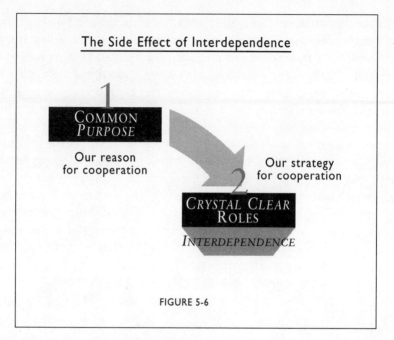

The Side Effect of Interdependence

1
COMMON
PURPOSE

Our reason
for cooperation

Our strategy
for cooperation

2
CRYSTAL CLEAR
ROLES

INTERDEPENDENCE

FIGURE 5-6

In the early 1960's an excellent movie, *The Defiant Ones,* starring Tony Curtis and Sidney Poitier, graphically portrayed the dilemma posed by interdependence. The story takes place in the early 1960's somewhere in the segregated South. The movie opens with a group of prisoners standing, rain-soaked, in a prison yard as guards move among them, pairing them with manacles and three-foot chains. Curtis and Poitier are chained together and loaded with several others into the back of a truck. These two prisoners couldn't have been more different. Beyond the difference of race, you quickly see big gaps in their values and personalities. Curtis plays a con man, a real weasel. Poitier gives the impression he is a man of values—steady, calm, and at peace with himself.

The credits are still rolling, and the rain is still falling as the truck pulls out of the yard toward its destination. Not far into the journey a distracted driver allows the truck to veer off the rain-soaked highway into a deep gully. With the exception of our two protagonists, everyone in the truck is apparently dead or unconscious. Curtis and Poitier emerge, shaken but alive. They quickly look to the trees illuminated by the overturned truck's headlights and then into each other's eyes. For one moment these two men have absolute unity of purpose, and they run for the tree line. Three feet inside the woods, Curtis takes a right and Poitier a left. These men come into a startled understanding of interdependence as each arrives at his respective end of the three-foot chain. Although they have everything to gain by cooperating, much of the film follows these two men fighting and arguing as they try to evade baying hounds, and overweight, cigar-smoking, shotgun-toting, Southern sheriffs.

Many contemporary management teams resemble these two adventurers, pulling against one another instead of pulling together. They buy into the promise of synergism and become interdependent, but because of a lack of trust, lack of alignment, or competitiveness, they elect to act independently. They create their own version of the *The Defiant Ones*.

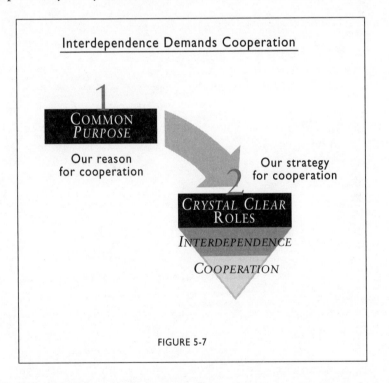

Interdependence Demands Cooperation

1
COMMON
PURPOSE

Our reason
for cooperation

Our strategy
for cooperation

2
CRYSTAL CLEAR
ROLES

INTERDEPENDENCE

COOPERATION

FIGURE 5-7

Interdependence demands cooperation (Figure 5-7). Note the prefix *co-* in *cooperation* and *collaborate*. *Co* means "with," "together," or "jointly." The prefix *syn* in *synergy* also means "together." Synergy is the product of cooperation. Common purpose was our reason for cooperation. Appropriate division of labor and clear roles was our strategy for cooperation. But our strategy introduces a side effect: interdependence. The next four characteristics of a high performance team are all designed to manage this side effect and produce the needed levels of cooperation.

- *Accepted leadership* provides the *structure* for cooperation (Chapter 6).

- *Effective processes* provide the *method* for cooperation (Chapter 7).

- *Solid relationships* provide the *climate* for cooperation (Chapter 8).

- *Excellent communication* provides the *means* for cooperation (Chapter 9).

THE BOTTOM LINE

To achieve exceptional results, high performance teams creatively divide the task and then cooperate like mad. When any complex task is divided, the roles assigned to various parts of the process must have the following qualities:

- Clear. The different roles on an effective team are crystal clear. Team members are clear not only about their role but also about the roles of their teammates.

- Complete. Ensure the roles in total cover the whole task. It is also important that everyone knows where the handoffs are in every team process.

- Compatible. Match roles to individual skills, interests, and experiences. Look beyond merely the functional background, as some of the most leveraged contributions will come from outside a person's functional expertise.

- Complementary. Make sure one role is "not in the way" of another.

- Consensual. The team should be clear about everyone's role and in agreement about it.

Dividing the task introduces interdependence. With interdependent roles both attitudes and boundaries must be carefully managed. The overarching attitude for team member roles is a thoughtful balance between individual responsibility and mutual accountability that conveys: "This is *my* part of *our* job."

High performance teams leverage the combination of team member roles. Principles for doing this include:

- Looking to the edge of expertise and encouraging input about everything from everyone.

- Reading the book on each team member and tapping into the entire pool of experience, knowledge, and skill rather than limiting input at the boundaries of their functional expertise.

- Proactively seeking input, particularly from the quieter team members who probably spent a large portion of the discussion time thinking about the issue. However, because of their nature, lack of confidence, or even the manner in which they have defined their role, they often hesitate to put forth their ideas.

- Ensuring the team has enough difference and the right kind of difference. The more different a team is, the smarter the team is IF (and that's a big if!) it can channel that difference productively against the problems, decisions, and tasks of the team.

MESSAGE TO TEAM LEADERS

A key role for team leaders is to facilitate the discussion about roles, particularly the issues around clarity. Don't forget team roles that are needed to support the team itself. Such roles would include tasks like facilitation, administration, communication, and any other task required by the team to get its job done. The process of achieving role clarity is accomplished through discussion. Lots of it.

Another role of a team leader is to balance the individual and collective aspects of each team member's work and recognition. Earlier I noted that high performance teams have a lot of stars/heroes on them. The team leader is the one with the spotlight so that when an individual team member plays a part in the collective score, he or she is recognized for that contribution. We have all appreciated a talented jazz group ensemble as we watch the leader nod his head toward the player working through a solo while at the same time raising his hand to encourage applause from the audience. An effective team leader acts in much the same manner.

Chapter Six

Accepted Leadership

Leadership at 37,000 Feet

Throughout those minutes of crisis for United Flight 232, Al Haynes demonstrated extraordinary leadership. As I reviewed the transcription of the cockpit voice recorder, I couldn't help being impressed with his calm, competent management of the crisis. The four men in the cockpit had a combined 103 years of flying experience, and Haynes did a masterful job in bringing their *collective* IQ to bear against their problem. Not a single thought or resource in that cockpit was wasted. Consensus ruled each move as Haynes made sure everyone's ideas were woven into their decisions about what to do and what not to do. There was no margin for mistakes in this situation. They couldn't afford to be wrong.

A few years earlier, an entirely different and more tragic result would have been likely. Between 60 and 80 percent of all plane crashes are blamed on cockpit error.[1] In many cases these errors are due to bad judgment or poor decision making on the part of one or several of the crew members, lack of skill in a critical situation, or breakdown in communications and teamwork among the crew members. However, in the

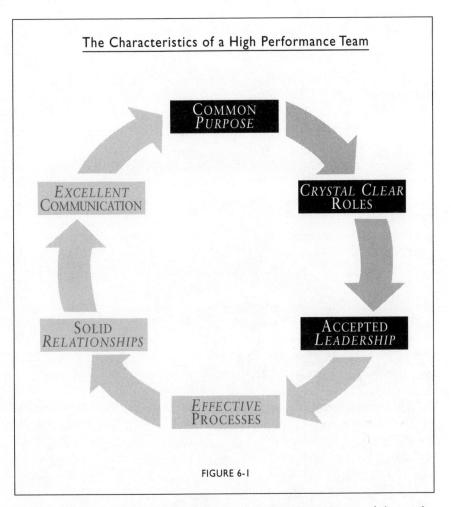

The Characteristics of a High Performance Team

COMMON PURPOSE

CRYSTAL CLEAR ROLES

EXCELLENT COMMUNICATION

ACCEPTED LEADERSHIP

SOLID RELATIONSHIPS

EFFECTIVE PROCESSES

FIGURE 6-1

early 1980's, mounting evidence indicated that a good part of the problem could be laid at the feet of airline captains themselves and their leadership style.

In the "old days," at the beginning of modern commercial aviation, the cockpit was under a totalitarian regime. Little or no teamwork existed, and the captain was known as "god." In these earlier times, airlines didn't have many procedures. The captain determined the routes, altitudes, and other details in a flight. The copilots weren't considered essential and were often called "stud" or "partner" because the captain forgot their names. Captains talked to captains; copilots talked to copilots. The focus of the copilot's job was to please the captain, who was never wrong.

One source of the problem can be found in the manner in which many of these captains received their original flight training. The military proved a fruitful recruiting ground for the airlines as they built their operations in the 1960's and 1970's. Therefore, many of these pilots were groomed in the combat settings of Korea and Vietnam. These macho, get-the-job-done individualists were ideal for pushing single-seat, high performance fighters into less-than-friendly situations. They were the rugged individualists immortalized by Tom Wolfe in his book *The Right Stuff*. Such individuals have a difficult time riding with a posse.

Captain Haynes was cut from this mold. Although he didn't experience combat, he was training in single-seat dive-bombers when the Korean war ended. As he explains it: "There was no one in the cockpit with me, no one telling me what to do or how to handle the situation." At 24 years old, he began working with United. "The first time I walked into a DC-6, I found the world's oldest man sitting next to me in the left seat. I had never seen a man that old fly an airplane. But, I'll tell you one thing; I wasn't going to question what that man said. If he said jump, you merely asked, how high? You did whatever he said because he was the captain, and he was the law."

This attitude stands in stark contrast to the type of leadership exhibited by Haynes in the transcripts of events during those fateful 41 minutes of Flight 232. He does not come across as a man who had all the answers and expected his underlings to carry them out quickly and without question. Haynes is a humble man, and getting the others involved in solving the problem seemed common sense to him. "Although we had 103 years of flying between us, not one minute of this experience was in trying to fly an airplane the way we were trying to fly that one. So why would I have any more of an idea of how to do it than the other three?"

But what he applied was more than common sense. When asked, Haynes is quick to point out that many of the leadership skills he applied that day were the product of a special training course, Command Leadership Resource Management (CLR),[2] a special crew-training strategy initiated by United in the 1980's. CLR had two primary objectives. The first goal was to teach junior crew members to be more assertive, training them to communicate and function as a team and to tap into the collective skills and experience of every crew member rather than relying only on the captain's skills.

The second objective was to modify the attitudes and leadership style of the captain to become more aligned with a team effort. Haynes summarized it this way: "CLR taught me to go find some help if you can't come up with the answer yourself and, on 232, that's what we did. It also taught the rest of the crew to assert themselves, to make their feelings known, to make sure that the captain understands what they are trying to say without fear of reprimand."

It would be safe to say that, over the last 20 years, both leadership and "followership" in the cockpits of America's airlines have been re-engineered. This effort has greatly increased the levels of communication and teamwork and, as a result, improved safety. We need to accomplish this same task in team-oriented organizations of the corporate community.

HIGH PERFORMANCE TEAMS NEED COMPETENT LEADERSHIP

High performance teams need clear, competent leadership. Rosabeth Moss Kanter writes: "True freedom is not the absence of structure—letting employees go off and do whatever they want—but rather a clear structure which enables people to work within established boundaries in an autonomous and creative way. It is important to establish for people, from the beginning, the ground rules and boundary conditions under which they will be working: what can they decide, what can't they decide? *Without structure, groups often flounder unproductively, and the members then conclude they are merely wasting their time. The fewer constraints given a team, the more time will be spent defining its structure rather than carrying out its task* . . . In short, leadership—the existence of people with power to mobilize others and to set constraints—is an important ingredient in making participation work."[3]

Notice what it is that Kanter says leaders provide: Structure (that is, constraints). Now to many of us, particularly those of us with temperaments that value freedom from control, this might sound a bit confining. However, when we understand the context in which we work today, we quickly realize that the concept of structure and constraint is a critical ingredient for both individual and team effectiveness.

As we have seen, over the years many organizations had become too structured, resulting in rigid, unresponsive structures in an environment that demands fluidity, speed, and responsiveness. Breaking down such barriers was needed, but as companies replace vertical hierarchies with horizontal networks, link traditional functions together with cross-functional teams, and form strategic alliances with customers and even competitors, they are confronted with levels of organizational ambiguity never before experienced in the corporate community. At General Electric, longtime CEO Jack Welch was determined to build a "boundaryless" company. A company, metaphorically speaking, with no walls. In such an organization, barriers between departments and functions become blurry and labels between salaried and hourly workers or between labor and management become irrelevant, providing no meaningful distinction between who is who and who does what.

Team life in such an ambiguous world requires better, and different, leadership rather than less. All boundaries aren't bad—just the impenetrable ones or those that exclude the presence or input needed to deliver exceptional results. In fact, boundaries are needed in any type of organizational setting. They provide a place that fosters a sense of identity and some semblance of stability in a very unstable world. These boundaries are more emotional than structural but no less real. However, they are more difficult to manage than those clearly drawn on an organization chart. They need to be carefully nurtured to ensure they provide the identity and protection we all need while at the same time not allowing them to become impermeable to needed input and perspective.

Leadership in such a setting requires the ability to balance the need to provide just the right amount of structure in an unstructured environment. Too much and the collaborative spirit will be stifled, too little and the team will flounder and become frustrated. As a result, the role of a team leader in today's work environment is very different from how we might have described it not too many years ago.

CONNECTING TEAMS TO TASKS

I have found that a good definition of leadership in any context might be a *person* influencing *people* to accomplish a *purpose* (Figure 6-2). This definition clearly identifies the critical components in leadership. It allows us to single out and discuss the attributes (for example,

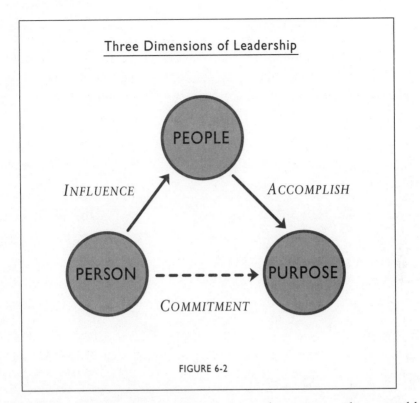

Three Dimensions of Leadership

PEOPLE

INFLUENCE

ACCOMPLISH

PERSON - - - - - - -> PURPOSE

COMMITMENT

FIGURE 6-2

character, competence, commitment, etc.) of a person others would willingly follow, the importance of knowing the skills, needs, and aspirations of those you would influence, and the nature of the task which we are called to accomplish.

In most organizational settings it is the leader who frames the task for the team and facilitates their discussion on its meaning and nature. In large measure it is the vision, commitment, and communication ability of the team leader that governs the "optics" through which individual team members see their task.

TEAMS MUST BE LED, NOT MANAGED

A clear team purpose is critical because it defines the results that set a team apart from any other type of group. Effective leaders understand the link between team and task and the power of goals to engender *exceptional* levels of cooperation. In organizational settings most groups achieve *acceptable* results (Figure 6-3). That is what people are

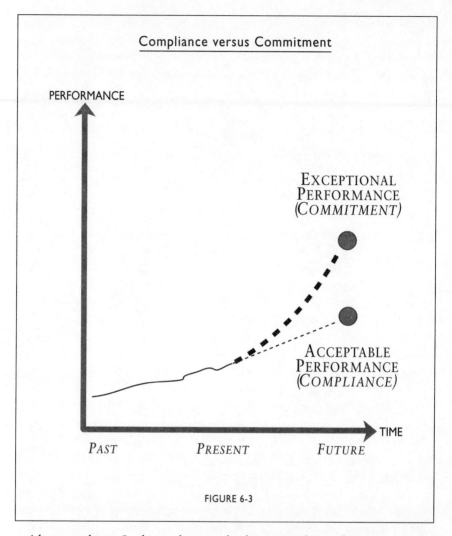

Compliance versus Commitment

PERFORMANCE

EXCEPTIONAL
PERFORMANCE
(*COMMITMENT*)

ACCEPTABLE
PERFORMANCE
(*COMPLIANCE*)

TIME

PAST   *PRESENT*   *FUTURE*

FIGURE 6-3

paid to produce. Such results are the basic product of management's ability to garner compliance to certain standards of performance. If individuals do not comply with those standards either because of attitude or ability, management will replace them with others who will, for that is what these individuals are paid to do.

Exceptional results however, are the product of that extra effort, initiative, creativity, and commitment people put out because they "want to" (Figure 6-3). They flow out of individual and collective commitment to the task of the team. While as a manager I can demand compliance, commitment (that is, the *choice* I make to cooperate at high levels) is volunteered. Leaders do not demand commitment but rather call it out of people. This is why teams must be led and not managed. One doesn't manage volunteers; one leads them. Effective leaders understand that command and control stifle the voluntary instincts of team members, and service and support release time.

In Figure 6-2 we saw that leadership is about influence. *Leadership* is the act of influencing others toward the accomplishment of a specific task or purpose. One source of influence can be found in a leader's formal authority as defined by the organization. However, the most effective form of influence is more informal. It flows out of the leader's mind-set about teams and people, skills, relationships, and resources. Although leaders are clearly committed to the purpose, success will be determined by the extent those being influenced accomplish the purpose. Effective leaders are those who rally the alignment of others to the task. They understand those they lead and are able to craft a definition of purpose that embraces the diverse interests and needs of individual team members. People buy into the purpose because, in the very truest sense, it is theirs.

Leaders who must rely on positional authority and autocratic style to achieve their ends seldom see the levels of performance shown to leaders who see their role as one of service and support. This concept is so important that it bears repeating: Teams are, in the very truest of terms, volunteers. Volunteers are not "managed" but demand leadership capable of calling out the levels of initiative and creativity that motivate exceptional levels of both individual and collective performance.

Because of the volunteer nature of teams, it is critically important that the team "accepts" their leader—that they support and respond to the team leader's efforts to provide direction, coordinate the collective work of the team, and set the tempo of its pace. However, in spite of its importance, our experience confirms that many team leaders are not up to the task. There are many reasons for such failure, ranging from inappropriate style and lack of skill to misguided mind-sets that fail to understand either the dynamic and potential of teams or of the people who staff them. Any of these problems can weaken the level of acceptance of leadership.

THE MIND-SET OF A TEAM LEADER

Regardless of the leadership skills of a leader, without a certain mind-set or perspective any efforts to call exceptional levels of commitment out of team members will fall on deaf ears. Our mind-set is the sum of our assumptions about the world around us. It's a fixed mental attitude or disposition that governs our interpretation and reactions to various situations. In most cases our mind-set is tacit and, like the lens of eyeglasses, we look right through it without understanding the influence it exerts on how we "see" the world.

Five qualities make up the mind-set of effective team leaders:

- *They appreciate the collective brilliance of a team.* In many instances teams don't work together so much as they think together. While in years past the focus was on division of labor, in today's world the focus is clearly on the division of knowledge. We have become a world of specialists, and great team leaders understand that the key to synergy is making it easier for the team to tap into the collective IQ. Ultimately team performance will be determined by the resourcefulness of the team, not its resources.

- *They believe in the power of diversity.* The more different a team is, the smarter it is. A team with a lot of diversity can surround problems and decisions with a wide spectrum of perspective, experience, skill, and knowledge. However, such differences can lead to strife as well as to synergy. The power of diversity must be first appreciated and then channeled productively against the mutual goals of the team.

- *They see team leadership as a role, not a position.* If a team leader wants to be "accepted" by the team, he or she must be seen as a servant leader. When people "accept" a leader, they are more willing to give power to the leader, that is, to empower the leader. I can picture some of you sliding to the edge of your chair over this issue. After all, isn't it the leader who should empower the employees and not the other way around? Well, yes and no. In this age of the knowledge worker, it's wise to treat every employee as a volunteer. As we have already discussed, this concept is particularly true with teams. Teams are, in the very truest sense, volunteer organizations. People empower leaders so that the leader is better able to serve them, the team members. Serving is a key role for the team leader.

In the corporate community, the term *servant-leader* was coined by Alan Greenleaf in his book by the same title.[4] He, in turn, got this idea from the New Testament and the teachings of Jesus Christ, who said, "You know that the rulers of the Gentiles lord it over them, and their high officials exercise authority over them. Not so with you. Instead, whoever wants to become great among you must be your servant . . ."[5]

Although this principle is ageless, in practice it is quite rare. Servant leadership is much more an attitude than a skill. Service and empowerment are inextricably linked (Figure 6-4). If the team members don't feel served, they will stop empowering (and accepting) the leader. If the leader doesn't feel empowered, it's quite likely that he or she will stop serving. Authoritative and controlling leaders are often insecure people attempting to take what they have not been given. Because they were not *given* acceptance (however they define it), they *demand* it. The key to becoming a servant leader is to see leadership as a *role* from which to serve, not a *position* to be served. Like any other team role, leadership is important, but no intrinsic merit falls to the individual who performs the role; it's the role itself that is important.

- *They see leadership and power as something to be released and shared rather than something to hold and control.* Highly effective leaders believe that there is leadership, creativity, energy, and initiative to be found in everyone. They work hard to read the book on every member of their team in order to understand and release the potential of each person. High performance teams liberate and leverage their "human resources" like no other type of group.

- *They understand teams are all about tasks.* Effective team leaders master the delicate balance needed between the task, the team, and individual team members. The motivation for the existence of team and the presence of team members is the task. If that is not accomplished, the team fails. On the other hand, if team leaders neglect the collective needs of the team or the individual needs

Service Leads to Acceptance

SERVE

EMPOWER/
ACCEPT

FIGURE 6-4

of its members, there is little chance they will exert exceptional levels of effort needed to accomplish the task.

THIS IS NOT YOUR FATHER'S LEADERSHIP STYLE

Over the past few years, few dimensions of organizational life have received as much call for change as that of leadership. Flatter corporate hierarchies resulting in widening of spans of control, new emphasis on teams and teamwork, increased use of information technology in the work area, and the advent of the "knowledge worker" are but a few of the changes that have challenged the older paradigms of leadership.

Bottlenecks, by definition, limit capacity. Under the old organizational paradigm too many leaders were bottlenecks of the intellectual and creative capacity of those they led. It was the leader who made decisions, set goals, solved problems, and established schedules. Under such a system, a group's output was limited by the capacity of the leader. Too often the group was nothing more than an extension of its leader, serving the interests for which he or she was held responsible.

As corporations have responded to intensifying competitive pressure by de-layering management levels and downsizing their operations, the demands on the typical manager have become even more severe as spans of control widened from 6-7 to 13-15 and, in many cases, as high as 25-30. Managers, in general, have become spread so thin you can almost see light through them, and the trend shows no sign of letting up. Coupled with the accelerating pace and scope of change in virtually every aspect of every business, there is no possible way managers with these wide spans can do their job the way they used to. They don't have the knowledge, time, or energy to stay on top of the details needed to "be in control."

The beauty of the modern, team-based organization when it is functioning properly is that productivity increases by moving these overworked managers from positions in which they channel work flow to roles in which they can facilitate the efforts of others. The bottlenecks are reduced or eliminated, and team leaders are seen as instrumental and contributing members to the collective product of the team.

The team on Flight 232 had only 41 minutes to achieve its mission. What if Captain Haynes had decided that he, and he alone, knew the right things to do, as well as how and when to do them? Instead, he operated on the premise that the four men in the cockpit were smarter than any one of them, no matter how smart any one might be. Haynes did whatever he could to bring their collective creativity to bear on the problem. They were manufacturing creativity. By becoming an effective facilitator, Haynes increased the capacity of the group to achieve their mission, thereby saving the lives of 189 people.

The leadership style demonstrated by Al Haynes would not be the logical first choice recommended by the experts. Conventional wisdom tells us that crisis is clearly the time for strong, directive leadership. There is no time for reflection or discussion. Immediate and decisive action is needed. This was certainly the preconception of the researchers at NASA who believed that airline incidents in which the crew had some influence to resolve were more likely to be resolved positively when the captain exercised strong authority in the cockpit. They checked their assumptions by putting crews through a series of incidents in simulators. As predicted, the captains responded in one of two ways, either becoming highly directive in style or being more consultative in approach, involving the other crew members in problem solving and decisions. What did not go as predicted were the results. NASA found that the captains using a more open, consultative style had greater success in getting their planes safely through the incident.[6]

Many leaders find it difficult to engage those whom they lead in the process. When the more directive pilots were asked why they had been so tough in their leadership style, a typical response was: "A crisis is no time for hand-holding."[7] Captain Haynes, on the other hand, found that crisis is a very good time for everyone to hold hands and collectively apply their skills and experience to the problem.

Leadership in a team environment is all about serving, facilitating, and releasing rather than taking charge and being in control. Figure 6-5 provides a summary of the difference between the old hierarchical paradigm of leadership and a leadership style better suited for the horizontal team-based structures of today.

We have found that in companies in which we assisted in developing team-based structures and cultures, between 30 and 35 percent of the managers found it difficult and often impossible to shift from the left-hand column of the following chart (Figure 6-5) to the right column. Not too long ago, I shared this observation with a group of corporate leaders. When I sat down, the individual next to me, a CEO of a Fortune 500 company, leaned over and said quietly, *"MacMillan, that's not been our experience. We have seen it as high as 60 percent of our managers who can't make the change!"*

THE ROLE OF THE TEAM LEADER

The role of a team leader, like the environment in which it's exercised, is very dynamic and must be adjusted for each specific situation on a moment-by-moment basis. However, in the very broadest terms, we might define it as follows:

- *Direction setter.* Ensuring clarity of direction for the team is a key role of the leader. Today's organizations and the teams within

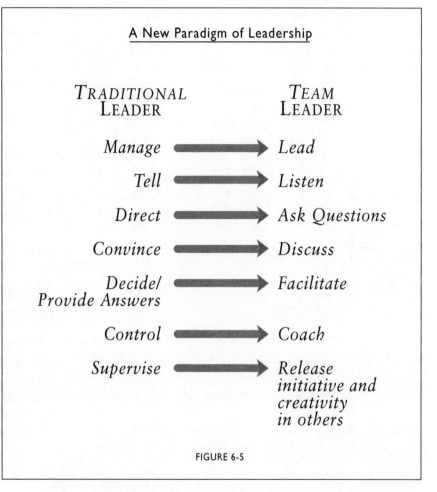

A New Paradigm of Leadership

TRADITIONAL LEADER		TEAM LEADER
Manage	⟶	Lead
Tell	⟶	Listen
Direct	⟶	Ask Questions
Convince	⟶	Discuss
Decide/ Provide Answers	⟶	Facilitate
Control	⟶	Coach
Supervise	⟶	Release initiative and creativity in others

FIGURE 6-5

them are buffeted by constant, high-velocity change. In such an environment it's important to maintain a sense of "magnetic North" so that we don't lose our bearings from constant change in both direction and pace. As the linking pin between the team and higher levels of management, the team leader not only facilitates the definition of the team purpose but also monitors progress and negotiates mid-course changes when needed. Earlier I noted that a key role of the team leader was to set constraints. This is very much a part of direction setting, for such constraints act much like riverbanks which set the boundaries and the direction of the river. Staying within those banks ensures that the river will be a powerful, productive force ultimately reaching its destination. Outside those banks, rivers accomplish little other than making a mess.

- *Boundary manager.* A team leader is the gatekeeper, assuring the team is effectively linked to the broader organizational environment that shapes its work. To serve their team well, team leaders must become consummate networkers. Kanter believes that in the business setting of today, the ability of managers to get things done depends more on the number of networks in which they are centrally involved than on their height in the hierarchy.[8] If the leader's negotiating and diplomatic skills are up to the task, such activities will be a significant contribution to the team, which is most likely connected to many other teams within the organization.

    Boundary management not only includes the interface with other teams but with upper management and the functional managers of team members as well. A deadline that must be renegotiated with upper management or resolving a conflict in priorities with the department manager of one of the team members all fall within boundary management issues for the team leader.

- *Facilitator.* For some, the word *facilitation* brings to mind meeting management, but that's not what I'm referring to here. Facilitation means to "make easier," and it involves a wide breadth of activities that might include facilitating problem solving when the team gets stuck, resolving conflict, and, probably most importantly, helping the team tap into its collective IQ.

    Facilitation not only requires a new mind-set but a new skill set as well. Successful team leaders see their role not as solvers of problems but rather as the people responsible for seeing that the problems get solved. This mind-set, coupled with an understanding of the skills and knowledge of various team members, opens up more creative possibilities than could ever be imagined by even the brightest, most experienced leader.

- *Negotiator.* Whether it's more time, equipment, funds, information, or even staff, the team leader is generally the one with responsibility for finding and negotiating for needed resources.

- *Coach.* An important role of the team leader is that of coach. Tom Peters defines *coaching* as "face-to-face leadership." To coach, he observes, is largely to facilitate. The most vital aspects of coaching are visibility, listening, limit setting, value shaping, and skill stretching.[9] Coaches must balance the need to develop the skills of each individual team member with the needs of the team as a whole. The ultimate responsibility of any coach is to build a winning team. They understand the importance of practice, watching game films, and goal setting that motivates the team to do everything a little bit better every day.

In summary, team leaders must be consummate jugglers. As a team leader, the more successful you are in involving the team in decision making and other key team processes, the more inclined team members will be to view you as a "member of the team." In most instances, however, team leaders retain some elements of their "official role" as team manager. They will often be one level higher in the hierarchy than the other team members. Frequently, they are still the ones who conduct performance appraisals for individual team members. Each of these differences reinforces the distinctiveness between the role of team leader and other team roles.

As team leader, you sit at a very interesting intersection of responsibilities and relationships (Figure 6-6). On one hand, you are the team gatekeeper and boundary manager, connecting the team to the broader organization and hierarchy. In this role, you must get both the marching orders for the team, as well as the resources to do the job. Hirshhorn reminds us that, on one hand, you must be a good corporate citizen linking the team to the corporate context and objectives. On the other hand, you need to protect and defend the team. You have pressure from below and from above.[10]

Within the team you must balance demands, sometimes conflicting, between individual team members and the task, between individual team members and the team, between the team and the task, and between the team and the larger organization. Again, you're a juggler. And if you drop one of these balls, you must invest in damage control. Typical examples might include:

- You fail to acknowledge the unique contribution of an individual on the team.

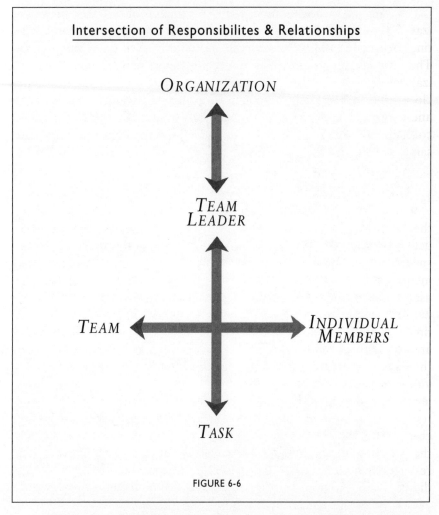

Intersection of Responsibilites & Relationships

ORGANIZATION

TEAM
LEADER

TEAM ← → INDIVIDUAL
MEMBERS

TASK

FIGURE 6-6

- You stress the task to the point that the team feels they are not appreciated by the organization.
- You side with the team, criticizing the "higher-ups" because those with resources higher in the hierarchy refuse to make them available.

The key to managing these trade-offs and contradictions that go with the role of team leadership is balance and a good sense of humor. Confident, self-aware leaders know their limitations. They understand that navigating through the paradoxical demands of the modern organization requires an understanding that sometimes we get it right, sometimes we don't, and we never get it right from everyone's perspective. The diversity, diverse interests, and competing needs of today's organizations seldom allow for "perfect" solutions. Our best hope is for a close fit. Effective leaders aren't held hostage to impossible standards and can chuckle at times at the expectation that two solid bodies (or conflicting ideas, goals, interests, etc.) can occupy the same space at the same time.

ACCEPTANCE IS EARNED, NOT DEMANDED

A few months ago I sat with a team leader who was lamenting on the difficulty of getting her team in gear. She was responsible for a product research effort that was designed to demonstrate the efficacy of a specific brand of medicine so the company could use the research finding in advertising claims. Her team members were all part-timers assigned from different functions. Some were to invest as much as 40 percent of their time, others as little as 5-10 percent. She had a difficult time getting consistent attendance at the team meetings. When they did attend, more energy was directed to side issues among team members than to the objectives of the meeting. After observation and a few interviews, it became clear that team members did not feel that their team leader had the "power" to get the needed resources and support from top management. Although this woman was an extremely capable chemist, she did not demonstrate the ability to communicate vision for the project to either upper management or to her team members. As a result, they were hesitant to invest their energies into something they didn't believe was going anywhere.

The qualifying adjective, "accepted," in our chapter title implies that there can be *unaccepted* leadership. I suspect that most of us have experienced situations in which a formal leader was not accepted by the group. Being assigned a formal leadership role in a group does not guarantee that the individual members in the group will loyally line up behind you. To be effective, you must be accepted by those you lead, and such acceptance is earned, not demanded.

When leadership is accepted, people are more responsive, more involved, and quicker to take initiative. Individual members are more supportive of the leader's efforts to provide leadership to the group.

They actively help the leader lead both themselves and the team as a whole. Over the years, I've observed that when I find an effective leader, I always find effective, willing followers as well—followers who go out of their way to help the leader lead.

Leadership acceptance will come easier when the team leader has a mind-set that reflects the value and potential of those he or she leads and sees the role of leadership as serving rather than being served. Having a clear understanding of the job of team leader coupled with an inclusive, facilitative style is also a major contributing factor in acceptance. I want to round out these observations with a brief overview of the attributes people look for in "accepted" leaders.

One extensive research effort on this topic asked managers to list the values, personal traits, or characteristics they look for and admire in leaders. More than 225 values, traits, and characteristics were identified. However, the vast majority of responses focused on four primary qualities:

1. Honest. Did they do what they said they were going to do?

2. Competent. Do they have the skills and knowledge to get us where we are going?

3. Visionary. Can they see past the horizon? Do they have a believable view of a desirable future?

4. Inspirational. Do they have a positive, enthusiastic, and energetic view about the future?

Taken together, these characteristics comprise what the experts refer to as "credibility," and credibility is the foundation for acceptance.[11] Ultimately leadership boils down to a relationship. High-quality relationships are based on trust—trust of one anothers' *competence* as well as *character*. Teams consist of interdependent relationships, and we will not be interdependent with those we do not trust. Trust is earned (more realistically it is lent) every time leaders do what they say they will do, do it with excellence, and do it with a spirit that conveys they serve and value those whom they lead.

START, STOP, AND CONTINUE—AN EXERCISE IN LEADERSHIP FEEDBACK

Leadership acceptance, like so many dimensions of team, is not an *on-off* concept but rather a matter of degree. Team members can strongly support and accept the leader, accept her with reservations, or totally reject her. Accepted leadership is so critical to overall team performance that anytime we can increase the level of acceptance, there is invariably a positive impact on the objectives the team is pursuing.

We have found few teams that have mastered straight talk to the point where they can candidly give the team leader feedback on how he or she, the team leader, is doing and how he or she could better serve the team. Sometimes it's because they are afraid of repercussions; often the hesitancy is motivated by not wanting to hurt the team leader's feelings. Frequently the lack of feedback stems from the fact that there is no forum or format to have such a dialogue.

Such a dialogue is possible and extremely insightful not only to the team leader but to the members as well. It must be initiated by the team leader or an outside facilitator and they, in introducing the exercise, must not only convey its purpose and value but also that the climate will be safe and conducive to candid discussion. One leader opened the exercise like this: "People, I need to know how I am doing as team leader and how I can do better, and I can't think of a more qualified group of people to give me this feedback. I would like you to spend some time this morning and develop the following list: Things I'm not doing that you would like me to start; things you would like me to stop doing, and things you like that you want me to keep doing. We will meet at ten this morning and I am going to ask you to share your thoughts using this format. Be candid. I won't faint from bad news. If you sense that I'm getting defensive, call me on it. While you're working on my list, I will develop a similar list with my thoughts for you as a team. See you at ten."

Typically, the team might come up with something like this:

- *Things we wish you would start doing*
  - Give us a better understanding of how upper management will evaluate our recommendations.

- Be clearer with us regarding decisions. Tell us in advance if we are merely providing input for a particular decision or if we are making it by consensus as a team.

- *Things we wish you would stop doing*
  - Exaggerating the consequences of missing a benchmark deadline by a few days. This project is on a three-year development track and we are always able to make up the days. When you position a two-day delay as catastrophic, it puts us under a lot of emotional pressure which, in turn, further impacts our performance and ability to hit the deadline.

- *Things we like and wish you would continue doing*
  - Having the entire team make the progress reports to the Management Committee. It gives us a chance to know them and how they are thinking about our work.
  - Celebrating benchmark accomplishments with the pizza parties.

When team leaders listen attentively, ask questions for clarity, and demonstrate they "got it," acceptance levels rise. This does not mean the leader must implement all of the suggestions. Often, he or she is not in a position to do so because of top management constraints. But at the very least it provides an opportunity to discuss and better understand the needs from both sides of the equation. As I noted above, the team leader provides similar feedback to the team: *"Here are some things you can do, as a team, to help me in my role as leader . . ."*

TASK-DRIVEN LEADERSHIP

Moment-by-moment leadership on high performance teams is *task-driven*. Actually, we find two types of leaders on a team: the *team leader*, who never changes, and *task leaders*, who change according to the needs of the situation. An outsider often has difficulty identifying the formal team leader on a high performance team. An outsider might walk by one moment to see Bob, the team leader, standing before the group, explaining the objectives of a newly assigned task. *Good leader*, the observer thinks, continuing on his way.

Moments later, Bob turns to a team member and says, "Mary, you're the most experienced finance person we have on this team; come on up and work us through a plan of attack for this project." As Mary facilitates the group discussion, our observer walks by again and thinks, *She's a great leader, but I thought* . . . Shaking his head, he continues past.

After Mary is finished, Bob turns to George and asks him, as team administrator, to explain the logistics and schedule. As he does so, the observer walks by one last time, thoroughly confused now as to who the team leader really is. In reality, there were several leaders in this situation, and Bob's role, as team leader, was *to facilitate* the change of task leadership between team members as the team developed its strategy.

One dimension of synergism embedded in every team in addition to its potentially higher collective IQ is the reservoir of leadership potential that resides in the team. There is a leader in every person. One major role of the team leader is to ensure the release of that leadership in the service of the team as he or she facilitates the constant change of task leadership as the team confronts different situations and elements of its task.

In our team workshops we sometimes blindfold the group and challenge them to assemble a portable dome tent without the benefit of sight. We don't tell how to do it, but merely drop a canvas bag full of tent and tent parts in the center of the group and assign a leader. In many groups at least one camper is familiar with tents, but seldom does the leader ask if anyone has experience with this sort of problem.

The blindfolds tend to make participants more passive in offering unsolicited input than would normally be the case and so, in many instances, this resource is wasted as the team flails about unproductively. In those few instances where the question is asked, leadership is almost immediately transferred to the experienced team member, who quickly explains to the rest of the group what a dome tent looks like and how to best organize to assemble it. In these rare cases the quantity and quality of leadership available to the team is greatly multiplied. Did the team leader abdicate? No. He or she facilitated task-driven leadership which reverted to the team leader at the completion of the task.

Task leadership occurs when individual team members provide direction out of their skills, functional expertise, and experience. With every team member contributing whatever leadership they can whenever it's needed, leadership becomes one more resource that can be leveraged by the team in the accomplishment of its mission.

THE BOTTOM LINE

High performance teams are supported by high performance leaders—team leaders who see their responsibility as a role from which to serve rather than a position to be served. These leaders could be better described as facilitators, networkers, resourcers, and boundary managers. They are attuned to the needs of the team and *serve* those needs willingly, knowing that the real "boss" of their team is the task.

Acceptance can't be demanded from followers. It must be volunteered. Team leaders who call high levels of commitment out of their followers are invariably seen by those followers to be servant leaders. Notice the order of the words—servanthood is "assumed," leadership is "bestowed." It is one's belief system that allows him or her to assume the role of a servant team leader:

- They appreciate the collective brilliance of a team.

- They believe in the power of diversity.

- They see team leadership as a role from which to serve, not a position to be served.

- They see leadership and power as something to be released and shared rather than something to hold and control.

- They understand teams are all about tasks and that they must master the delicate balance needed between the task, the team, and individual team members.

MESSAGE TO TEAM LEADERS

In every respect, this entire chapter has been a message to team leaders. If I had to add anything, it would be that team leadership may be the most challenging of all leadership roles. In this arena, the team leader must lay aside his or her mantle of *positional* leader and take on the role of a *servant* leader, serving the task of the team as well as the individual members.

CHAPTER SEVEN

Effective Team Processes

THE POWER OF A PROCESS

The DC-10 is one of the first aircraft designed to rely solely on hydraulic, as opposed to mechanical, linkage between the cockpit and the plane's control surfaces. DC-10s, with their three independent hydraulic systems, are constructed in such a way that it is considered a billion-to-one odds that complete hydraulic failure could occur. United Flight 232 proved to be that one-in-a-billion experience.

Once Captain Haynes and his crew realized their precarious situation following the explosion, the crew began executing a series of well-defined processes that played a key role in helping them get the plane on the ground. Although the plane did crash, Captain Haynes believes these processes were vital for containing the damage, preventing a complete disaster, and saving many lives. He calls them "standard operating procedures" or SOPs—a series of procedures worked out in advance, practiced, and applied with concerted diligence in a particular situation.[1]

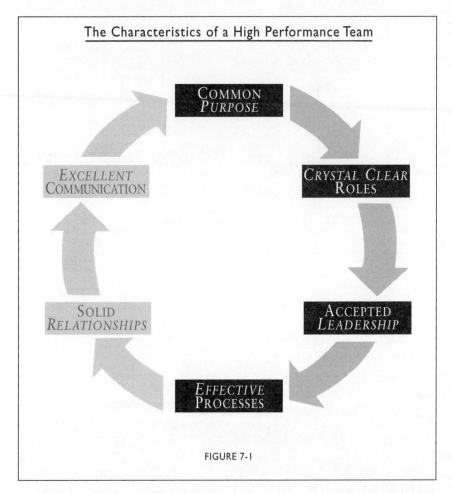

The Characteristics of a High Performance Team

COMMON
PURPOSE

CRYSTAL CLEAR
ROLES

EXCELLENT
COMMUNICATION

ACCEPTED
LEADERSHIP

SOLID
RELATIONSHIPS

EFFECTIVE
PROCESSES

FIGURE 7-1

Captain Al Haynes described the role of process for a flight team: "None of us really like standard operating procedures, especially pilots. They don't like being told how to do their job or how they should fly their airplane. But standard operating procedures are absolutely essential, if for no other reason than for a foundation on which to build. On United we have emergency and regular procedures that are in the book for us to follow in case of an irregular procedure on the airplane, an engine failure and so forth. Usually by the time you follow the checklist down the row, you have isolated your problem. In our particular case, when we got to the bottom of the page, we were still 35,000 feet in the air with no idea of how to fly the airplane. But by going down that list

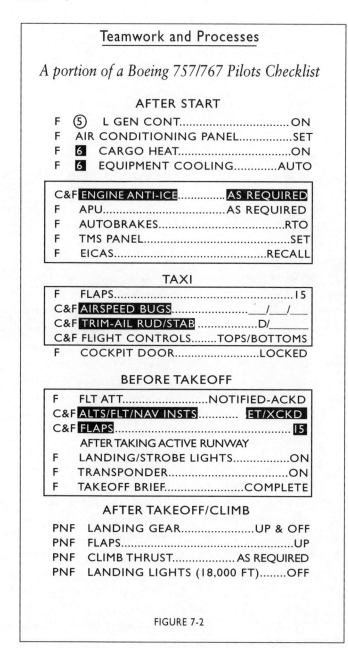

Teamwork and Processes

A portion of a Boeing 757/767 Pilots Checklist

AFTER START
F ⑤ L GEN CONT..................................ON
F AIR CONDITIONING PANEL................SET
F **6** CARGO HEAT....................................ON
F **6** EQUIPMENT COOLING.............AUTO

C&F ENGINE ANTI-ICE.............AS REQUIRED
F APU.................................AS REQUIRED
F AUTOBRAKES..................................RTO
F TMS PANEL....................................SET
F EICAS......................................RECALL

TAXI
F FLAPS..15
C&F AIRSPEED BUGS......................___/___/___
C&F TRIM-AIL RUD/STAB................D/_____
C&F FLIGHT CONTROLS........TOPS/BOTTOMS
F COCKPIT DOOR.........................LOCKED

BEFORE TAKEOFF
F FLT ATT.........................NOTIFIED-ACKD
C&F ALTS/FLT/NAV INSTS............ ET/XCKD
C&F FLAPS...15
AFTER TAKING ACTIVE RUNWAY
F LANDING/STROBE LIGHTS.................ON
F TRANSPONDER....................................ON
F TAKEOFF BRIEF......................COMPLETE

AFTER TAKEOFF/CLIMB
PNF LANDING GEAR.....................UP & OFF
PNF FLAPS...UP
PNF CLIMB THRUST.................. AS REQUIRED
PNF LANDING LIGHTS (18,000 FT)........OFF

FIGURE 7-2

as far as we could, we built a foundation of information from the standard operating procedures that allowed us to begin to experiment on our own. The SOPs were extremely important. We may think it's a pain sometimes, but it is essential that you follow standard procedures so that you are all working the same way—so that you are all following the same line of reasoning."[2]

Rule number one, for instance, is that someone must continue flying the plane while other crew members work on a problem. That's why co-pilot Bill Records kept the controls when United 232's engine blew. That's also why some flights fail. The airline industry has witnessed many disastrous incidents in which everyone attended to a problem, but no one flew the plane.

Next Haynes and second officer Dvorak began going through the checklist, the process for tackling a certain problem. According to Haynes, pilots are taught not to do anything from memory.

The operation of a modern airplane is a superb illustration of team-work and processes. The whole system is process driven; checklists are critical. Figure 7-2 provides an example of a portion of a checklist used with the Boeing 757/767 series aircraft. Generally there are two manuals that define just about everything you would want to know about flying a commercial jetliner. The pilot's operating manual covers every-thing about the plane itself and how to operate it—flight instruments, fuel, hydraulics, fire protection, oxygen, and landing gear, among other topics. A reference manual covers the elements that aren't part of the aircraft itself, such as safety procedures, passenger comfort, cockpit decorum, scheduling, and other issues. These two manuals contain the prescribed processes by which flight teams operate.

Having such predetermined processes reduces the need for planning (particularly in a crisis situation), encourages confidence, predictability, and precision among the crew, discourages unsafe practices, careless-ness, and complacency. But we're not talking about robots here. These same processes promote flexibility, professionalism, and good judg-ment. When Haynes and his crew realized SOPs wouldn't help in this situation, they were prepared to develop alternative solutions.

Other factors that contributed to their achievement were creative, out-of-the-box thinking and a willingness to take risks and try some-thing new. Many feel that process and creativity are in conflict, believ-ing that creativity needs spontaneity and unstructured approaches. No doubt, a lot of creativity is a by-product of informal, spontaneous thinking. In this instance, the foundation for such innovation was the core processes that had been hammered into the heads of the crew over the course of many years. When the procedures didn't work, as in this crisis, the team had the confidence to explore some very inventive, unorthodox experiments. As I reviewed the cockpit voice recorder transcript, I found the crew testing one process after another. When a process was unsuccessful, they identified what they had just learned and begun to design a new process, including taking advantage of unexpected opportunities.

At 3:28 P.M. twelve minutes after the explosion on United 232, a United captain, flying as a passenger in first class, tells a flight attendant who he is and asks her to tell the captain he is aboard and willing to help if needed. His name is Dennis (Denny) Fitch, and he is an instructor and check airman for the DC-10. As a check airman, his task is to fly with and evaluate DC-10 crews for United. He was off duty at the time and heading back to his home base in Chicago, having just finished an evaluation of another DC-10 crew.

Upon hearing about Fitch, Al Haynes tells the flight attendant to have him come up to the cockpit. He is looking for all of the information and resources he can get his hands on, and it occurs to him that possibly this airman might have some information they don't have.

Although Fitch arrives in the cockpit in civilian clothes (without a uniform), it is quickly apparent from his questions and demeanor that he is an asset. Haynes not only accepts Fitch's offer but quickly briefs him on the situation and sets him to work. Haynes explains that they don't have any controls and asks Fitch to return to the passenger cabin to determine if he can see any external damage to the airplane through the cabin windows. Fitch returns in a few minutes and reports that, aside from the fact that the ailerons are sticking up, he can't tell much.

Seeing Haynes' and Records' struggle with the yoke, and Dvorak's preoccupation with managing radio communications, Fitch immediately asks what he can do to help. At the captain's request he takes the throttles. Fitch kneels behind the console between the captain and co-pilot and works the throttles on their command. Captain Haynes later described the process: "Fitch began to move the throttles in response to our directions to bring a wing up or let the nose down. He would add or subtract power, and pretty soon we were working as a team. Every time we'd move the yoke, one pilot would say 'left' or 'right,' 'back' or 'forward.' Then the other pilot would move the yoke that way, and

Denny Fitch would respond accordingly with the throttles. Denny began to experiment, and pretty soon he figured out what he needed to do to help us." It turns out to be a critical task because, unknown to them at this time, the yoke was having no effect and it was only the throttles that were steering and controlling the airplane.

Calling "right" or "left" as they moved the yokes greatly enhanced the communication and coordination in their efforts, even if, in hindsight, the yoke wasn't having any actual effect on the control of the aircraft. In some respects this procedure had much the same effect as that of a coxswain calling out the beat in a crew boat. It made it easier for the individual team members to move together.

Everyone had clear roles within the process. Captain Haynes and Records worked the yokes, Fitch worked the throttles, and Dvorak coordinated radio communications. It was Dvorak who shared the situation with the passengers, explaining that because of an engine failure, they would be a little late arriving in Chicago. Although roles were crystal clear, the process was evolving moment by moment. Everyone felt free to take the initiative to suggest process improvements and help in any other person's area.

Having well-defined, agreed-upon processes makes perfect sense in many situations. Teams and processes go together. Many professions take processes for granted. It would never occur to a surgical team, construction crew, string quartet, film crew, or the team on the flight deck of Flight 232 to approach their tasks without clearly defined processes. The playbook of a football team or the score sheet of a string quartet clearly outlines their process.

Business teams have processes as well. Instead of a run off tackle or executing the scene in Act II, business processes would include activities like designing a new product, hiring new team members, making a major sales presentation, completing the monthly financial reports, making a decision, having a meeting, and any other activities we take in pursuit of our mission. Hopefully, in each of these processes, each of us has a clear, specific role based on our function, skills, and expertise. However, too often in team situations such processes are often inadequate, ill defined, or missing entirely. I find there are four common barriers to developing effective team processes:

1. *Unclear need.* Actors wouldn't think of going on stage without a script and lots of rehearsal. But, for some reason, many teams in

business settings attempt to "wing it"; they will make a major presentation to a new client with little effort to coordinate themselves around the objective. They don't stop and agree about where to start, how to proceed, and who will do what and when. The concept of practice and debriefing after the presentation is given little thought. Time is the issue as they rush off to prepare for the next new client presentation in which they often make the same mistakes.

In spite of such pitfalls due to hasty or ill-conceived processes, these teams continue to speed along, never slowing to evaluate their methods. They seem blind to the need to evaluate not just the substance of the task and their results, but also the processes involved.

2. *Lack of time.* Not long ago I was asked to facilitate a conflict between two departmental teams which were at loggerheads over how to allocate and divide a series of common costs the larger organization had assessed each department. After interviewing the key executives in each group, I met with one of the department heads to give him my initial impressions. "MacMillan, we really need your help on this thing. It has cost us tons of hours and a lot of emotional energy." I explained that my first thoughts were that the issue was pretty straightforward and there appeared to be several solutions that might meet their needs. In fact, it appeared to be so straightforward that I wondered why they hadn't addressed the problem themselves. "Time!" the executive shot back. "The clock was running."

"When is it not running?" I responded. I could tell in his sheepish grin that he got the point. The clock is always running. In Western culture, particularly in the U.S., we have a problem with time. Our society promotes 30-second hamburgers and One-Hour Martinizing. We live in a very impatient society in which instant is preferred over merely fast. We have time to do things again but not to do them right the first time. There is a propensity for action that often precludes taking the time to plan and agree upon our processes.

3. *Process evolution versus design.* I grew up in a beachfront house on beautiful Puget Sound. Every morning of my childhood I awakened to a view of the sound and the Olympic Mountains in the distance. My parents bought the house for the setting, not its architecture. Many years before we arrived, it was a two-room summer cottage.

Then the owners added a bedroom and a storage area. Their children later added a family room and an entire second floor. The subsequent owners remodeled again and added a third floor and then, after some years, my family bought it. The house was great for kids. It was like living in a maze. With no master plan, every project was an "add-on" or "fix." You even had to go outside and around the side of the house to reach bedrooms on the first floor. My brother and I, who occupied the rooms, didn't mind the detour. Because of the hassle of getting there, we didn't have many parental room inspections. After a number of years, my parents finally came to grips with starting over. One more "fix," and the whole structure would surely come tumbling down around our shoulders.

I see many processes that remind me of my childhood home, processes that are a product of evolution rather than design. Because the process is there, even though it doesn't work very well, we keep right on using it. Every once in a while we might apply a "fix," but it's clear there was no master plan in its origins. The urgency of current operating demands conspires to keep a more complete redesign of this process in the cool part of our to-do list. When you have numerous processes that have evolved in such a fashion or systems that, although once effective, have grown cumbersome and inefficient, the organization loses its responsiveness. Lethargy abounds, as though a giant tapeworm were sapping the organizational vitality. More energy is devoted to doing it again to correct mistakes, assign blame, and resolve conflicts than to serving customers and building the business.

What is the logical solution? Do you continue to spend three hours having a one-hour meeting? Or go home every night feeling tense about the relationships with the accounting department because they never get the accounts receivable report out in time? Do you experience stress watching your competition consistently beat you to market with new products? Have you ever spent a few hours (or days and even months if the issue is important enough) designing a process that efficiently and effectively addresses those issues?

4. *Management opposition.* Building team-based organizations means organizing around processes rather than departments and functions. In today's world, almost all work to meet customer demands cuts across multiple departments. Initiating well-defined, effective

processes has a very liberating effect in an organizational setting. Everyone knows what to do and how to do it. They can monitor their efforts to see if the expected output occurs and take remedial action when needed. They can take initiative to improve the system whenever anyone comes up with a better idea. However, such liberty is challenging to insecure managers who believe everyone needs them to tell them what to do. In these situations, the process is often there, but "there" is in the manager's head. The process is like a map, and the person with the map is the person with power.

Manager resistance can come from myriad factors—concern over job security, personality, role confusion, perceived loss of freedom, and lack of skill. However, when supervisors see the power and potential that can be found in releasing the creative initiative of the team around a well-designed work process, they quickly become the champions of such efforts. A concerted effort to provide assurances of job security, role clarity, good communication, and time will bring many of the resisting managers into alignment with the new paradigm of organization.

Although teams work well within vertical hierarchies, a vertical mind-set becomes a liability when it comes to processes. Processes are invariably horizontal, and when one places too much emphasis on the vertical dimension of the organization, to the point where boundaries become barriers, these processes quickly become blocked, convoluted, and inefficient. The vertical and horizontal dimensions of an organization must reflect an appropriate balance, with horizontal processes generating results and the vertical hierarchy accounting for them.

New Wine, Old Wineskins

Recently a client came to us when conflict between two internal teams had grown to the point where it was affecting overall business results. These two departments were responsible for selling and providing financing to the construction industry. One department (Sales) sold the financing services to prospective clients, the other (Underwriting) processed the application, analyzed the deal, and recommended acceptance and on what terms. The entire procedure was so slow that many potentially qualified clients became frustrated and found other sources for their financing. Both departments were convinced they knew the roots of the problem: the other department! The Sales group claimed that Underwriting was incompetent and didn't honor their turnaround commitments. Underwriting felt that the Sales department was too motivated by their potential commissions on a deal and, as a result, brought in high-risk deals (which took a lot more time to process) and incomplete applications. Motives were challenged, and relationships were rapidly deteriorating. As communication worsened, the application flow slowed even more.

What had been viewed as a relational problem was actually a product of poor process. Several years before, the company had pioneered a new form of financing that proved very successful. One of the benefits of this new product was that it was also applicable to many other types of construction projects than the original product. For all practical purposes they had totally transformed the nature of their product and the types of customers who bought it, but they continued to use the old process with adaptations made on the fly. Over the years they had taken up the slack by working harder and longer, but now there was no slack left and work quality and relationships were the first victims. It was beginning to affect even the bottom line.

The New Testament contains a parable about the futility of putting new wine into an old wineskin. In those days people stored wine in animal-skin containers, not bottles. Because the new wine was still fermenting, it would continue to release gases, putting pressure on the skin. A new skin had the flexibility to withstand this pressure, but an older skin, stiff with age, would burst. A similar parable could be told of the organization above when they attempted to put new circumstances (in this case new product and client type) into old processes.

Processes are the "how" we go about achieving the "what" in our purpose. They are a sequence of step-by-step actions designed to produce a desired outcome. The word *designed* in this definition is an important qualifier. Processes, like any other dimension of organizational life, must be addressed with a determined intentionality. Often there is too little "design" in our processes. We are quick to equate any process activity with little thought about which might be the best activities and what might be the best sequence. In many situations, activities are relatively unconnected with the outputs we really seek. The result is often a lot of activity but little accomplishment. Even effective processes become ineffective over time as circumstances change. When this happens the organizational dominoes begin to fall. Business results suffer when traditional processes cease to fit current realities, roles drift out of alignment, relationships become strained, and miscommunication occurs.

WORKING TOGETHER AND THINKING TOGETHER

Over the past ten years, the emphasis on re-engineering and total quality management has contributed to increased awareness on the part of teams as to the importance of process. Many teams have made great strides in approaching their basic work processes with the intentionality needed to achieve exceptional results. However, many, even after investing in their basic work processes, still feel frustrated in their attempts to achieve the synergies they desire. Because synergy is found in both the work and wisdom of the team, we have found it is very helpful for teams to divide their processes into two categories: implementation processes and thinking processes.

Implementation processes are the executional processes that drive business results. Examples might be manufacturing amplifier components, selling products, and underwriting insurance policies. Thinking processes are frameworks that allow a team to collectively discuss, think, and decide about issues. Thinking processes are activities like planning, decision making, problem solving, and conflict resolution.

In today's world of cross-functional teams, we must be able to think together with the same degree of skill with which we hope to work together. Cross-functional teams are an acknowledgement of the fact that in a world of knowledge workers, we divide knowledge much in the same way that we used to divide labor. Synergy, in many respects, will be determined by a team's ability to think together—to leverage the diverse functional expertise available to the team to higher levels of creativity and effectiveness. The collective IQ of the team is often best seen in the team's thinking processes.

However, we have found that it is the thinking processes of a team that are most often ignored. One reason is that we have a difficult time seeing these activities as processes. After all, what does it take to have an effective meeting or to make a decision anyway? Many team processes like decision making, meeting management, and planning appear to be so easy that we believe we can just jump into the activity with little thought about how to best organize our collective efforts. It isn't long before we find that appearances were deceiving. Without a well-defined method and ground rules, these processes quickly become ruled by the most articulate, assertive, or argumentative in the group. The collective IQ never gets into the game. The fruit of such endeavors is often frustration, anger, poor decisions, wasted time, and confirmation to the more reflective members that, in the future, they would rather do the work alone. As with any process, when people have a common approach to thinking processes from decision making to meeting management, they find it easier to work as a team.

HIGH PERFORMANCE TEAMS
ARE PROCESS FANATICS

High performance teams are very intentional about both their work and thinking processes. They are clear about what processes they need and then they map and master them.

Mapping your processes (making them visible). The first step in the design of any process is to clearly describe the desired output, whether it's an effectively run meeting that produces high-quality decisions or a product design process that delivers new product in half the time of the current method. Secondly, identify the specific actions (steps in the process) that will bring about this outcome. Finally, identify who on the team is responsible for each action or step in the process. Whether a list of ground rules or a map, the process on paper becomes *visible* to all team members. What we are attempting to accomplish, the steps we need to take, and individual responsibilities become clear. Making the process visible allows the team to quickly *see* inefficient areas of the process or unproductive activity and to "re-engineer" the process accordingly.

Mastering your processes (making them better). Effective teams watch the process game films. After making and implementing a major decision, the team would take a few minutes and debrief (Figure 7-3). How effective was our decision? If we had to do it again, what would we do differently? What changes in our decision process would allow us to make future decisions faster and more effectively? Please note that unless the process is written down and made visible in some way, it would be virtually impossible to evaluate how well the team is implementing it. They would have no

FIGURE 7-3

standards of performance and comparison that would even let them ask the question. This team would have the same discussions about their work processes—a sales team might discuss how well they rolled out a new product to their customers and how they could do it better, an engineering team might analyze and improve their design process.

In both designing and evaluating processes, these teams would pay particular attention to passing the "process baton." Processes should be designed to facilitate the exchange of the baton, the movement of responsibility from one person to another. Careful design will then make it evident when and why the baton is dropped. I suspect many of us have been in or seen situations like that in Figure 7-4. Those poor guys not only dropped the baton; they lost it!

In the Bleachers

You what!!? I can't believe this! Now think. When was the last time you had it in your hand?!"

FIGURE 7-4

TURNING PRINCIPLE INTO PRACTICE—THE MEETING

Several years ago I was asked to work with a special team (I'll call them the Strategy Team) of a large corporation. The team, which consisted of 15 members from two separate departments, had collapsed under the strain of broken relationships as two of the functional areas represented were locked in major conflict. Infighting was intense, and the consequences were painful. Team members felt frustrated, rejected, and misunderstood. As a result, they withdrew from one another. When apart, they disparaged members of the other group, challenging either their competence or character. Business results suffered as other people from other departments were drawn into the fray. They were becoming angry with the inability of team members from these two departments to "get their respective acts together."

I worked with the team for a number of months. And over the course of several off-site sessions and a good number of small group and individual meetings, the rift began to close. A beachhead of trust was established, making communication more effective, and even this relief in the tension created a visibly better work climate. This improvement, in turn, motivated even more communication and the first tentative steps in collaboration.

This particular management team was responsible for the corporation's primary product and marketing decisions—decisions that were generally made in a monthly strategy meeting. Because of the team breakdown described above, several months had passed since they had held one of these meetings, despite their importance. Meetings had just been too painful and only aggravated the relational problem. When necessary, decisions had been made in smaller, more informal, ad hoc settings. They were getting by, but only getting by. As relationships became healthier, the first thing they decided to do was to resurrect the monthly strategy meeting and request my help to work through how to keep these meetings positive and productive.

If your team meetings have not been as effective as you feel they could be, you might gain some insight for improvement from the process used by this strategy team. One of the first steps was to clarify the team's mission and, subsequently, the mission of this meeting. Next we evaluated meetings up to that point. I had each of them rate the overall quality of their meetings on a scale of 1 to 100 (with 100 as the best possible score). I also had them rate decision quality in the same manner. The results were predictable. The average score for meetings was 41. (That's not as bad as it seems—the national average is 47![3]) Decision quality, evaluated on the same scale, rated 46. Looking at the bright side, the group had significant opportunity for growth.

Team Meeting Evaluation[4]

	NOT AT ALL DESCRIPTIVE 1	SELDOM DESCRIPTIVE 2	SOMEWHAT DESCRIPTIVE 3	OFTEN DESCRIPTIVE 4	VERY DESCRIPTIVE 5
1. The purpose and objectives of our meetings are clearly defined before we meet.	☐	☐	☐	☐	☐
2. Our meetings tend to start on time.	☐	☐	☐	☐	☐
3. Our meetings tend to end on time.	☐	☐	☐	☐	☐
4. Those attending have the authority necessary to make needed decisions.	☐	☐	☐	☐	☐
5. We review progress during the course of our meeting.	☐	☐	☐	☐	☐
6. We have agreed on a systematic process to make decisions.	☐	☐	☐	☐	☐
7. The individuals who attend the meetings have to be there (e.g., to give data, make decisions, etc.) and they feel the time involvement is worthwhile.	☐	☐	☐	☐	☐
8. We start meetings with a clear statement of objectives.	☐	☐	☐	☐	☐
9. People come prepared (i.e., completed pre-work, etc.).	☐	☐	☐	☐	☐
10. We stay on course and don't allow the participants to get off the subject.	☐	☐	☐	☐	☐
11. Participants have a clear understanding of their roles in the meeting.	☐	☐	☐	☐	☐
12. People retain interest and attention during the meeting.	☐	☐	☐	☐	☐

FIGURE 7-5

	NOT AT ALL DESCRIPTIVE	SELDOM DESCRIPTIVE	SOMEWHAT DESCRIPTIVE	OFTEN DESCRIPTIVE	VERY DESCRIPTIVE
	1	2	3	4	5
13. We "conserve" decisions and ideas that are generated in the meetings through effective use of minutes, memos, etc.	☐	☐	☐	☐	☐
14. Our meetings generally *allocate the proper amount of time for the subject at hand.*	☐	☐	☐	☐	☐
15. *We follow up and implement decision made in our meetings.*	☐	☐	☐	☐	☐
16. *We have a clear set of meeting ground rules that outline participant rules and responsibilities.*	☐	☐	☐	☐	☐
17. *Presenters for agenda items* make it clear how they want us to listen (i.e., for feedback, decision making, etc.).	☐	☐	☐	☐	☐
18. If a regularly scheduled meeting is not needed, we will cancel it.	☐	☐	☐	☐	☐
19. FYI material that can be effectively communicated by memo or e-mail is not covered at our meetings.	☐	☐	☐	☐	☐
20. Presenters make effective use of presentation tools (e.g., PowerPoint, overheads, flip charts, handouts, etc.)	☐	☐	☐	☐	☐

Scoring: *Assign a value of 1 to all marks in column 1, a 2 to column 2 marks and so on through column 5. Next total your overall score which will fall somewhere between 20 and 100. How did you do?*

more than 80 — *"Excellent! I love these meetings!"*
66–80 — *"Pretty good but we can improve."*
51–65 — *"Mundane, I'll send my assistant."*
36–50 — *"Painful experience—just send me a memo."*
20–35 — *"Dismally poor. Don't send me anything!"*

How did other team members score this survey? Is there agreement on areas needing improvement? What specific actions will you take to improve meeting effectiveness?

FIGURE 7-5

Next they completed a short survey detailing specific problems that hampered meeting effectiveness (Figure 7-5). They discussed the survey results, emphasizing items with low scores and the root causes, and

Strategy Team Meeting Ground Rules

MEETING SCHEDULE

1. When there is no reason to meet, we will not meet.
2. Attendance will be limited to our regular members. We will invite others to attend only when their expertise is needed.
3. Meetings will start and end on time.

AGENDA AND MINUTES

1. We will limit our topics only to those that fit our team mission statement.
2. We will prepare the agenda for the next meeting at the end of each team meeting.
3. Each agenda item will include topics, outcome frames for each topic, time allotments, presenters, and required decision makers.
4. A final agenda, complete with prework, will be issued one week before each meeting.
5. Each meeting will begin with a brief status report of progress since the previous meeting.
6. Each team member will take his or her turn at being recorder for the meeting. Minutes will be finalized by the recorder with 48 hours of the meeting and will be e-mailed to each team member.

MEETING GROUND RULES

1. We will respect each other's competence, opinions, and contributions at all times.
2. No side conversations are allowed.
3. Silence is hearty acquiescence.
4. Off the track (out of frame) topics that are nonetheless important will be noted on a flip chart for future reference.
5. We will address issues, not personalities. Personal attacks will not be tolerated.
6. We will be prepared for each meeting (having read the prework) and will stay for the entire meeting.
7. We will commit to be candid and open with one another.
8. Each meeting will have a facilitator to assist the team process.
9. We will briefly evaluate each meeting for efficiency and effectiveness in the interest of continuous improvement.

FIGURE 7-6

then laid out the ground rules for running future meetings (Figure 7-6). These guidelines established their meeting process.

Did it work? Note their last ground rule (Figure 7-6), which says they will evaluate each meeting for efficiency and effectiveness, in the interest of continuous improvement. They did this faithfully, publishing those scores in the meeting minutes. Every six months, or more often if necessary, they spent an hour asking how they were doing. They looked at their score and asked how they could improve. They reviewed their ground rules and edited them accordingly. Scores from the first nine months of their effort are shown in Figure 7-7.

This is an excellent example of a team process in action. They designed their process and made it visible with a set of written ground rules. They monitored and measured both the process and results and continuously improved in both areas. What the chart in Figure 7-7 doesn't show is that they were also able to cut their average meeting

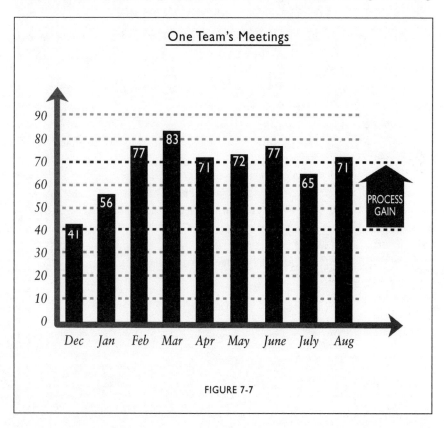

FIGURE 7-7

time by 50 percent and increase the average score for decision effectiveness to between 75 and 80 on a scale of 1 to 100. That's a process gain!

THE BOTTOM LINE

A team can be no more effective than its processes and the ability of the team to execute them well. Most teams have two basic types of processes—work implementation processes and thinking processes. Work processes are the core processes that accomplish the team's primary mission. For example, sell the product. Thinking processes are process frameworks that facilitate the thinking and discussion of the team as they resolve issues. Too often teams overlook the existence and importance of thinking processes, which need to be addressed with the same degree of deliberateness the team invests in their work processes.

MESSAGE TO TEAM LEADERS

The pressure to get work done in this no-time, high-urgency world tends to eliminate any thought of taking a few moments to ask, "How are we doing and how can we do better?" Team leaders have the power to create time for evaluation by reminding the team that it's OK to call time out to ask those questions.

Every organization, including teams, has two primary objectives: build the business and build organizational capacity (for example, leadership, systems, processes, etc.). They must build the business today or go out of business today; they must build the organization today or go out of business tomorrow. Effective leaders are able to manage the tensions of these two objectives and ensure that the team regularly addresses its processes. They understand that processes are the best vehicle through which the team both works together and thinks together, and the team cannot perform any better than its processes will allow it to.

CHAPTER EIGHT

Solid Relationships

T he crew of UAL 232 weren't best friends. In fact, they didn't know one another all that well. Captain Haynes had flown six times during the previous 90 days with Bill Records, unusually frequent in the scheduling scheme of any commercial airline. It was Dudly Dvorak's first month flying a DC-10. As a crew, these three men had flown one four-day set together prior to this assignment, and Captain Haynes had never met Denny Fitch before he came forward to the flight deck to help during the incident. Yet these individuals related to one another in a crisis to achieve exceptional levels of teamwork.

I asked Captain Haynes if having an opportunity to fly several times with his copilot over the previous several months was a factor in their success in getting the plane on the ground. I suspected that even a little foundation of relationship would increase their confidence and communication. His answer surprised me. "It's hard to say," he responded. "I did have confidence in Bill because I had flown with him before, but I have a great deal of confidence in United Airlines' training. I feel very comfortable with any copilot United says is OK to fly on the line. Everybody can fly the airplane, or they wouldn't be there." As to how four nearly complete strangers worked so effectively together under so much stress, he had an answer for that as well: Standard Operating Procedures. "That's how the four of us communicated so well when we

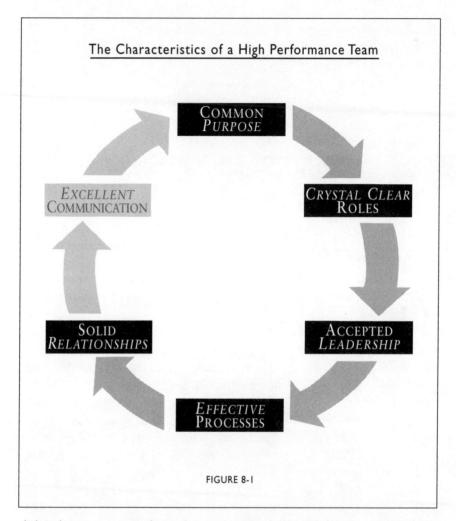

The Characteristics of a High Performance Team

FIGURE 8-1

didn't know one another," he said. "We followed standard operating procedures."

On reading this, some might think: If all a team needs for effective performance is a good process and trust in the system (in this case, United's ability to train and qualify pilots), then why do teams put so much energy into building relationships? If we read between the lines of Captain Haynes's remarks, we would find some determinative content about relationships. Haynes wasn't saying that relationship wasn't important, but rather that it is the nature of the relationship that counts. Effective team leaders understand the relational qualities needed for high levels of team effectiveness and work diligently to build team cultures that foster those qualities.

CHUMS VS. COLLEAGUES

In the world of teams and teamwork I often find the belief that to work and communicate effectively, team members must be close comrades. In fact, this is a common misperception. Although team members don't need to know one another very well personally to perform as a team, they do need to know one another's abilities and potential contributions.

In many technically oriented or highly structured jobs, the procedures are well developed and clear. The specialists who perform them or certain parts of the larger process are well trained, rehearsed, and often certified. Commercial airline pilots or a surgical team performing angioplasty or even open-heart surgery would certainly fall into this category.

I have had an opportunity to produce several films and have watched with wonder as diverse groups of specialists, many strangers, come together in some of the most choreographed, high performance teamwork I've ever witnessed. Sound engineers, lighting specialists, gaffers, grips, set designers, make-up artists, costume designers, caterers, and actors, all under the leadership of a director, come together for an almost seamless production. The script provides the overall game plan, and the unions or guilds of each specialty represented on the crew attest to the competence of their representatives. In such instances, specialists, on short notice, contribute their unique expertise and knowledge, complete the task and disperse, going on to their next assignments. They perform well, not because they like one another or even know one another, but because they know how to work together.

Relationships do indeed play an important part on high performance teams. But the kind of relationship necessary for a team's performance differs markedly from friendship.

Friendship is, among other things, built on compatibility of interests, shared values, and alignment of other relational and philosophical dimensions. In contrast, team synergy is born out of the differences between team members. The more distinctive the diversity among the team, the more options they have to creatively deploy themselves against goals, decisions, problems, and opportunities. The result-oriented nature of a Division VP; the measured, analytical nature of a Finance representative; the optimism, energy, and creativity of an employee from Sales; and the systematic, process orientation of the representative from Customer Service all combine into something greater than the sum of the individual contributions. However, if mismanaged, these differences will lead to strife rather than synergy.

DIFFERENCES DO MAKE A DIFFERENCE

Several years ago *The New York Times* ran an entertaining article about a growing number of corporations that were taking their management teams mushing—you know, snow, dogs, sleds, cold. One of the mushing enthusiasts observed many parallels between teams of dogs and teams of people:

Each dog is an individual. They can be ornery, but each has a role to play. The challenge is to get them to work together.

The dogs are bred for speed and endurance, not looks. They're smaller than might be expected, weighing 35 to 50 pounds. But they know their business. If you're not doing your part—maybe getting off the sled and pushing up a hill—they turn around and look at you, wondering if you know what you're doing. You realize that they are training you.

Some of the dogs resemble definite corporate types. There's Wyoming, the leader who never seems to have any fun. If the team stops and the other dogs start playing, he just stands there, his brown eyes focused on the trail ahead. On the other hand, there are the leaders Gillis and Sag, sisters who keep up team morale by such antics as jumping in the sled when no one is looking.

The lead dog is not necessarily the alpha male. Smoky is the leader of the group, and he's the wheel dog, the one closest to the sled. He's respected because he works his buns off. When Smoky says, others do. I may say 'whoa!' but they only stop if Smoky barks.

Five rather small dogs can be very powerful. If you can get a team pulling together in one direction, you can get enormous power out of them.[1]

What a great illustration about cooperation in the face of contrast and difference. I can't include a chapter on team relationships without at least mentioning the topic of diversity. Putting it on the table as an issue, a critical one, is all I can do, for the subject is so broad in scope and complex in nature, to adequately address it would require another book.[2]

Diversity, as an issue of importance, was first sighted on the corporate radar screens in the 1970's. Over 20 years later, American organizations are still wrestling with it. Some observers would say the results have been mixed at best. Others, possibly more pragmatic, would express disappointment in the gap between reality and expectations. Roosevelt Thomas, founder of The American Institute for Managing Diversity, notes that between the mid-1980's and mid-1990's, he has seen little change in the effectiveness of organizations in managing diversity. "Organizations," he concludes, "still do not work well for the non-traditional worker."[3]

Denial, debate, or any other strategy to delay or deflect the onslaught of diversity is naïve. We are becoming so diverse in the make-up of the workforce that anything other than effectively embracing it would be organizational suicide. A 1987 study funded by the U. S. Department of Labor projected that 25 million people would join the American workforce between 1987 and 2000. Of these new workers, only 15 percent will be young, white males, once the mainstay of American business. Women will make up 61 percent, and minorities will account for 29 percent (minority women were counted twice).[4]

The first thing that comes to mind when the topic of diversity is raised are the issues of gender and race within the workforce. Certainly, when it comes to differences, those two have the lion's share of media attention. But they only represent the tip of the iceberg. Diversity encompasses all differences among coworkers, and the typical organization is characterized by race, gender, generational, physical, mental, functional specialty, stylistic and personality differences, to name a few. All of these combined can either lead to synergy and competitive advantage or to strife and discord.

In his book *Redefining Diversity*, Thomas observes that when confronted with differences, people respond in one or several well-defined actions.[5]

1. *Inclusion.* Acknowledge the issue and develop a strategy to increase target-group members at all hierarchical levels. This is generally the principle that undergirds most affirmative action efforts.

2. *Denial.* Deny that differences even exist. When the issue of difference is put on the table, the message is that differences will not, in any way, affect how the organization treats people. Merit and performance are what count. Sweeping differences under the carpet doesn't make them go away.

3. *Assimilation.* Expect that those who are different and in the minority will somehow learn to be like the majority.

   Charles Garfield describes the insidiousness of assimilation, explaining that its basic proposition stems from the philosophy: "If you can't beat 'em, join 'em." It involves inventing a new artificial self that takes on the appearance and mannerisms of the majority group. This philosophy robs people of their basic identities and, ultimately, their self-esteem. It's a sword that cuts both ways—assimilators lose their identities, and the organization loses the creativity, energy, and contribution of these workers. Garfield provides an excellent illustration of assimilation and its potential consequences with an observation by Michelle Hunt, then vice president of People at Herman Miller: "I think women for a long time, particularly in management, were told to play the game the way the man plays it, and that's the way to get ahead. The problem with that is then you are not adding value. If I'm attempting to think like a man, then what am I bringing to the table?"[6]

4. *Suppression.* Encourage those with differences to hide them and not manifest them. Unlike denial, suppression acknowledges the differences, but discourages their expression "for the good of the enterprise."

5. *Isolation.* Include people or organizational entities with differences, but separate them from the majority so they won't contaminate the culture with new or radical ideas.

6. *Tolerance.* Live and let live. Individuals or entities with differences are included, but not valued. Their presence is accepted, even sought out, but not their ideas and contribution. Those who

"tolerate" are seen by the tolerated as arrogant and condescending. It's unlikely that in such a culture the "tolerated" will reciprocate with their highest and best effort.

7. *Build relationships.* Overcome differences through good relationships. The focus is on similarities, with the hope of avoiding the challenges associated with differences. Thomas correctly observes that most team-building sessions stress this dimension of relationship.[7] I have found that creativity and synergy flow from leveraging differences rather than combining likenesses.

8. *Foster mutual adaptation.* Accept and understand differences and diversity, realizing that all parties may be called on to accommodate and to adapt. Mutual adaptation enhances a team's ability to deal with the complexity of diversity. To some extent this is one of the most challenging dimensions of diversity. Most of us will go to great lengths to avoid complexity and to keep things simple and manageable. For example, the use of stereotypes, an inflexible, uniform way of describing people who aren't like you, is a way of keeping life from getting too complex.

The lack of diversity is harmful to the vitality of a healthy team ecosystem—the climate needed to engender creativity and insight. For it is the diversity of experiences, perspectives, and skills that introduces increased quantities of creative solutions. When those differences exist, if we embrace any of the eight strategies above other than number eight, mutual adaptation, we sever the path to enhanced levels of team communication, originality, and innovation.

For the team leader there are several important insights needed to effectively manage diversity in a team setting:

- *Be clear and honest about your own feelings*; if you hold bias or prejudice toward differences, it will be unlikely that you can create an environment that will have the synergistic cohesiveness needed by the team.

- *Don't be naïve about diversity*; either the positive or negative effects: become clear about the positive contributions of diversity. Diversity is not good just because it's the law, it's good because it's good business. The more different a team is, the smarter it is. Your task as team leader is to help the team realize they have greater potential if they can capitalize on their differences. Be just as clear about the effects of prejudice and bias. When prejudice between team members is present within the team, it's as though a hockey team voluntarily decided to place one or two of their members in the penalty box, and attempted to compete effectively against the opposing team with fewer players.

- *Keep things on the table and in the light.* If diversity is hampering the team's ability to communicate or work effectively together, move toward your own resistance to confront a sensitive issue and bring it before the team. "I sense that we are not generating the level of creativity we need to have in this meeting; do any of you have suggestions on what may be hindering us or what might get us unstuck?"

- *Don't confuse diversity with lack of unity in the team's mission and values.* Those are non-negotiable.

CREATING SOLID RELATIONSHIPS

We choose the word *solid* to define effective team relationships because they must be able to withstand the jolts and turbulence of day-to-day interaction, misunderstandings, dropped balls, disagreements, and bad-hair days. Six qualities are essential in building solid relationships.

Trust

Trust is the essential quality in any team relationship. Team members will not work interdependently with anyone they do not trust. And without interdependence there can be no effective division of the task, no leverage of the gifts and skills of individual team members, and therefore, no synergy. No trust, no relationship, no team.

In a team relationship, as in any relationship, we trust people because we are comfortable with both their *character* and *competence*. By *character*, I mean our perception of another person's motives, values, honesty, or moral fiber. *Competence*, on the other hand, refers to the capability, knowledge, and skill of a team member in general, and specifically as it impacts his or her assigned role. If we don't trust both a team member's character and competence, it is unlikely that we will put our desired goals, performance appraisal, compensation, or career into that person's care.

Trust is difficult to define, for it is more an emotional and intuitive concept than a concrete one. It is more than simply confidence based on calculation and experience.[8] Sometimes we trust another person without any evidence they are worthy of trust. Our intuition or instinct tells us this person is trustworthy. Occasionally our instincts are misguided, and the object of our trust proves unworthy of the gift. And that's what trust is, a gift. We can decide to give, to withhold trust, or even to withdraw it if the recipient is undeserving. To emphasize this nature of trusting even further, it's often said that we don't give people our trust; we just lend it to them.

Douglas McGregor, the author who introduced the concept of Theory X and Theory Y as a means of explaining different management behaviors, shares what trust means to him: "I know you will not—deliberately (*character*) or accidentally (*competence*), consciously or unconsciously—take unfair advantage of me." It means: "I can put my situation at the moment, my status, and self-esteem in this group, our relationship, my job, my career, even my life in your hands with complete confidence."[9] Trust is a measurement of my sense of safety with you.

Would you accept interdependence with someone with whom you had that level of trust? Immediately we see that trust is a relative concept. It's not a matter of whether we trust a certain individual, but *how much* we trust him. Additionally, trust must be established on an individual basis. Although we might place our trust in the team, that trust is invested one person at a time. I, as a team member, must build trust with every other member of the team on an individual basis and vice versa.

For many years people have used the metaphor of a bank account to describe the dynamic nature of trust in a relationship. Assume you are a new member of a team. Because trust is really lent to another, picture yourself as a bank, a bank in which the other team members can decide to make deposits (that is, lend you their trust) and withdrawals (Figure 8-2). As a new team member, you need to convince every other team member to make trust deposits in you to build up a positive balance. Over time, no matter how reliable and competent you are, you will make mistakes and the team members will make withdrawals. If, however, you have established and maintain a sufficient balance, some withdrawals can be made without endangering the relationship needed for effective teaming.

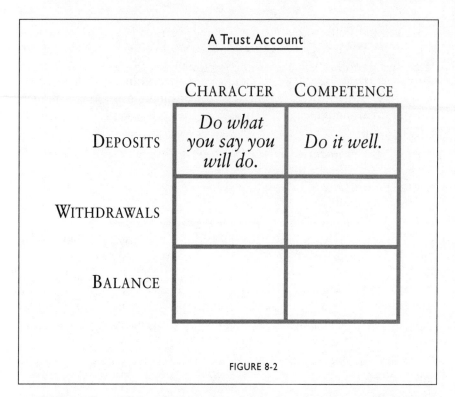

FIGURE 8-2

High performance teams are like finely tuned racing engines—heat and friction are natural by-products of the work. Trust is a necessary lubricant, and therefore team members need to be vigilant in making sure there is enough to do the job.

Our behavior may be the most critical factor used by others in their decision to "lend" trust to us, as our actions reflect our character. When we honor our commitments and do what we say we will do, others will be inclined to deposit their trust with us. Another way to motivate deposits on the character side of the ledger is self-disclosure, taking the initiative to share what's on our mind, our motives, or concerns. If people perceive we are closed or hiding something, they are unlikely to reciprocate with a high level of trust. A deposit of competence might be doing what we do with excellence. Withdrawals would be the opposites of deposits, such as failing to follow through on a commitment, or coming to a meeting unprepared.

Trust is extremely fragile, and although building it can take extensive amounts of time over the course of many personal interactions, it can be destroyed (withdrawn) within seconds. Trust accounts can be overdrawn and even closed. Consider the implications on performance and team climate when one or several members of a team have overdrawn accounts. Several years ago I was invited to lunch by a group of regional managers of a large national consumer products company. Each of these managers was responsible for an entirely different product line, and the only thing they had in common was the region for which they were responsible. Their product lines had little relationship to each other, and in some cases their customer bases were different as well. The question they wanted to discuss was why and how a group of independent, autonomous division managers should cooperate.

I used the metaphor of international trading as an example of independent, self-sufficient parties "choosing" to cooperate through trade. They liked the metaphor, and we were soon embroiled in a discussion on the trade goods different regional managers brought to the table. They each had different skills and interests, and it wasn't long before they could make out the faint outlines of a team beginning to form. As I was saying my good-byes after lunch, several of the managers took me off to the side to ask a perplexing question. "What happens if no one wants to trade with a person?" they asked. They went on to explain that most of the other managers did not trust one particular manager. Over the years he had done some things that eroded their ability to work with him. Here was a forming team and one of the accounts was already closed. Sadly, the untrusted team member was unaware of the feeling of his colleagues. Even sadder, this had been going on for years, and no one had ever taken the risk of letting this fellow know he was overdrawing his account. He was subtly kept on the outside of things because none of the other team members wanted to be in a position of interdependency with him. The result was that the team was always playing a man short in a very competitive industry.

Understanding

Even though team members don't need to know one another all that well personally, they do need to have a mutual understanding of one another's job and potential contribution. Indeed, the deeper the level of understanding, the greater the potential for effective collaborative effort, particularly in the less structured, ambiguous circumstances confronted by most management or cross-functional teams. Understanding is a key step to trust, and trust is a key element for interdependence and team effort. In the typical cross-functional business team, there is no certification as to the competence of other team members. Thus getting to know one another plays an important role in developing trust.

Understanding can be expedited by creating opportunities for team members to get to know one another. Because trust is so foundational to any team effort, we generally build such opportunities into our team development strategies as early as possible. With a little creativity you can find many ways to jump-start interpersonal understanding. One avenue might be an outdoor adventure such as white-water rafting, in which participants learn the value of teamwork while gaining keen insight into the nature, skills, attitudes, humor, and personalities of their teammates.

For situations in which we don't have the time or resources for such an expedition, many creative and inexpensive exercises can accomplish the same objective. For example, in classroom settings, we often use a "Coat-of-Arms" exercise. Each person is given a flip chart sheet and a set of colored markers and asked to design and draw a coat of arms that will most clearly communicate what they want others to know about them. To ensure some consistency of feedback, we list a number of suggestions to get participants started, such as the most important accomplishment of their life, the single value from which they never budge, and three words they'd like people to say about them at their funeral. Every one of these sessions has been characterized by insight, increased understanding, and a tremendous amount of laughter.

Another popular way to gain quick insight into the nature of our teammates is through personality instruments. Several educational instruments are designed for use in such settings. Team Resources publishes one developed specifically for the purpose of helping teammates get to know one another better. It's based on the DISC concept and entitled *The Personal DISCernment Inventory*.[10] Another well-known instrument is the Myers-Briggs Type Indicator (MBTI).[11] These tests have an enduring benefit, for they give the team the vocabulary to talk about personality and its impact on how people make decisions, resolve conflicts, and communicate.

Again, the more you and I understand about one another in a team setting, the quicker we will build trust, if this understanding is supported with mutual character and competence deposits. This understanding helps me put a positive spin on my assumptions about your motives. I am able to replace conjecture with observation and insight. In summary, effective teams experience a healthy level of intimacy ("into-me-see").

Acceptance

Acceptance is the bridge that connects differences. To accept is to approve of someone, even though that person may be very unlike us. It's easy to accept someone who's like us, but accepting those who are different in values, experiences, manner, and gifts is more difficult. Basic training in the U.S. Army gave me my first taste of both the challenge and benefits of blending a group of people from tremendously diverse backgrounds into a highly collaborative unit. It was obvious in the first moments that the U.S. Army was not concerned about homogeneity. There were tall kids, short kids, rich ones, poor ones, and several from every possible ethnic background. Education spread the gamut as well. Wanting to give us all at least one thing in common, the Army immediately shaved our heads.

We didn't enter the experience with open minds, but as the weeks wore on and our bodies wore down, one exercise after another in unfamiliar and trying circumstances began to make differences in language and manner seem less important. If that kid with the tattoos and angry countenance could help me get over a 14-foot wall and away from an even less savory drill sergeant with a bad attitude, he'd be my friend forever! Over the course of eight weeks of shared experiences, a sense of mission and comradeship born out of surviving a series of tough assignments made differences seem not so unimportant when those differences helped the rest of us accomplish our mission. In fact, during the eight weeks, emotions migrated from anxiety to acceptance, and then to appreciation for each member's unique contribution to the unit. As I reflect on this experience, I wonder if the greatest loss of the mandatory draft is losing an appreciation for the diversity that is so representative of our country.

In many respects the face of business at the turn of the century is beginning to look very much like that platoon of recruits in 1968. Over the years the country has become considerably more diverse in almost every respect. We had best master the art of acceptance if we ever hope to achieve high levels of team effectiveness in organizational settings.

Respect

In a team setting, everyone brings something to the table. Without that something, what we are attempting to accomplish will not be possible. Every team member and his or her contribution is essential. High performance teams treat the input of every member with respect and appreciation, showing no partiality for one person's role over that of any other.

To respect someone in a team setting means to show honor and esteem for his or her contribution. We must acknowledge that we need one another and we must show equal concern for every member. If one member suffers, we all suffer. If one member is honored, we are all honored. We are a team. It was respect in the cockpit of UAL 232 that motivated quality listening to every idea regardless of who voiced it. Al Haynes reflected his respect for others when he denied he was a hero and paid a tribute to the team: "Just a group of people who did their job. . . . Everyone kicked in and offered assistance without being told. We have a lot of experience here and it showed up in the cockpit."

One of my partners is fond of telling the story about a particular cross-functional sales team of one of our clients. This team, like others with the company, included several retail support people, the group responsible for ensuring customer shelves were stocked and straight after product arrived. Most sales teams in this company considered the retail support function to be outside the team: people to whom they gave orders and direction but not really a part of the in-group. This one team always invited their retail support reps to team meetings and any other team function. They constantly thanked the reps for doing a great job and complimented them on their skill and contribution. Little wonder that the stores in the territory of this team were always spic-and-span and stood in stark contrast to those served by other retail reps.

Courtesy

Courtesy is one of the most visible indicators of team relationships. As a consultant, I have often been asked by team leaders what I thought of their teams after spending a very short time (sometimes just minutes) observing the team working together. Most often, I draw my conclusions based on two things: first, the clarity of the process (if any) the team uses to attack their task, and secondly, the level of courtesy among team members as they address one another, listen, and respond.

Of particular interest is how the team members treat one another when the team is under stress.

We find a great example of courtesy during crisis in Flight 232. Captain Haynes and Bill Records had their hands on the steering column. Dudley Dvorak, the engineer, monitored the radios. Denny Fitch, a United captain who had come forward to help, was between Haynes and Records, working the throttles with both hands. About 22 minutes into the 41-minute incident, Al Haynes realized he hadn't introduced himself to the volunteer pilot. He turned in his seat, extended his right hand and said, "I'm Al Haynes."

Fitch responded: "Hi, Al, Denny Fitch."

Al Haynes: "How do you do, Denny?"

Denny Fitch: "I'll tell you what, we'll have a beer when this is all done."

Al Haynes: "Well, I don't drink, but I'll sure have one this time."

This team consistently demonstrated amazing courtesy under pressure. For example, when the plane was within sight of the airport, less than two minutes from impact, Al Haynes tells the tower flight controller, "We'll be with you shortly. Thanks a lot for your help." This example stands in stark contrast to several similar transcripts of aircraft incidents I reviewed. Throughout the incident, the cockpit voice recorder transcript reveals intent listening and courteous responses and the absence of profanity.

Courtesy is often the manifestation of trust, acceptance, and respect. We demonstrate courtesy by graciousness, consideration for one another, sincerity, listening, how we talk about teammates who aren't present, and the type of humor we use when jesting with one another. Have you ever been in a group situation in which the humor consisted of cutting remarks, making fun of one another in a subtle or not so subtle manner? Although masked as humor, such comments don't fool anyone. The team may appear to be relationally solid and at ease with one another, but in reality it is fragile and fractured. The relationships on such a team probably couldn't withstand the strain of much stress.

Mutual Accountability

The final relational quality I find indispensable in a team setting is mutual accountability. When effectively practiced, accountability can be very liberating for both the team and the individual team members. The climate will resound with the understanding that we are all in this together and will succeed or fail as a team. It creates the freedom for team members to proactively share ideas and needs, and to ask for help. In the case of the latter, effective team accountability is like an early warning system that can alert the team if it is getting behind or off course when an individual team member gets stuck, overloaded, or over their head. It makes it easy for team members to yell for help. It also makes it more comfortable for team members to share ideas and suggestions to others outside of their area of expertise or responsibility.

Accountability doesn't come easily to people raised in a culture that values the rugged individualist and free spirit. Many view it as a constraint or imposition into their affairs, rather than a contributing element of effective teamwork. As a result, although the concept is often mentioned in team settings, it is seldom defined and rarely practiced.

To be accountable is to be answerable. It's an implied obligation to give an account of one's actions, progress, or results. Notice the qualifying adjective: "*mutual.*" We are more comfortable being accountable to an organizational superior. Accountability has been a cornerstone in the traditional hierarchical organizations. But being accountable to my peers and colleagues, . . . what does that entail? "*I don't want someone sticking their nose into my territory. What do they know about it anyway? I'm the finance expert on this team! Don't they trust me?*"

It makes perfect sense that others would want to know how you are doing on your part of the job, because in an interdependent situation, if *you* don't succeed, then *we* don't succeed. As a team, we will hold one another not only responsible for progress and results, but for upholding team ground rules and operating principles as well.

Team members may resist the concept of accountability for several reasons. First, they may see their job as their job, rather than their part of the larger task. Secondly, they may be afraid of the consequences of poor performance. If the team merely uses accountability as a disciplinary strategy, team members will soon discover that openness is painful. They will become less open and forthcoming in expressing their needs. The third barrier is poor relationships—who would want to be accountable to individuals they did not trust, respect, or accept, or vice versa? Finally, holding one another mutually accountable requires sensitivity and skill. How do we create an atmosphere that allows people to be honest about needs, shortcomings, mistakes, and does not challenge them personally or put them on the defensive?

One way to help the team develop an accountable environment is to ensure that everyone understands what mutual accountability is, why it's important, and how we, as a team, actually go about holding one another accountable. For a team to really embrace the concept of accountability, they must believe that it will be within a supportive environment.

OPERATING PRINCIPLES—RELATIONAL GROUND RULES FOR TEAMS

High performance teams understand that good relationships on a team are not natural, but rather the product of determination and hard work. Many effective teams have discovered the benefits of having the team develop and agree to a list of explicit operating principles that define how they will expect team members to behave when interacting with one another. Figure 8-3 provides an example of operating principles developed by a senior leadership team. Notice that they express each item in the present tense rather than saying, "we will." They wanted to ensure that each member understood that this was how we should be treating one another today versus good intentions for the future. I have seen a lot of such lists, and although most have tremendous similarity, every team has its own twist that reflects its history, culture, and special needs.

Being explicit with such principles facilitates the ability for team members to hold one another accountable for healthy behaviors as well as progress and results in their area of responsibility. Several years ago I facilitated a series of strategic planning sessions for the top management team of a privately held corporation owned by the managers themselves. As I do in most such situations, I had the team agree on their operating principles, which would later prove critically important.

For several years they had worked hard to build the revenue and value of the firm. They succeeded in their efforts to the point where another company offered to buy my client for an extraordinary amount of money relative to the size of the firm. This opportunity would make each member of the management team financially independent.

As is often the case with corporate acquisitions, after the first blush of excitement, the hard work of negotiation and due diligence began. In

Team Operating Principles

We *are open and honest with one another*

We treat each other with dignity and respect

We listen to and respect each other's ideas and opinions

We hold confidences

We honor our commitments

We support and invest in each other's development

We routinely critique our processes

We have fun

FIGURE 8-3

one meeting near the end of nearly four months of negotiations (and the end of our patience), the team was discussing an ongoing concern of the CEO. Throughout the process he had expressed concern for the current employees after the sale because the purchaser was headquartered in another state and was sure to consolidate part of the operations. The CFO had been unusually quiet during the discussion but suddenly sat up straight, pounded his fist on the table, and challenged the CEO in no uncertain terms. "Bob, you are just trying to derail this sale. You just can't let go of your baby even though we all have a piece of the company!" He then got up and stormed over to the window, staring out with his back turned toward the group. The rest of the team quietly stared down at their shoes. The outburst was out of character for the CFO, and no one knew what to do or say. You could have heard a pin drop.

As facilitator, my mind was rushing. *Should I intervene? What should I do to get the meeting back on track?* At that point, a young executive, in fact the newest and least senior member of the team, turned to the CFO. "Don," he said, "you broke our ground rules. You are reading Bob's mind and ascribing motives." Don didn't respond. He kept on staring out the window. The rest of the team continued to examine their shoes with renewed interest. A moment later he turned and said, "Bob, David's right. I violated our principles. I apologize. It's just that we are so close and you keep pushing back on this location issue."

Bob responded, "Don, I forgive you. I understand the pressure we're all under. Let's be clear about my intentions. I am committed to this sale and won't do anything to derail it. I just want to make sure we don't leave anything on the table regarding our employees." They got back to work and closed the deal the following month.

This example surfaces two important issues about operating principles. First, the time to develop them is when there doesn't appear to be any need for them. They are often most useful in times of stress, but then it's too late to call time out and develop the list. Secondly, operating principles level the playing field for team members. They allow team members to have a powerful impact even when they are not in a powerful position. David leveraged the power of operating principles, and he was the least senior of the team.

Team leaders, developing team operating principles is something you can facilitate with your team. You need only a flip chart and 30 to 45 minutes of discussion time. The exercise involves five simple steps:

1. Explain the purpose of team operating principles to the team (that is, this is a list of the ground rules that we, as a team, want to be characteristic of our relationship and interactions). It is important for the team to understand that any team member may "blow the whistle" if a ground rule is broken.

2. Using the flip chart so everyone can track the discussion, brainstorm as a group which principles the team wants to be descriptive

of your relationship. Like any brainstorming session, don't attempt to fine-tune the wording merely capture the ideas as accurately as possible.

3. Assign the one or two best wordsmiths on the team to take this input and rework it with the objective of reflecting the team's intentions within the clearest possible fashion.

4. As a team, review the finished product, making any additional changes needed to capture the full intent of the team.

5. As team leader, look for opportunities to model the principles as well as opportunities to reinforce the principle if it is violated. I have found that once a team sees how the principles can be used to reinforce healthy behavior with no negative side effects, other members will begin to take the initiative to speak out.

THE BOTTOM LINE

Teammates don't have to be best friends. In fact, the diversity and differences among the individual team members will probably preclude close friendships. However, the relationships must be solid enough to withstand the turbulence of day-to-day interaction, misunderstandings, and an occasional bad day. Solid team relationships provide the climate needed for high levels of cooperation and are characterized by trust, acceptance, respect, understanding, and courtesy.

Finally, to effectively cover the role assignments of the team and to ensure the needed inventory of perspectives, experience, and skills, the team must seek out, recruit, and unleash the creative aspects of diversity. Differences must be seen as value added in a team environment.

MESSAGE TO TEAM LEADERS

Trust is the glue in any relationship and is clearly the non-negotiable element of interdependent relationships. We will not be interdependent with those we don't trust. Trust is somewhat like a thermometer, reflecting the current state of a relationship. Unlike a thermostat, a thermometer can't be used to set a desired temperature level; it merely displays the current level. You can't mandate the level of trust; you can only attempt to create an environment and opportunities that will facilitate its development among the members of your team. Providing time for interaction, formal and informal, as well as shared experiences in which teammates can see one another in action helps individuals get to know one another better. Assuming these insights are positive, such knowledge will foster higher levels of trust.

Ensure that the team understands all of the qualities that describe a solid relationship and their contribution to team effectiveness. Take time, as a team, to talk about them. For example, sometime during a team meeting or over lunch discuss the following questions:

- What is acceptance?

- What does it look like in practice? How would a person know if they were accepted or unaccepted?

- Why is acceptance important in a team setting?

- What are the implications for a team when one or several members don't feel accepted?

Over time, work through discussions of the other qualities (respect, appreciation, courtesy, and mutual accountability). I'll predict the discussions will be so rich that it will take several sessions to complete one and you will return to these themes again and again.

Reinforce the practice of these qualities in the day-to-day interactions of the team. In instances where a team member consistently violates the tenets needed to maintain healthy team relationships, get that person off to the side and help her understand the impact and implications of her behavior. As a leader, remember that one of the most significant strategies for building the qualities of solid relationships into the relational fabric of the team is for you, the team leader, to model them. Let team members see them in practice.

Finally, ensure that the team takes the time to develop and use team operating principles—a list of specific behaviors that the team wants to be descriptive of its interactions and relationships.

CHAPTER NINE

Excellent Communication

L et's return to our real-life example of teamwork on United Flight
232. Note how the officers, though struggling to land the disabled aircraft, continued to communicate with one another throughout the
ordeal. We'll focus on two minutes of their interaction as transcribed
from the cockpit voice recorder. At this point, they are less than six
minutes from impact.

15:53:49	CO-PILOT RECORDS	Let's just see if we can get a shallow descent, Al.
15:53:51	CAPTAIN HAYNES	That's what I'm trying to do, . . . Trying to stop . . . (*unintelligible but probably referring to the oscillations caused by the frozen auto pilot as it attempted to continue to fly the plane as though nothing was wrong*) . . . get this thing under control, . . . when it starts up, push.
	RECORDS	OK.
15:53:58	RECORDS	Here we go, . . . push hard, . . . push hard.

	FITCH	When the speed bleeds back you'll catch it . . . Now where do you want to go?
15:54:09	HAYNES	. . . want to keep turning right, . . . want to go to the airport.
	FITCH	You want to go to the airport?
	HAYNES	I want to get as close to the airport as we can.
	FITCH	OK.
15:54:13	HAYNES	If we have to set this thing in the dirt, we set it in the dirt.
15:54:19	UNKNOWN	Speed's too slow.
15:54:22	UNKNOWN	Watch the angle.
15:54:34	HAYNES to RECORDS	Get on the air and tell them we have about four minutes to go.
	RECORDS to flight control	We've got about three or four minutes to go, it looks like.
	HAYNES to DUDLEY DVORAK, the second officer	Get on the PA system and tell the passengers.
15:54:41	Sound of PA announcement	We have four minutes to touch-down—Four minutes to touchdown.
15:54:45	FITCH	Which way do you want to go?
	HAYNES	Right, right, right. We gotta go right.
	UNKNOWN	Speed up.
15:54:48	FITCH	Airport's down there . . . got it.
15:54:50	HAYNES	Don't see it yet.
15:54:53	RECORDS	As soon as it starts down, *the oscillation forcing the nose of the plane down* . . . back we go, *pull the steering column back.*
15:55:00	UNKNOWN	Not too much back . . . the bank.
	RECORDS	OK, now you can bring them up.
15:55:08	UNKNOWN	Keep turning . . . keep turning . . . keep turning.
15:55:18	RECORDS	There's the airport.

Despite a highly stressful situation these men stayed remarkably calm. They had no time for mistakes and little margin for error, and they communicated clearly and succinctly. They took time to clarify and verify. Communication among the team members in this situation demanded high standards of excellence, and they achieved it.

Effective teams always outperform other types of groups in creativity, problem solving, and decision making. Such performance is possible only to the extent that they are able to tap into the collective brilliance of the group. This is done through communication that engenders creativity and discovery and productively resolves differences and conflicts. Effective teams have a repertoire of many types and

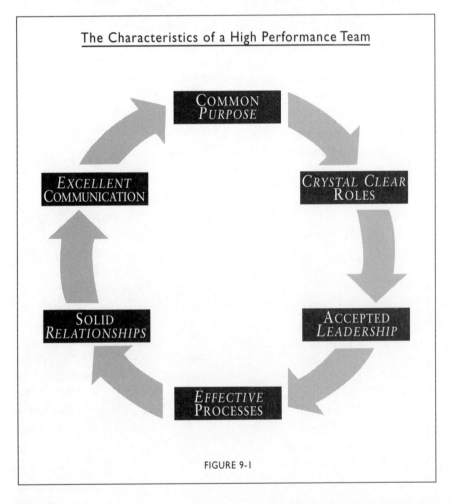

The Characteristics of a High Performance Team

COMMON PURPOSE

CRYSTAL CLEAR ROLES

ACCEPTED LEADERSHIP

EFFECTIVE PROCESSES

SOLID RELATIONSHIPS

EXCELLENT COMMUNICATION

FIGURE 9-1

levels of team communication, each demanding a special set of skills. Operational or executional exchanges like what went on in the cockpit of United Flight 232 are generally direct, straightforward, and filled with the technical shorthand typical of that milieu. In these situations, the emphasis is on clarity, accuracy, and efficiency.

In other instances, a team might find itself working through a specific team-thinking process like problem solving or decision making in which the conversation becomes looser and less pointed but is still channeled by the steps and principles of the specific process. The communication involved with discovery processes like planning, brainstorming, and conflict resolution involves much broader and less structured forms of interaction. It's this process of productive discussion and dialogue that high performance teams can mine for the synergy embedded in the collective wisdom of the team. But the valuable stores of synergy are not to be found lying exposed on the surface of the effort; they are the product of hard work and skillful exploration.

WHEN I NOD MY HEAD, HIT IT!

Effective communication enables a team to achieve exceptional results. However, most teams find that barriers to communication are legion—barriers such as incomplete or disorganized information, too much data, poor timing, or the wrong vehicle for the message. Not surprisingly, only the most astute, pragmatic, and persistent teams overcome them.

I'm often reminded of the story of a blacksmith who said to his apprentice: "Take this hammer. I'll take these tongs, reach into the forge and grasp the horseshoe, putting it on the anvil. When I nod my head, you hit it."

Communication appears to be deceptively easy. However, most of us carry a major misconception about the process: that communication is primarily message sending. Communication does not take place until someone receives the message and understands it *as the sender intended.* The most eloquent speech or the most beautifully composed letter isn't a successful communication if it misses the mark.

At Lake Havasu, Arizona, stands a bridge whose origins stem from 13th century England. U.S. developers purchased the bridge in 1968 and painstakingly dismantled it brick by brick. It was then shipped to Arizona and reconstructed.

That's the way we communicate. But instead of bricks, we use verbal and nonverbal symbols. I take an idea or picture in my head, dismantle it and send it over to you word by word, gesture by gesture, inflection by inflection.

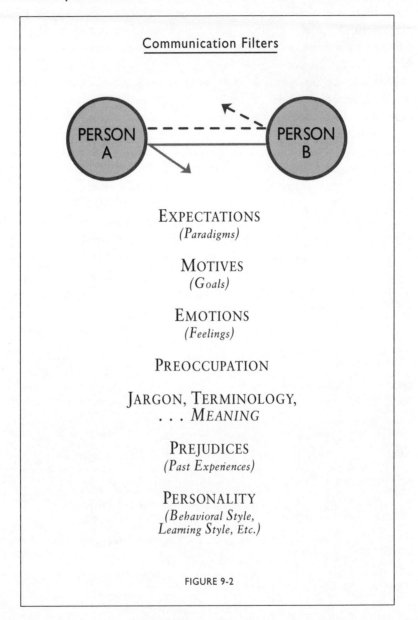

FIGURE 9-2

Unfortunately, I may have sent you a marble temple, but you think you received a mud hut, and often neither of us know that what I sent is not what you received. The biggest problem with communication is the assumption that it has taken place. Like the bricks, words must navigate their way through a lot of debris that filters, distorts and blunts the intent of a message (Figure 9-2). The current state of the receiver's emotions, motives, preoccupations, expectations, prejudices, and personality are only a few of the barriers that must be hurdled.

Each of us has a preference for how we give and receive information—how we communicate. Most of the time, we assume that everyone else likes to exchange ideas the same way. If we are a "cut-to-the-chase," bottom-line communicator, we can't understand why anyone would want to be buried in details. On the other hand, if we can't make a decision without all the facts, we want to know everything about the "how" before we consider the "what." Differences in personal style can impose formidable barriers to communication. Understanding differences in personal style and adapting to our audience's own style is critical to getting a message across. As in a buyer-seller relationship, the sender of the communication (seller) must connect with the receiver (buyer) and meet that person's need before communication (the sale) can take place.

In most spoken communication, we must take into account that words alone account for only 7 to 10 percent of the message (Figure 9-3). Vocalics (tone, inflection, volume, speed) account for 35 percent of the message, and body language makes up the remaining 55 percent.[1] All too rarely have we mastered the ability to listen effectively to both the *music* and the *words*.

Therefore, we need to choose the right medium

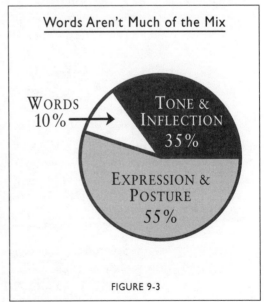

Words Aren't Much of the Mix

WORDS 10% → TONE & INFLECTION 35%

EXPRESSION & POSTURE 55%

FIGURE 9-3

for our message, remembering that face-to-face communication is the richest form because we can draw on the resources of words, body language, voice, or even the physical arena itself to deliver our ideas. At the same time, we can receive a constant update on how the audience is receiving our message and can make midcourse corrections if we're going astray.

For that reason, messages that are sensitive or unwelcome may demand this channel, while information of a general, unemotional nature works well with a leaner method of delivery. When we put things in writing, for example, we lose everything but the words. An e-mail is perhaps the stripped-down version of written communication (but without the spontaneity of spoken communication). It's all too easy to hit the "send" button before we've really had the chance to think about the effect on the audience. Although informal, e-mail is still written communication. It's permanent, and once out of our hands is beyond our control.

Further, some people hide behind e-mail to avoid the discomfort that face-to-face communication can produce, in the case of an unpleasant topic.

Phone mail also has its pitfalls. Although we have the benefit of voice inflection and tone, we need to use phone mail primarily for the transfer of unemotional information.

Teams that communicate successfully understand the importance of choosing the right channel for the right message.

So Much Information, So Little Time

Now, take this insight and compound it with the distributed work force of the 21st century.

First of all, we're all suffering from information overload. Our desks and credenzas are piled high with a stack of periodicals that we'll read "when we get around to it." We've seen and heard three iterations of *Headline News* by 7:00 A.M. Our attention spans are less than half what they were in the 1960's. We have more choices of ways to deliver messages, but we have perhaps less control over the quality of those messages.

A complex number of communication networks must be established and maintained in a team setting. In a hierarchical structure in which the chains of command and communication are rigidly adhered to, the

communication process can be pretty straightforward. Information largely flows in one direction with little opportunity for dialogue.

But a team setting stresses horizontal interaction. Every person is "connected" to every other person on the team as well as to a lot of people who aren't. The numbers of communication possibilities proliferate geometrically (Figure 9-4). Horizontal communication carries the price tag of complexity and increased risk of misunderstanding. As we consider these impediments, the astounding fact is not that communication is difficult, but rather that there is any communication at all!

LISTENING ISN'T JUST WAITING TO TALK

No team can communicate successfully without highly developed listening skills among team members. Most experts would agree that

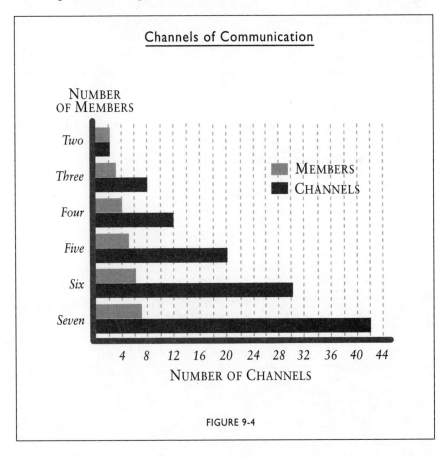

FIGURE 9-4

listening is the most overlooked and underused component of communication. Although listening comprises about 45 percent of the communication process, we have little or no formal training in this important skill.

Further, in our culture, we tend to view listening as passive behavior. How many times have we said, "I'm going to that meeting, but I won't participate. I'll just listen"? We see power as resting in the hands of the one who has the floor at the moment. In many cases, one's position in the company determines how carefully we listen to that person.

Almost every expert on the subject tells us that to be a good listener, we have to decide that listening is important. We have to learn to *want* to listen and take the proper steps to create a healthy listening environment. Eliminate those internal and external distractions that interfere with our ability to concentrate on what someone is telling us. Turn away from the computer, turn off your cell phone, close the door to your office, get out from behind your desk, and sit at a conference table.

Not only external, physical distractions hamper listening; internal ones do as well. You may have just gotten some bad news and aren't in the mood to hear about the latest sales projections.

You can always tell someone that it's not a good time and that you would like to schedule a time when you can give the subject your full attention. That approach is far better than what we do all too often—pretend to listen while our minds are elsewhere.

Further, we often make the mistake of treating listening as merely waiting for our turn to talk. While other team members are making their points, we're preparing our rebuttal. It takes practice and discipline to withhold the urge to jump in with our opinion and really concentrate on what the other person is saying.

Good listeners ask questions to clarify understanding and to let the speaker know that we are paying attention. And good listeners also "listen" with their body language as well as their auditory systems. They make eye contact, lean forward, nod their heads, use any number of gestures and behaviors that signal attentiveness. In addition, as they focus on the speaker, they listen with their eyes, by observing the demeanor and body language of the speaker, and they pay particular attention to what isn't being said.

Successful teams take listening seriously and make sure that everyone on the team listens holistically: with the senses, the mind, and the emotions.

TOO MUCH TEAM—TOO LITTLE UNDERSTANDING

For the most part group cohesiveness is a desirable team attribute but too much of a good thing can be a bad thing. Sometimes groups can develop such high levels of cohesiveness that the desire for uniformity and unanimity becomes stronger than the need for the wisest and most objective solutions. Such a state is often called *groupthink*, a term coined by Irving L. Janis.

Groupthink explains how well-intentioned, well-informed groups "collectively" make poor decisions. Janis identifies eight symptoms that may indicate the presence of too much conformity.[2]

- *An illusion of invulnerability, shared by all or most of the members, which creates excessive optimism and encourages the group to take extreme risks.* A top management team of a company with an exceptionally large market share might be tempted to assume that increasing competitive inroads into their territory will never be able to challenge their leading position. Can you say General Motors?

- *An unquestioned belief in the group's inherent morality, inclining members to ignore the ethical or moral consequences of their decisions.* Michael Milken's antics in the structuring and marketing of junk bond issues in the late 1980's or the questionable tactics of the Microsoft leadership team in squashing potential competition might fall into this category.

- *Collective efforts to rationalize in order to discount warnings or other information that might lead members to reconsider their assumptions.* This might be the group equivalent of a paradigm. Everyone contributes to reinforcing the dike to hold out reality. In many respects, this was the case with Lyndon Johnson's inner circle as they became increasingly enmeshed in the escalation of the Vietnam War.

- *Stereotyped views of the enemy or competition, portraying them as evil, weak, or stupid.* "We can't fail. Those guys couldn't think their way out of a wet paper bag!"

- *Self-censorship of deviations from the apparent group consensus.* "I don't want to rock the boat. After all, the rest seem so confident. It must just be me." Five of the seven people around the table might be having these thoughts, but no one speaks out, and this leads to another symptom . . .

- *A shared illusion of unanimity that puts tremendous pressure on individual group members to conform to the majority view.*

- *Direct pressure on any member who expresses arguments against the group's assumptions, illusions, or commitments.* Such dissent is clearly not what we would expect from a "loyal" team member.

- *Self-appointed mind-guards who act as the group whip to bring dissenting members into conformity with the group's or leader's position.* The executive vice president of one of our clients played such a role. If there was dissension regarding a significant issue during the executive team meeting, he would later meet with the dissenter and gently communicate, "Bill (the CEO) is concerned about your attitude. I'm sure he's wondering if you are still with the team." Bill hadn't actually sent this messenger, but there was clearly a tacit understanding between him and the EVP that the message was to be sent.

When groupthink occurs, the group isolates itself from the outside world and the information it contains. They accept positive, reinforcing signals while, at the same time, ignoring or rationalizing contrary evidence. The group "norm" is one of conformity at any price. Team members become unwilling to "rock the boat" and criticize ideas or suggestions voiced by others.

Groupthink stifles the possibility of suspending one's assumptions. In fact, its whole purpose is to elevate and protect those assumptions from any assault by logic. Creative and synergistic communication is doomed within groups infected with the symptoms of groupthink. Any new or unusual notions quickly fall victim to the group's terminal sense of certainty.

Janis suggests several remedies for this condition:

- Encourage group members to take on the role of critical evalua-tors and encourage sharing objections within the discussion.

- Make sure the leader doesn't "overlead" and show strong par-tiality to one solution or course of action. He or she should with-hold their ideas at first, letting others express their opinions and encouraging new ideas or approaches to the issue and should encourage, protect, and listen to minority views.

I experienced this situation several years ago in a planning ses-sion I was facilitating for a new client. I wasn't an hour into the planning session before I knew we were in trouble. In many years of facilitating strategic planning sessions, I had never seen such a responsive group of managers. The problem was, they were responding only to the CEO. If she smiled or nodded at some-thing I'd say, 14 other heads would smile or nod in unison. If her face reflected concentration or concern as she wrote a thought down in her notebook, 14 managers would seriously make their entries as well.

When she had retained my services, the CEO explained that increasing competition forced a more planned approach to their business efforts. "Just as importantly," she exclaimed, "I've finally put together the perfect management team." I don't know how she was defining team, but this group didn't meet my stan-dards. She is one of the brightest, most capable people I have ever met. After nearly 30 years in the industry, she knew practically every facet of the business. She could do virtually every job in the company better than anyone else and was quick to remind them of that at the first hint of trouble. But her strategy of team devel-opment consisted of "trading out" anyone who would push back or voice a contrary opinion. Such people were replaced with "team players." This wasn't a team, but rather one exceptionally strong person with 14 very responsive assistants. A better term for this type of interaction might be "leaderthink!"

- Invite outside experts and observers and provide opportunities for them to express their opinions not only about the subject under discussion, but also about the group dynamics and process.

- Hold "second-chance" meetings after consensus is apparently achieved, giving team members an opportunity to express their doubts or concerns.

The ancient Persians applied this principle in a unique fashion. According to Herodotus, writing about 450 B.C., they would make a decision with careful, serious deliberation and then reconsider the matter under the influence of wine. I'm not suggesting that this is an appropriate strategy, but we can appreciate that such an approach might allow second thoughts to flow more freely.[3]

EXCEPTIONAL TEAMWORK DEMANDS EXCEPTIONAL COMMUNICATION

High performance teams escape the gravitational force of group-think. They develop high levels of trust among team members as well as in their communication processes. Defensive mechanisms are left behind in the pursuit of the most creative and productive courses of action. They have mastered the art of "straight talk," which allows them to be tough on the issues without blowing team relationships out of the water. Such talk is characterized by clear, straightforward communication that could be described as open, honest, timely, and accurate.

As with many of the characteristics of effective teams, great communication is a combination of both skill and willingness. In discussing the complexities and barriers to communication above, I suggested a number of ideas that would increase the effectiveness of team communication. Let me suggest a few additional strategies that would encourage creative communication in team settings.

Regardless of mission, almost every team must plan, set priorities, solve problems, generate and examine new ideas, and make decisions. Productive communication processes can assist teams in each of these tasks. Two time-tested processes—brainstorming and the nominal group technique—have proven highly effective in helping teams generate and assess ideas.

Brainstorming

Brainstorming is an unstructured free association process intended to generate as many ideas and alternatives as possible. Generally, brainstorming sessions are governed by some essential ground rules:

- *No criticizing others' ideas.* You cannot use phrases like "that won't work," "we tried that years ago," or "that doesn't sound feasible." These kinds of comments will inhibit other group members from making their comments freely and tend to move the group in unproductive directions.

- *Be creative; do some freewheeling.* All ideas or comments, no matter how absurd, are recorded. The group members should be free to move around, to explore the materials provided for the session, and to arrange themselves into subgroups whenever such groups seem appropriate.

- *Emphasize quantity of ideas over quality.* You will evaluate ideas later. In a brainstorming session, the goal is to generate as many ideas as possible. As one engineer put it, "It only takes one good idea out of thousands to save us millions."

- *Combine ideas; hitchhike on one anothers' ideas.* Many really creative ideas are sparked in one person's mind by something someone else says.

- *Include non-specialists in the group.* When working on an engineering problem, for example, include someone from accounting, information systems, and so on. These diverse elements often contribute provocative questions and comments, and can often be vital to the success of the brainstorming effort.

Brainstorming separates the idea generating phase from the evaluation phase, thus reducing fears of criticism and increasing a participant's willingness to risk suggesting off-the-wall ideas.

Nominal Group Technique (NGT)

Like brainstorming, NGT assists a group in developing a lot of ideas in a short time. Its more structured approach is helpful when a group is less confident or feeling some uncertainty about individuals with different status within the group (e.g., a superior). Thus, the technique "nominalizes" the group by creating the perception of a more level and safer playing field on which to discuss an issue.

In many respects the process and principles are similar to brainstorming, but instead of orally introducing ideas in a freewheeling and spontaneous fashion, each member writes down his or her ideas (as many as possible) on a sheet of paper. After everyone has finished, the facilitator will go around the group, asking each individual his or her first idea to the question at hand. After the facilitator has completed the first round, the group begins a second and then a third, continuing until everyone has expressed satisfaction that all of their ideas are listed.

The next step is to clarify any questions about an item on the list (still without evaluation). At this point, the facilitator could give each participant a card and ask him or her to rank order the top five items. These are tallied, and the ideas with the most consideration become the topics of discussion and evaluation.

CONFLICT JUST MEANS YOU'RE COMMUNICATING

In any team situation, one barrier that challenges the team's ability to communicate clearly is the issue of conflict and the frequent misunderstanding about it. Frequently in team workshops, I ask participants to write down the first idea that comes to their mind when I say a certain word. When their pencils are poised I say, "Conflict." In return I most often hear things like "fight," "anger," "lose," "hurt," "pain," and "fear." "If this is the way people feel about conflict," I ask, "how do they most typically handle it?" Their responses are both quick and consistent: "Avoid it." That's exactly what many people do. After being hurt by destructive conflict, we get the picture that conflict is something to be avoided. But the price of peace is high, because conflict is often a door to creativity, consensus, and commitment.

Clear communication *always* leads to conflict, and the clearer the communication the faster we arrive at it. Most people sense this intuitively. When there is the potential for disagreement, they create a gap between how they feel versus what they say. If we see conflict as a negative force to be avoided, and most people do, then we tend to "murk" up the communication.

A new paradigm is needed that doesn't see conflict as good or bad but as an indication of difference in interests, opinions, and points of view. Mary Parker Follett laid the foundation for more effective conflict resolution strategies of today when, nearly 70 years ago, she observed that conflict cannot be avoided and therefore must be managed and made to work for us.[4]

For conflict to be productive, it must first move through five distinct phases of interaction (Figure 9-5). First, we must clarify the facts or the issues over which we disagree. In most points of disagreement we put

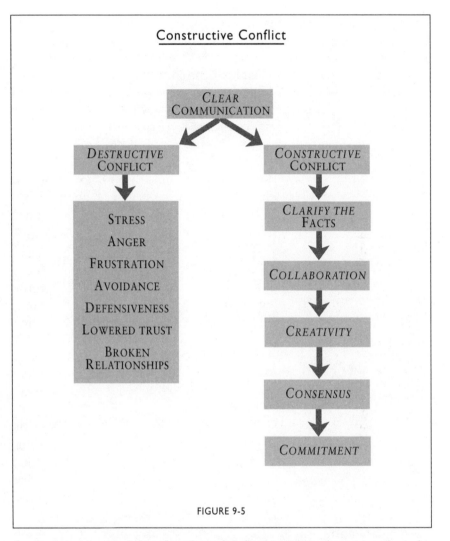

Constructive Conflict

CLEAR COMMUNICATION

DESTRUCTIVE CONFLICT

STRESS

ANGER

FRUSTRATION

AVOIDANCE

DEFENSIVENESS

LOWERED TRUST

BROKEN RELATIONSHIPS

CONSTRUCTIVE CONFLICT

CLARIFY THE FACTS

COLLABORATION

CREATIVITY

CONSENSUS

COMMITMENT

FIGURE 9-5

forth a position and then fortify and defend it. The other party does the same. The positions are either offensive or defensive, and the more one is forced to defend a position, the more difficult it becomes to "suspend our assumptions." Like an iceberg, what's under the water line is what really counts. Our underlying interests and motives live beneath the surface, and without trust, we are unlikely to reveal them to others. When trust is present, however, we are more open and reveal the fundamental needs driving us to push for one position or another.

Clarification leads to collaboration, in which the team can work collectively to engineer higher level solutions that escape the magnetic pull of compromise. Many see compromise as the high side of conflict resolution but, in reality, it is a tepid resolution to difference. It is a so-so outcome that basically says, "If we're going to be unhappy about this conclusion, let's be equally unhappy." Follett observed that, because in compromise we give up part of our desire, conflict is bound to surface again or in another form as we later attempt to attain the whole of our desire.[5]

Collaboration introduces the possibility of synergism or creativity needed to discover a win-win solution that more adequately meets the needs of all parties. Again Follett pioneers a creative insight for repositioning conflict. She explains that compromise does not create, but rather deals with what already exists. However, an integrative solution creates something new.[6] Thus the creative dimension of conflict is introduced.

With a win-win solution we can gain consensus and consequently commitment that channels the team's energy into execution unencumbered by unresolved conflict. In this way, conflict opens the door to creativity, consensus, and commitment. If the group has an unhealthy view of conflict or doesn't have the skills or process by which to manage it constructively, they will never attain the realm of synergistic communication and the exceptional levels of performance it supports.

Just How Good Is Our Communication?

In Chapter 7, I provided a meeting evaluation survey. It included a number of questions about communication. The Team Communications Inventory below will serve a similar purpose but with a broader look at overall team communication. We have found that this type of inventory does an excellent job of priming the pump of discussion about communication and how to make it better.

Back to the Beginning

If you review the Team Wheel, you will find that we have returned to *Common Purpose*, the first characteristic of a high performance team. The connection is intentional, for a team cannot maintain unity of purpose without exceptionally good communication among team members. A familiar story from the Old Testament provides a good example of this principle. In Genesis, Chapter 11, we find "Babel Engineering" building a high rise and embroiled in a divine zoning infraction. God had told the people to scatter, but they rebelled and decided instead to build a high tower. In heaven, as God watched events unfold below, he observed, "because they speak with one language, nothing which they propose to do will be impossible for them."[7] (If only that could be said of the typical team!) God opposed their purpose in building the tower, and his strategy to thwart it was to confuse their language. Once they lost the ability to understand one another, they quickly lost their sense of purpose as well and scattered as God first intended. Confused communication and unity of purpose cannot live together.

THE BOTTOM LINE

George Bernard Shaw summed it up well when he observed that the biggest problem with communication is the assumption that it has taken place. Effective communication enables a team to achieve exceptional results. However, most teams find that barriers to communication are legion. Barriers such as incomplete or disorganized information, too much data, poor timing, or the wrong vehicle for the message all conspire to block team communication. Not surprisingly, only the most astute, pragmatic, and persistent teams overcome them, for they understand that . . .

* Communication is the very means of cooperation.

* Communication appears to be deceptively easy. As a result we often fall prey to the misconception that it has taken place when it has not.

* We tend to focus most of our energy on the sending part of communication and little on the receiving side. We would be well-served by reversing our emphasis.

* The power of a team is found in the collective IQ of the group. However, in some circumstances unhealthy group dynamics like "groupthink" can thwart effective team communication and thinking.

* Clear communication inevitably leads to conflict. Teams need to master the art of conflict resolution in order to maintain the high

Team Communications Inventory

	NOT AT ALL DESCRIPTIVE	SELDOM DESCRIPTIVE	SOMEWHAT DESCRIPTIVE	OFTEN DESCRIPTIVE	VERY DESCRIPTIVE
	1	2	3	4	5

1. We value and encourage the input of everyone in any discussion. ☐ ☐ ☐ ☐ ☐

2. We are active listeners — We listen with our ears, eyes, minds, and hearts (listen for both words and music) ☐ ☐ ☐ ☐ ☐

3. We make effective use of the creative tools to surface the best ideas (brainstorming, nominal group technique, etc.). ☐ ☐ ☐ ☐ ☐

4. We keep each others' confidences. We do not indiscriminately copy, forward or communicate messages that may be sensitive to sender. ☐ ☐ ☐ ☐ ☐

5. We pay attention to what is *not* being said. ☐ ☐ ☐ ☐ ☐

6. We encourage constructive criticism and questioning of ideas. ☐ ☐ ☐ ☐ ☐

7. We listen to each other with the same respect and courtesy that we show clients or the CEO. ☐ ☐ ☐ ☐ ☐

8. We have discussed and decided the appropriate channels (i.e., in-person, written, fax, voice mail, e-mail, etc.) for different topics and types of communication. ☐ ☐ ☐ ☐ ☐

9. We have discussed the different communication channels (i.e., in-person, written, fax, voice mail, e-mail, etc.) preferred by different team members. ☐ ☐ ☐ ☐ ☐

	NOT AT ALL DESCRIPTIVE	SELDOM DESCRIPTIVE	SOMEWHAT DESCRIPTIVE	OFTEN DESCRIPTIVE	VERY DESCRIPTIVE
	1	2	3	4	5
10. We do our best to create a positive attitude and "interpersonal slack" for miscommunications in this fast track, communicate-on-the-fly world of ours.	☐	☐	☐	☐	☐
11. We have a safe team environment that encourages open, clear communication.	☐	☐	☐	☐	☐
12. Team members feel "listened to."	☐	☐	☐	☐	☐
13. Team members feel connected and have a sense they know what is going on in the team.	☐	☐	☐	☐	☐
14. We have a clearly defined process for handling conflict that everyone follows.	☐	☐	☐	☐	☐
15. As a team we have mastered the art of "straight-talk"— We are tough on issues but not tough on people.	☐	☐	☐	☐	☐
16. We never attack each other's personality or character.	☐	☐	☐	☐	☐
17. We make written documents reader-friendly and easy to follow.	☐	☐	☐	☐	☐
18. Topic, importance/urgency and desired action (e.g., act on, decide, respond, file, FYI, etc.) are immediately clear to readers.	☐	☐	☐	☐	☐
19. We avoid overloading each other with e-mails and voice mails (indiscriminate use of FYI).	☐	☐	☐	☐	☐
20. Topic, priority and desired action is immediately clear in both e-mail and voice mail.	☐	☐	☐	☐	☐

Scoring: *Assign a value of 1 to all marks in column 1, a 2 to column 2 marks and so on through column 5. Next total our overall score which will fall somewhere between 20 and 100.*

80–100— *As clear as good lead crystal*
60–79— *Not bad, but could be better*
40–59— *"Say again..."*
30–39— *Message fragments and static*
Less than 30— *Huh?*

levels of straight talk needed to coordinate collective efforts and find synergy.

- Teams must sit down on a regular basis and assess the quality of their communication. What's working? What's not working? How can we do better?

MESSAGE TO TEAM LEADERS

The team leader is the one member of the team most able to create a team environment conducive to excellent communication and hostile to groupthink. There are several specific elements of such an environment that can be meaningfully influenced with good leadership:

- *Proactively attempt to build solid relationships among team members.* "Why did you put relationships before communication?" we are constantly asked. "Isn't good communication needed to build solid relationships?" One could make that argument, for these two dimensions of team are closely connected. However, in our experience relationship generally leads communication. For example, the level of trust determines how open we will be in our communication. If a person does not trust another, they will not be vulnerable and transparent and the possibility of misunderstanding and misinterpretation increases. Low trust situations weaken the connection between what we *feel* and what we *say*. Other team members pick up on this lack of trust on their intuitive radar screens, raise their defensive shields, and respond in kind. Trust and communication spiral down together.

  Secondly, research has found that when team members feel respected by the group, they are much more likely to risk voicing contrary opinions to ideas, directions, and conclusions with which they disagree. Team members who do not feel respected or accepted by the team are more likely to be subdued in their feedback and thus promote the possibility of groupthink.[8]

- *Model active listening.* One of my partners, formerly with Procter and Gamble, is fond of recounting a story of a meeting he was in that included John Pepper, the CEO of P&G. A group of managers was having an interactive session in which they would present their strategies and ideas. Every now and then Pepper would ask a question, and when the individual began to respond, Pepper would physically turn his chair to face the person so that he was looking directly at him or her, giving his undivided attention. No one was confused about whether or not the CEO was listening. Not only did Pepper gain better understanding of the issues through such intense listening, he paid great respect to the speaker in doing so. He also modeled the standard for listening to the other managers in the room.

- *Put ideas on trial for their lives.* In a recent team strategy session a client organization decided to pursue a radically different manufacturing strategy for their products. A subgroup of the team was selected to develop the proposed idea in more detail, including financial projections. When they were finished, a second subgroup was assigned to go off and destroy the idea—to find its weak points, test the assumptions, and challenge the logic. Certainly such rigor is not often called for, but the principle is a good one in situations that are very risky and/or expensive. At least assess the risk of major decisions in a way that gives the team opportunities to voice their concerns. I have found that the following three questions do a good job of surfacing risk issues:

  * What is the worst thing that could go wrong with this idea/decision?

  * How bad would that be on a scale of 1 to 100? (100 = very bad)

  * What is the probability it could happen?

- *Engage everyone, all the time.* In facilitating team discussions, decision-making, or problem-solving sessions, reach out to the edge of the group where the quieter, more reflective team members tend to be found. Proactively seek input from those who might not feel this is "their area."

- *Regularly review the state of team communications.* Use a survey like the one provided above or just put the issue on the table for general discussion, but don't leave the table without one feasible idea to make communications better.

Excellent communication doesn't just happen naturally. It is a product of process, skill, climate, relationship, and hard work. One of the most important roles of leadership is to cultivate these variables with a determined intentionality motivated by the understanding that a team can move no faster than the speed of its communication. In the same respect, the limits of team work products will be defined by the quality of communication among team members and between the team and the larger organization.

PART THREE

Turning Principle into Practice: Building the Team

CHAPTER TEN

The Path to High Performance Teamwork

THE MEETING

8:13 A.M., West Board Room, Fifth Floor

Steve Geiger had just finished listing the meeting objectives on the white board and now sat at the end of the table going over his notes one last time. He was preparing for a session with his management team to work through a new structure that would better support his firm's new field sales strategy. In Steve's mind they only needed to make a few changes, and he fully expected to be finished by lunch. After all, this was a seasoned group of executives who generally achieved high results.

The various departments in his division worked well together when necessary. But, for the most part, they supported field sales as individual departments responding to local requests of one type or another. The new corporate strategy would emphasize the national programs to a much greater degree, and the current structure of his division would need to be better aligned to meet the demands of this new approach.

Steve felt that a good plan would be to create a new department comprised of small parts of the three current departments. This arrangement would consolidate the people concerned with national events under one director. Not only would the shortened lines of communication give them faster response times, but a new department would also open a promotion opportunity for one of his top managers. In this age of flat organizations, any type of promotion would boost morale.

This is going to be a slam dunk, thought Steve, as he finished highlighting his thoughts on the yellow pad. The most people any one department would lose would be three. Furthermore, without exception, every one of these directors had complained that the national initiatives invariably created more trouble than they were worth and hindered their departments from serving their local markets in a timely manner. "In fact," he concluded as the first person was entering the room, "we'll probably be out of here by ten."

9:45 A.M., West Board Room, Fifth Floor

Over an hour later, Steve had not even put his suggestions on the table. He had started the meeting by outlining their objectives and soliciting ideas on how to best structure the division to support the new strategy. Sharon Gibbons suggested they really didn't need a new department, but thought the "most economical" approach would be to transfer the needed staff to her group. Ed Haley was reviewing, for the third time, his thoughts concerning Sharon's suggestions. "I'm not sure this is the most efficient way to organize this," Ed concluded. "It would seem that the most logical place to position that portion of marketing would be to leave it with me. That would minimize change on the part of staff, and the field is used to coming to my department for those requests as well." Bob Smally nodded in agreement. Twenty minutes earlier, he had made a similar observation about the group. Steve looked at his watch. "So much for the slam dunk," he concluded quietly in his head. "At this rate we'll be lucky to get out of here by Friday."

5:50 P.M., an Office Suite, Seventh Floor

Steve looked pensively out of his window. He tried to spend a few minutes at the end of every day, reflecting on the day's events, considering the next day's activities, and just generally decompressing before heading home to his family. However, tonight he wasn't decompressing very fast. What had appeared to be such a simple, straightforward task had turned into a major brouhaha as his "team" fought over various pieces of the structure. Actually, *fighting* wasn't the correct description. Everyone was exceptionally polite and logical. Terms like *economical*, *effective*, and *efficient* were tossed back and forth across the board-room table in a most civil manner.

By the end of the day, the team was worn to a frazzle from all of the high diplomacy used to disguise their resistance. When it became clear that they weren't going to resolve the issue in one day, they agreed to reconvene with fresh minds Wednesday morning. Steve wasn't sure what had gone wrong. Although cordial, there was little, if any, effort to resolve this issue in a manner that would best serve the interests of the company. Beneath the polite rhetoric, self-interest reigned supreme. *I don't understand it*, he thought as he pushed back from his desk. *How did we get so bogged down on such a simple issue?*

Steve was frustrated. The members had been carefully selected, they had the individual skills needed to get the job done, and they had invested nearly a week over the past year in team training with outside facilitators. He had stumbled into a typical group problem—lots of skill but little in the way of willingness to deploy that skill against the larger mutual goals of the team.

THE TWO COMPONENTS OF COOPERATION

A few years ago in the midst of a team development workshop, I had just finished explaining that cooperation could best be described as a continuum rather than merely an on-or-off affair. During a coffee break, several of the participants gathered around me to comment on the concept. One made the observation that the continuum concept was a good picture of what teamwork was all about. Another ventured that a more accurate picture of the continuum would be to draw it vertically rather than horizontally. "Like a ladder leaning against a wall," she explained, "cooperation is an uphill battle!" The others were nodding in agreement when someone asked, "If it's so difficult, what does it take to get to the top?"

Two things happened at this point. First, I realized that I wasn't going to get coffee during this coffee break, and, second, a full-blown discussion was launched that would give me and the other participants new insight into the issues of teams and teamwork. As I played the role of scribe at the flip chart, we began to build a list of ingredients necessary to climb this ladder to the heights of effective collaboration. That evening, after the participants had departed for dinner, I was gathering up my teaching materials and preparing for the next day. I paused for a moment at the flip chart, reflecting on the conversation from earlier that afternoon. As I read through the qualities that would describe a team capable of climbing to the "top" of the continuum, I realized that they fell into two broad categories—the *willingness* to cooperate, and the *skill* of cooperation.

Willingness
to cooperate deals with the issue of motivation.
Examples include commitment to team goals, energy, creativity, willingness to subordinate individual results to those needed by the team, a sense of alignment between individual and team goals, and the initiative to help others.

Skill
in cooperation deals with our ability to "team up" in accomplishing tasks.
Examples include goal setting, communication, decision making, and problem solving.

Willingness to cooperate is a critical first step in any team effort. Remember, cooperation is a choice. Teamwork is hard work, and teams are always made up of volunteers. If they don't come up with a good answer to the question "Why should we cooperate?" it's unlikely they will. A good answer to this critical question is needed to develop the commitment and motivational levels necessary to get the team through the inevitable tough spots.

Skill is the second dimension in cooperation. I'm not referring to the technical or functional expertise each individual brings to the team, but rather the ability of the group to blend those skills in the process of "teaming up" in *accomplishing* tasks. This would include the skills of being able to effectively and efficiently mobilize the gifts, skills, and experiences of team members in various team processes like goal setting, problem solving, decision making, and conflict resolution.

By understanding how skill and willingness work together in cooperation, we can begin to build a model of group development (Figure 10-1). The vertical axis represents the willingness component; the horizontal measures skill. Theoretically, these dimensions of cooperation would be independent. All of us can think of instances in which we have seen a group of people with a great attitude and willingness to collaborate, but for one reason or another they lacked the skill to coordinate their efforts. A new Broadway play in the first few weeks of rehearsal or a football team in spring practice would be good examples. Correspondingly, there are instances where the reverse is true—instances in which individuals who had the ability to cooperate were unwilling because of a competitive spirit, lack of commitment to the team task, or some other reason that caused them to believe the interests of the team were counter to their own.

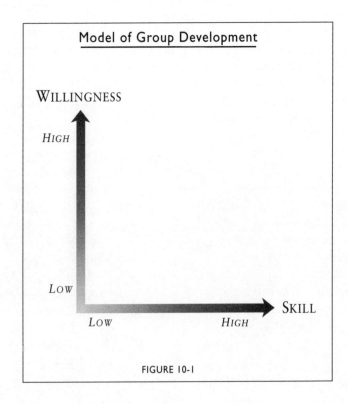

FIGURE 10-1

GROUP DEVELOPMENT

Seeing cooperation as two dimensions expands our understanding of how teams develop. If teams can identify their level of cooperation in terms of willingness and skill, then they can better design strategies to increase their effectiveness. Not every team is the same. Whereas Steve's group was high in skill but low in willingness, another group might be just the opposite. Consequently the strategy you need to encourage one team will be quite different from the other.

Most observers of group development have noticed that over time groups tend to move through four to five predictable stages of development. Our conclusions have been no different.[1] In 1981, we developed a survey instrument that assists teams in evaluating their stage of development. Refined over the past 19 years, this instrument, *The Team Profile®*, has been completed by several thousand people representing hundreds of teams.[2]

The results have shown us four primary stages of healthy team development—the Basic Group, Adolescent Team, Learning Team, and the High Performance Team. Although groups tend to move through these stages in sequence, the boundaries between them are not clear-cut. Like any model, it depicts a simplicity not found in everyday life. In real-life situations, one stage blends into the next. A group may exhibit characteristics of more than one stage, particularly as they make the transition between stages.

In addition to four healthy stages, we have identified four other types of groups that are at best dysfunctional. Groups exhibiting these characteristics—Confused Crowd, Unruly Mob, Warring Factions, and Individual Stars—have little or no chance of developing into productive, synergistic teams. Such groups will require major surgery to get them on the healthy track or perhaps may need to be disbanded altogether.

Once you are familiar with the characteristics of each stage of group development, you will be better able to identify where your team is and design strategies needed for growth.

Stages of Team Development

These stages present a simplistic picture of a complex issue. In reality, a group may exhibit characteristics of more than one stage.

BASIC GROUP — *Person-Centered*
The major distinction of a group (versus a team) is that the results are additive. Each additional person adds one more unit of output (the same amount of output the individual could produce alone). Both willingness and skill in cooperation is relatively low, just enough to keep the group together.

ADOLESCENT TEAM — *People-Centered*
This stage takes the first step toward teamwork. The focus is on getting to know the other team members—their strengths, weaknesses, and unique contributions to the team. Through this knowledge and the process of sharing it, trust builds, as does willingness to subordinate individual interests to a greater possibility.

LEARNING TEAM — *Process-Centered*
Generally, this is the second phase of team development. Having gotten to know the members, trust and willingness have grown to the point that the team begins to openly discuss process or skill areas. They then determine how they can cooperate more effectively.

HIGH PERFORMANCE TEAM — *Purpose-Centered*
This team can balance the tensions between people and task, between individual initiative and collaboration, between clear division of labor and commitment to the whole task. Flexibility, adaptation, and responsiveness characterize this team, and the results are exceptional.

INDIVIDUAL STARS — *Self-Centered*
This group demonstrates a high skill level to cooperate. They know how to do it. However, they are not willing to subordinate individual goals, interests, and needs to that cooperative effort. The competence is there, but it is blocked by competitive or distrustful attitudes.

CONFUSED CROWD — *Reasonably High Willingness, Very Low Skill*
Here the issue is basically one of competence. Even though the motivation is positive, members are stepping on one another's toes and running in circles in efforts to cooperate. The overall result is that less gets done together than if the individual were working alone.

WARRING FACTIONS — *Very Low Willingness, Reasonably High Skill*
Competition or lack of trust creates hostile, competitive environments. The result is inevitably a group of interdependent people acting independently.

UNRULY MOB — *Very Low Willingness, Very Low Skill*
This situation is anarchy at worst, chaos at best. We recommend immediate evacuation of the area.

FIGURE 10-2A

Stages of Team Development

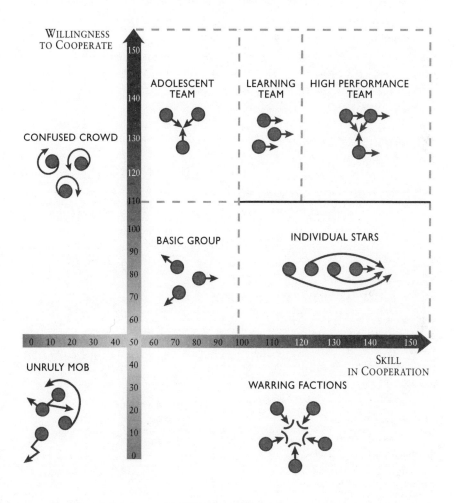

FIGURE 10-2B

THE STEPS AND MISSTEPS TO
HIGH PERFORMANCE

The Basic Group

This is the most common type of group found in most organizational settings. With a little orientation and reasonable thought in assigning team members, we can safely say the Basic Group is home plate, the starting place of the typical team. Many, if not most, groups never proceed beyond this stage of development. Although most members enter the group with positive expectations, they are also anxious and concerned about personal interests and needs. In this first stage, the core concern is that of alignment. Members ask themselves, consciously or subconsciously, "Is this group going where I want to go? Are they going to do what I want to do? Is participation with this group in my best interest?" Because of a lack of good answers to these questions at this point, the willingness to cooperate is low. Skill in cooperation is also low due to the inexperience of the group in working together.

In Figure 10-3, note that the graphic objects represent individual group members. Notice the different direction of the arrows. This symbolizes the lack of alignment regarding goals and aspirations of group members. The focus of their attention is on their own self-interests. Until team members become committed to the overall team objective, there is little chance they will get to the next stage of development.

Structure for this group usually comes from an outside, higher authority such as the department manager who put the team together and assigned its task. Things are done in a somewhat mechanistic, by-the-book manner. Feelings and true opinions are not expressed openly because there are too many unknowns. Members are wary of other team members, new processes, and repercussions from being too open.

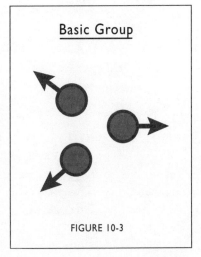

Basic Group

FIGURE 10-3

Therefore, we find a lot of listening and watching as group members attempt to size up the situation and one another.

With good leadership and a clear task, this group often appears to outsiders as effective and, to a limited extent, they are. However, close examination would show their results to be additive rather than synergistic. Like the football team in spring practice or the first few days of rehearsal with a new repertory group, the basic talent might be there, but the power of this group lies in its *potential* rather than its *current* performance.

The Adolescent Team

If and when team members become somewhat convinced that being a member of this team is in their best interests, they begin to move into the second stage of development, the *adolescent team*. Having wrestled with and resolved the issue of alignment, the team members become willing to risk being more open, expressing personal concerns and feelings with greater candor. Attention begins to turn from personal to interpersonal concerns, as evidenced by the direction of the arrows in Figure 10-4.

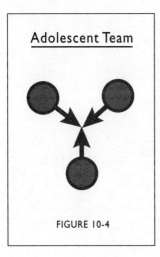

Adolescent Team

FIGURE 10-4

Trust is the core issue at this stage. The focus of team members is on getting to know their co-workers—their strengths, weaknesses, and unique contributions to the team. Through this knowledge and the process of sharing it, trust begins to build, and with it, *willingness* to subordinate individual interests to a greater possibility.

As the team members grow in their knowledge and trust of one another, also they are gaining a more accurate picture of the scope of the task and beginning to question the ability of this group to achieve their original expectations. As the curiosity and preoccupation of getting to know one another begins to fade, the team begins to turn toward the task.

The Learning Team

Once the team has generally resolved the issues of alignment and trust, they are able to move on to the task itself (Figure 10-5). It's not as though they don't already have one, but at this stage they begin to recast the work in their own terms and take ownership of it. When the task is fully grasped, the next issue is figuring out how to accomplish it. Building on the trust and willingness developed earlier, the team begins to openly discuss the processes and skills needed to accomplish the task. Roles are discussed and clarified. Missing or inadequate processes are identified and addressed. The team is asking: "How can we cooperate more effectively?"

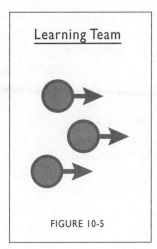

Learning Team

FIGURE 10-5

It is at this stage of development that the focus of the learning team turns toward the skill dimension of cooperation. Without the trust and interpersonal relationships established previously, the team would have difficulty discussing task and process with the needed levels of openness. For example, if I walk into a teammate's office and explain that I need the financial reports earlier in the month and in a different format, she might suggest that I take a long walk on a short dock. That's her area, and I should mind my own business. But if we have gotten to know one another and established some trust, she will be more open to listening, knowing that my concern is about how the team can do the job better and not merely to further my personal interests.

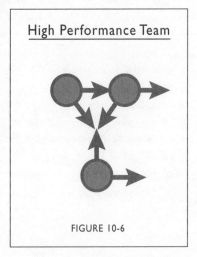

High Performance Team

FIGURE 10-6

The High Performance Team

At this point in its development, the team can balance the tensions between people and purpose (Figure 10-6), between individual initiative and collaboration, between clear division of labor and commitment to the whole task. Flexibility, adaptation, and responsiveness characterize this team. Although the amount of synergy found in team results has been on the increase as the team has moved through one stage of development to another, it's a specific agenda item for this team at almost every meeting. "How are we doing?" and "How can we do better?" are the two most frequently asked questions. They are in touch with both the task and one another and have learned to manage both. It is this group of people that is described with the accolade High Performance Team.

It's Not All Roses: Four Unhealthy Stages

Figure 10-2-B introduces the possibility of both willingness and skill being not only low but also negative. Many of us have experienced situations in which individuals expressed a low inclination to cooperate and were clearly negative, even hostile, about it. Similarly, over the years, I've seen groups whose composition was so poor that the skills needed to cooperate were absent or so low that they actually worked against one another.

A classic example occurred in Philadelphia in the early 1800's. At that time there was no central city fire department. Rather, there were independent fire brigades who competed vigorously to be the first to a fire. Fueling this rivalry was the fact that the fire brigade that responded the fastest and put out the fire was the only one who received the financial remuneration from the carrier who insured the property. Competition was so intense that the different brigades would often sabotage one another and even go so far as to hide fire hydrants. This situation continued until 1817, when the fire brigades themselves realized that the bedlam and chaos couldn't continue and they united to form the Fire Association of Philadelphia.[3]

Confused Crowd

FIGURE 10-7

Figures 10-2-A and 10-2-B give brief overviews of four different types of "groups," three of which are floundering in the dysfunctional portion of the matrix.

Confused Crowd

This group (Figure 10-7) has the best of intentions and a great attitude, but they do not have the skills needed to effectively combine and coordinate their collective efforts. Notice that the skill levels are in the negative portion of the continuum. In this case, skill is lacking to the point of dysfunction. This problem could stem from inadequate training for current team members or even team composition (you can't have a string quartet without a violinist).

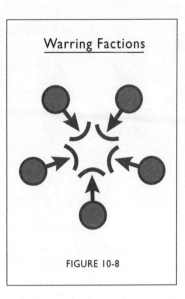

Warring Factions

FIGURE 10-8

Warring Factions

This group (Figure 10-8) is characterized by high levels of competition, internal politics, or lack of trust. The skill to cooperate is there, but relationships have been so bruised and broken that there is little chance individuals will subordinate their interests to the greater needs of the group. At this point, it is unlikely that anyone would take the risk of being interdependent with those other untrustworthy people. The group isn't cooperating and doesn't want to.

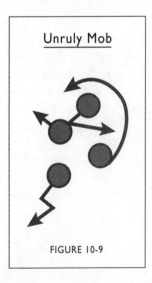

Unruly Mob

FIGURE 10-9

Unruly Mob

This group (Figure 10-9) scores in the negative range of both skill and willingness and, yes, we have seen people score their teams in this area. I worked with a large professional services firm in which several teams described themselves as unruly mobs. For the most part these were technical specialists, consultants

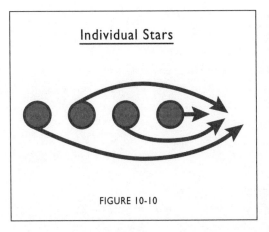

Individual Stars

FIGURE 10-10

who operated independently on client assignments. Their compensation was based on their individual billable hours, and that's where they put their energy.

During the last few years competitive pressures and a restructuring of many of their clients demanded a more team-oriented approach in which a broader range of functional expertise could be made available to clients in a more integrated fashion. Twenty years of working alone and "doing it my way" coupled with the old compensation plan thwarted the company's attempts to form teams. Consultants were "assigned" to specific customer teams, who were told that collaboration was the wave of the future. Management might as well have been speaking to a stone wall.

Individual Stars

These group (Figure 10-10) members are highly skilled, but are in it for themselves, not the team: thus the title, *Individual Stars*. Steve Geiger, our troubled executive at the beginning of this chapter, was dealing with just such a group. This group has low willingness but medium to high skill. Remember, skill refers not to their individual technical skills but to the skills needed to cooperate. Only when it's to their distinct advantage do they use those technical skills in a collaborative fashion. Individual Stars are like professional cyclists. In a long race, cyclists "draft" one another to save energy. Drafting is when one cyclist stays close behind another and lets the vacuum formed behind the first rider pull the other along a little, saving the second rider considerable energy. Over the course of the race they may trade places a few times, but near the finish, it's every person for himself or herself.

Sometimes the members of an *Adolescent Team* see the results of a group of *Individual Stars* and express envy that these results appear to come with so much ease in contrast to the frustration and hard work they experience. However, whereas the *Adolescent Team* has considerable potential for improvement, the *Individual Stars* have gone about as far as they can go. Notice the solid line separating the *Stars* from the teams above in Figure 10-2B. Over the years, as we have surveyed teams, we have not found one instance where a group, having established such a pattern of behavior, suddenly came to its senses and decided to cooperate fully. At this point, competitive spirits are too high and trust too low to allow such a change in direction. The hardness of these attitudes seems to form a type of attitudinal glass ceiling above which they cannot (better yet, *will not*) rise.

Confused Crowds are often the result of inadequate thinking about team mission, whereas groups described as *Warring Factions* or *Unruly Mobs* could be the result of poor staffing decisions. Such groups can also be the product of growth in the wrong direction as, over time, competition and/or conflict continue unchecked. The popular movie *The War of Roses* was based on the principle that mismanaged conflict tends to escalate and intensify. The result is that the relational fabric needed for trust and communication is torn to the point where it becomes impossible to repair.

Most groups start as a *Basic Group*. Although this is the starting place of most teams, growth is not assured. In fact, in our model of team development, only three of the groups attain the accolade "Team." Team development is the product of asking and answering some very tough questions as well as a lot of hard work. We estimate that 60 to 70 percent of all groups will not develop into teams. When growth does occur, it's one step at a time. The group needs time to work through the issues in each stage of development (Basic Group—Adolescent Team—Learning Team—High Performance Team).

This first stage of development can last for several hours or for the lifetime of the group. How long depends on the size and the complexity of the task, the quality of leadership, and the understanding and expectations of the members going into the experience. The bigger and more complex the task, the longer it will take the members to work through the issues of alignment. However, if the task is well defined and the rationale for their assignment to the group is clearly explained to the individual members, the pace of progress will be greatly enhanced.

A DEVELOPMENTAL PICTURE OF FOUR TEAMS

Figure 10-11 shows a number of scores for *The Team Profile®* from actual work groups. Let's see what we can glean about their teams. First, Group A presents a typical profile for a new or young group. This is generally where every group starts and often stays.

Team B has dealt with the issues that allow it to move to higher stages of development. I will discuss these issues in the next chapter. They seem to be in consensus that they are somewhere between an Adolescent Team and a Learning Team.

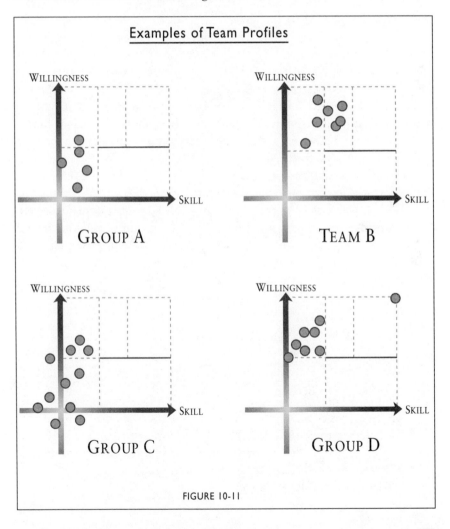

FIGURE 10-11

Group C is having a rough time and it is reflected in the team members' description of where they feel their team is. This was an Economic Development team for a southeastern state, in which members who represented every county had the task of encouraging outside industry (for example, Mercedes, BMW, etc.) to come to their state. They were great on the front end of the process. However, if a company expressed interest, the team members quickly started squabbling about the specific county that would be best for the enterprise. In some cases they went straight to the inquiring company, behind the backs of other team members, to make the case for *their* county. Regardless of their strategies, it was always apparent to outsiders that this wasn't a team but rather *Warring Factions*. They have yet to convince a major industry to relocate to their state.

Finally, Group D. As so often happens, several members of the team have materially different perspectives where the team is developmentally. The person in the lower left is somewhat concerned about the state of "teamness," whereas the team member in the upper right thinks things couldn't be better. Who is right? Without discussion and more information, it's hard to tell. We all tend to see the world, not as it is, but as we are. Think of how interesting this discussion would be, especially with the inputs of the other teammates included.

The same insights apply for growth in other phases as well. Understanding that there are specific stages of team development and knowing the characteristics of those stages can greatly enhance the probability of growth. Armed with such insight, teams can take the initiative to address the critical issues and questions of growth.

THE BOTTOM LINE

If we are going to build high performance teams, then it is imperative that we become familiar with the stages of group development and the principles that help or hinder growth from one stage to the next. We can use the relationship between the team's willingness to cooperate and its skill in cooperating to define the different stages of team development.

- There are two dimensions to cooperation: *willingness* to cooperate and *skill* in cooperating.

- Interaction between these two dimensions describes different stages of team development.

- Growth from one stage of development to another is not guaranteed. Seventy percent of all groups stay groups and never attain true "teamhood."

- The path to high performance must pass through each of the other stages of team development.

MESSAGE TO TEAM LEADERS

The ability of the group to navigate successfully from one stage of development to the next improves with effective leadership. A leader is someone who knows the road ahead, in this case the path towards greater team effectiveness—helping your team understand that there are different stages of development and that growth from one stage to another is a critical step in team development. Secondly, the team must come to grips about where it is and where it wants to go developmentally. The next chapter will go into detail about what you, as team leader, can do to foster team development from one stage to another.

CHAPTER ELEVEN

Achieving the Summit of High Performance Teamwork

Higho performance teamwork has an element of magic. Over the years I have asked people who had been members of great teams how they were able to capture such effectiveness and what feelings went with it. Many said they didn't know, that "it just happened." I remember a runner telling me that periodically when he ran long distances and physical and emotional conditions were just right, he would experience a condition runners call "runner's high." It is a feeling of unbelievable exhilaration, well-being, and physical stamina. He said that when this happens he feels that he can run forever and that often establishes his "personal bests" when it occurs. We find such feelings in group settings as well.

Bill Russell, the star and mainstay of the Boston Celtics for many years, wrote the following in his memoirs: "Every so often a Celtic game would heat up so much that it became more than a physical or even mental game and would be magical. The feeling is difficult to describe . . . When it happened I could feel my play rise to a new level. . . . The game would move so fast that every fake, cut, and pass would be surprising, and yet nothing would surprise me. It was almost like we were moving in slow motion. During those spells, I could almost sense how the next play would develop and where the next shot would be taken . . ."[1]

Peter Senge shares a similar illustration about a jazz ensemble. "There is a phrase in jazz, 'being in the groove,' that suggests the state when the ensemble 'plays as one.' These experiences are very difficult to put into words—jazz musicians talk about them in almost mystical terms. The music flows through you rather than from you."[2]

"In the groove." "Runners high." "Mystical." These are not the day-in-day-out experiences of any team, not even the best team. However, high performance teams experience their version of this phenomenon more often than other teams. Other types of "groups" seldom, if ever, know what it's like to work at this level of synergy. Positive team experiences, for most of us, appear as infrequent and seemingly random events in our lives. But with some effort, teams can progress toward and reach this goal. As we come to understand and consistently apply the principles of teamwork, we become better able to take charge and create situations in which such experiences would become more probable. United Flight 232 showed how time and energy invested toward training pilots to team up paid off in the long run. High performance doesn't just happen. It takes thought and planning to develop groups into mature high performance teams.

THE PATH TO INCREASED TEAM EFFECTIVENESS

Let's look again at the stages of team development (Figure 11-1). Notice I have added a curve that represents a team's path of growth in cooperation. Our research indicates that although willingness and skill are theoretically independent, they are somewhat connected in practice. We consistently found that when teams grow, willingness invariably precedes skill.

As willingness increases it appears to "pull" skill up behind it. This fits intuitively because when our motivation to cooperate grows, we become more open to investing the hard work to increase the skills needed to cooperate. We won't put the effort into developing the skill unless we believe it's worth it. Thus, as Figure 11-1 shows, the development curve for team effectiveness appears to be first *up* and then *right,* with willingness pulling skill behind it.

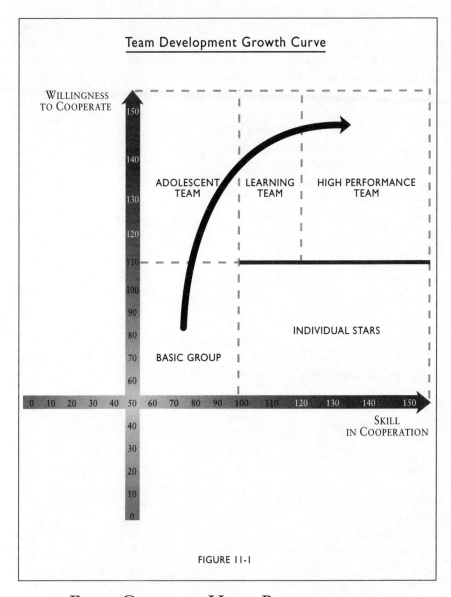

FIGURE 11-1

FOUR GATES TO HIGH PERFORMANCE

Teams who want to progress up the Team Development Curve must work through a series of important questions and issues. The answers to these questions materially affect a person's ability to integrate and work effectively as a contributing member of the team. The picture that comes to my mind is that of a group of fellow travelers on a pilgrimage to find a great treasure. They must navigate a steep path and difficult terrain. Periodically along the way, large, formidable gates bar their route, preventing them from advancing to the next stage of their journey. The gate can only be opened with the answer to a complex riddle or question. The team leader plays a critical role in determining the pace and progress of the team. He or she will act as guide, coach, facilitator, and encourager as the team progresses along the path and confronts the challenge of each issue.

The team must address four primary issues or questions. The first two questions are asked and answered individually in the quiet of one's own mind. The second two questions are addressed collectively as a group.

1. Alignment—Why am I here?

2. Relationship—Who are you and why are you here?

3. Task—What shall we do?

4. Strategy—How shall we do it?

Not long ago, I was observing a product development team. The team was in the thick of a day-long strategy session and had long forgotten that I was in the back of the room. As the morning wore on, it was clear that a number of the team members were not engaged in the process. In fact, one woman spent most of the time facing away from the group looking out the window. This withdrawal by some individuals was not lost on the rest of the team. Throughout the morning, the number of glances between team members increased, as did the overall tension in the room. It was because of this type of behavior that the team leader had asked us to attend. About midmorning, the team leader gently confronted the woman gazing out the window. *"Julie, are you with us today?"* Julie, turned and countered, *"I'm here but I don't want to be. I don't want to be on this team. I was told by my manager that I had to be on it!"* You could have heard a pin drop.

Julie and, in some respects, the team itself, had not yet worked through the foundational issues I described above. If they had been addressed, the answer was not sufficient. In this case, Julie had not found a good answer to the question: "Why am I here?" She probably didn't arrive in the group with a list of questions to be answered. She didn't even know she had questions. Most likely, she, as well as others in the same situation, attribute tension, nervousness, and unsettledness to being in a new and strange situation. However, it's more than a new environment. If teams don't address these issues, the tensions and disassociation will continue long after the situation is no longer new. In fact, I have seen many older teams that have never grappled with these issues and, as a result, never lived up to expectations.

An example of just such a situation involved a new product development team formed as part of a strategic alliance between two large electronics firms. After nearly a year of effort the team was hopelessly behind on its commitments to the sponsoring parent companies. The team began the initiative with a burst of energy and unbridled optimism. It had been tasked with the responsibility of developing the next-generation technology for a major portion of their two companies' future business. This was a tremendous opportunity for those assigned to the project.

A year later when we began to work with them, the atmosphere and attitudes had changed dramatically. Team members were frustrated, angry, and even fearful. Fearful that the sponsors would change teams or even shut down the project; frustrated and angry at other team members because, after all, it was their fault. The root cause was that these key questions had never been addressed. Team members had never wrestled with their individual and collective alignment to the project's deliverables. They hadn't taken the time to get to know and build trust with teammates from the other company. At the beginning of the project, when it was a merely a matter of getting established and flying all over the world gathering resources and research, these things didn't seem important. However, under the pressure of real work and non-negotiable deadlines the issues of alignment and trust loomed very large indeed.

With no alternative but to call timeout and regroup, the team convened in our conference room and began to work through foundational questions. Why are we here . . . really? What are each of us bringing to the table and why is that crucial to the success of the project? What are the essential elements of the task and what is each team member's role in that task? What is our overarching strategy? What is our action plan for getting caught up? We could see the agony of spending this time reflected in many of their faces. If we could have read their minds, we would have heard them screaming, "We don't have time for this! We're too far behind and need to be working." But they endured and, over the course of a few days, we noticed an exceptional improvement in the quality of communication. They soon got back on track, having discovered that an aligned team with high levels of trust moves a lot faster than the confused crowd that had met four months earlier in our conference room.

These questions address the critical issues for each stage of healthy development—alignment, relationship, task, and strategy.[3]

As you can see in Figure 11-2, when a question is resolved satisfactorily, an individual moves on to the next question. If left unresolved, continued development is challenged as members fall back or even fall out. Although in reality these issues are not so crisp and separate as portrayed in the model, they are highly interdependent and tend to be resolved in a sequential manner. In general, one must resolve the first issues before effectively engaging the latter ones. For example, setting goals before alignment and trust have been established can lead to unrealistic, formalized goals which have little hope of achievement because of the lack of the necessary levels of commitment or confidence.[4]

1. Alignment—Why Am I Here?

The core issues in this first question are those of belonging and alignment, and the focus is on the individual team member. The first question is invariably, "Do I belong here?" I want to know if I can play in this league and make a worthwhile contribution. All of us have experienced the disorientation of walking into the wrong classroom, knocking on the wrong door, or sitting in someone else's seat in the theater or on an airplane. One who cannot establish a sense of belonging and membership in a group setting will feel the same way. Fear, anxiety, withdrawal, and even defensiveness will motivate his or her responses to team initiatives.

This disquiet will lead to other questions related to your initial involvement with a particular team: "Do I want to be here? Is this group doing something that is important to me? Can I do better on my own or with another group?" The issue behind these questions is that of alignment, the condition that occurs when I perceive that by contributing to the team's goals, I am making a direct contribution to my own as well.

If the team member can answer these questions positively, he or she begins to develop a sense of belonging and membership that provides a

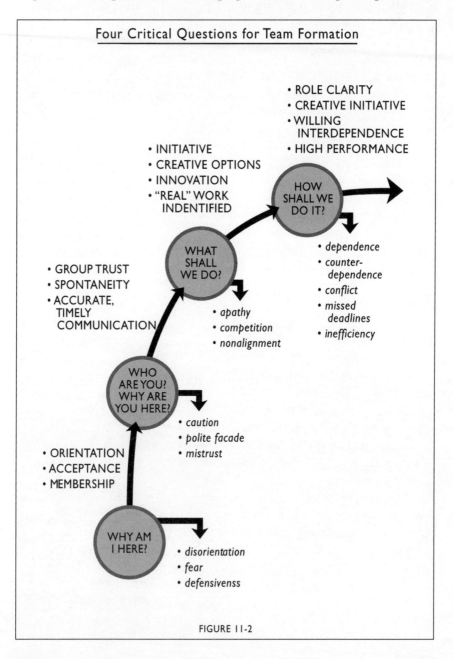

Four Critical Questions for Team Formation

- ROLE CLARITY
- CREATIVE INITIATIVE
- WILLING INTERDEPENDENCE
- HIGH PERFORMANCE

- INITIATIVE
- CREATIVE OPTIONS
- INNOVATION
- "REAL" WORK INDENTIFIED

HOW SHALL WE DO IT?

WHAT SHALL WE DO?

- *dependence*
- *counter-dependence*
- *conflict*
- *missed deadlines*
- *inefficiency*

- GROUP TRUST
- SPONTANEITY
- ACCURATE, TIMELY COMMUNICATION

- *apathy*
- *competition*
- *nonalignment*

WHO ARE YOU? WHY ARE YOU HERE?

- *caution*
- *polite facade*
- *mistrust*

- ORIENTATION
- ACCEPTANCE
- MEMBERSHIP

WHY AM I HERE?

- *disorientation*
- *fear*
- *defensivenss*

FIGURE 11-2

critical foundation for the commitment needed to achieve high levels of performance. Successful resolution of these issues frees team members to begin to confront questions of interpersonal relationships and task.

Savvy team leaders ensure that each team member is clear about the team task and understands why its accomplishment is important not only to the organization but also to him or her as an individual. New team leaders often assume that because this is a team, everything must be done in a team setting. But with the issue of alignment, you must make sure that you spend quality time communicating with individual members. Alignment is a personal decision. Even when you get every team member to agree on the destination of the team, it's quite likely they each go there for different reasons. It's not unusual for a seasoned team leader to take a new team member off to the side for a discussion along these lines:

> *Bob, let me take a few minutes and explain why the mission of this team is so important. I'd also like to share with you why you are here, why you're so important to the team, and why achieving these goals might be important to you.*

2. Relationship—Who Are You and Why Are You Here?

Here the core issue is relationship, and therefore the focus is on the other team members. Who are you? Can I rely on you? Are you competent? Are you committed to the task? Do you have a hidden agenda? If team members can answer these questions positively, trust begins to develop. As a result, communication becomes more open. The quality of communication will determine our ability to work through the task and strategy issues that lie ahead. Without trust, I will certainly be unwilling to put my success at risk by becoming interdependent with you. Communication, the primary means of cooperation, is almost always the first victim of low trust. Openness will be replaced with caution, polite facades, and calculated responses.

Although we ask this question individually, it is answered collectively. The team leader might take a few minutes to review with new team members the backgrounds and roles of the other team members, but then must create opportunities for team members to get to know one another. Trust flows out of knowledge. It might be something as simple as a team meeting in which the background of each team member is explained along with his or her role and the importance of that role to the team. More intense team experiences might include off-site team workshops in which specific exercises are crafted to give team members an opportunity to share experiences and exchange information. Building trust takes time and can't be achieved in a single team workshop. But the seeds of trust can be planted in such settings. The point is that taking the initiative in providing opportunities for team members to gain insight into one another's character and competence will certainly increase the probability and pace of team development.

3. Task—What Shall We Do?

Having worked through the foundational issues of alignment, and trust, the team now begins to focus on the task. Even when a team is given a clear mandate from above about its work objectives, invariably it has some latitude to tailor the group's definition of what they will do. Team members need to be unified about their task. If not, energy will be wasted on strife rather than synergistically achieving clear, mutually agreed upon goals.

Consider this situation described by Allan Drexler: "When a team has not addressed clearly what it should be doing, . . . its interactions tend to be marked by either apathy or irrelevant competition. Watch a meeting of a group with unresolved task issues, and you will notice a lot of arguments and bickering about things that do not matter that much. You will also notice that some members are tuned out, uninterested, and disengaged. These 'fight-or-flight' symptoms tend to persist until the group reconnects with its real task issue and develops a consensus about its work. Teams that do not move beyond this stage rarely find or sustain the energy to perform at a high level. Their energies dissipate over many tangential or conflicting activities, or become invested in competition for dominance in setting the groups' direction."[5]

Sound familiar? In synergistic relationships team members often describe their experiences as "energizing." They credit team involvement for creating energy they didn't know they had. Members leave group meetings invigorated, not drained and frustrated.

Team leaders must take time to ensure that every team member clearly understands the team task in detail. The higher the level of understanding, the greater their ability, individually and collectively, to take initiative in accomplishing that task. Apathy about teamwork generally is an indicator of lack of alignment or lack of understanding of the task. Do not push the team boat off from the dock unless you are certain that every team member is aligned with the team mission—that they believe that achieving this mission is clearly in their best interests.

4. Strategy—How Shall We Do It?

This final question addresses strategy or a specific action plan for accomplishing a task. This is where choices are made concerning roles and responsibilities. If these choices are not resolved successfully, members express their frustration in one of two ways. Some might respond passively, failing to engage proactively and energetically in team activities and decisions. They disavow any personal responsibility for team results. Others are more animated. These people often express their displeasure in more hostile, antagonistic ways. They criticize and complain, never offering better alternatives.

When the team can successfully define its specific approach to the task as well as the roles and responsibilities of the individual team members, it has established a solid foundation for high performance teamwork.

It is only after the team clarifies the task that they can wrestle effectively with roles and action plans. It is at this stage that the team asks questions: What specifically will we do? Who will do what and in what sequence? How do different parts of the task (roles) fit together in an integrated fashion? How will we make decisions? In Chapter 5, I outlined several specific steps team leaders can take to ensure that tracks are laid for this stage. Additionally, many teams have found that flowcharting is an excellent tool to describe individual roles and activities in a clear, comprehensive "picture."[6]

CLIMBING THE CURVE

Again, I want to emphasize that in reality the dividing lines between these issues are not so distinct and clear. It's unlikely that an individual will "nail down" his or her conclusions to one question before moving on to the next. Preliminary conclusions may provide enough motivation for the individual to move on to the next question. Over time one may revisit these core issues many times as information changes or becomes clearer.

Every member of the group will ask these questions. The answers should be tailored to each member's needs, goals, and values. The first two questions are generally evaluated on a private, personal basis. The second two, task and strategy, are frequently discussed formally as a team. Even here the answers must make sense individually. We might all decide to get in the same boat and work as a team to get to a particular

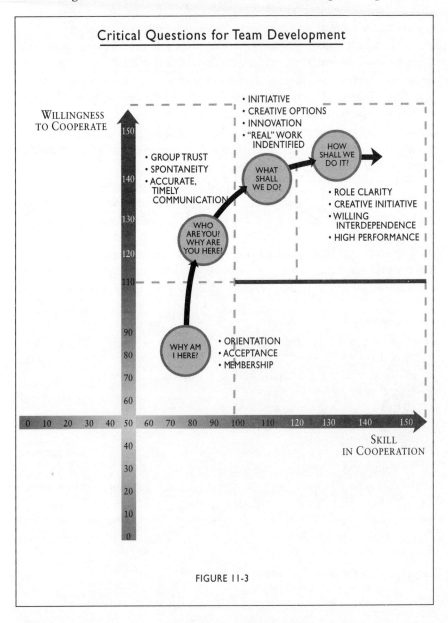

FIGURE 11-3

destination, but each of us may be going there for entirely different reasons. Even when the questions are not overtly on the table, it's important for the team to understand that they are still there and must be answered. Wise team leaders take the time to make sure that corporately and individually these issues are addressed and resolved. Otherwise, when the going gets tough, and it always does, individual team members may not have the conviction to stick it out.

Each of these questions resides in a particular stage of team development. Figure 11-3 shows how these two ideas come together by blending Figures 11-1 and 11-2. Growth from one stage of team development is not assured. In fact, most groups never develop into teams at all. Team leaders can significantly influence both the probability of growth as well as its pace by first understanding the development model and its underlying dynamic and then proactively investing in team development on both individual and group levels.

Largely through ignorance, many teams never address these questions and spend most of their time drifting through a fog of ineffectiveness characterized by defensiveness, mistrust, game-playing, and politics, apathy, competition, and conflict. Team leaders must anticipate these questions and take the initiative to help each individual team member address them.

THE BOTTOM LINE

Team development only occurs as the team becomes more willing to cooperate and more skilled in their cooperation. Skill is motivated by willingness, and willingness is motivated by some good answers to four key questions—questions that must be asked both individually and collectively:

Individually

1. Alignment—Why am *I* here? Is this group going where *I* want to go? Can *I* do better with this group than *I* can alone?

   Focus: Individual team member

2. Relationship—Who are *you*? Why are *you* here? Are *you* committed? Are *you* competent? Can I trust *you*?

   Focus: Other team members

CHAPTER ELEVEN: ACHIEVING THE SUMMIT OF HIGH PERFORMANCE TEAMWORK   207

Collectively

3. Task—*What* shall we do?

   Focus: Team task

4. Strategy—*How* shall we do it?

   Focus: Strategy

MESSAGE TO TEAM LEADERS

Growth from one stage of team development to the next is not assured. In fact, most groups never develop into teams at all. Team leaders can significantly influence the probability of growth as well as its pace by first understanding the development model and then productively investing in team development on both individual team member and group levels.

Note the need for attention to individual team members. Cooperation is a choice made on an *individual* basis. Effective team leaders work creatively with *each* team member to ensure they understand the following issues:

- Why this task is important to the organization.
- Why this team task is important to them personally.
- Why they (their role) are important to the team.
- Who the other team members are and why they are important to the mission of the team.

Alignment cannot be achieved with one good speech from the bridge of the ship—it is established one person at a time. Even though everyone is in the same boat, heading in the same direction, it's quite likely they are going there for different reasons. Yes, working through these issues one person at a time is time consuming, but not as time consuming and frustrating as dealing with lack of alignment when the boat is in the middle of a storm, part way to its destination.

CHAPTER TWELVE

Pitfalls in the Path to High Performance

The best-attended session every year at the International Conference on Work Teams is "Why Teams Fail." According to *USA Today*, it's been standing room only for eight years. As we move into a new century the team trend is even hotter, and with virtually every Fortune 500 company having some version of teams on their roster, and tension is starting to show.[1] One Mercer Management study found that only 13 percent of 179 teams surveyed received high ratings for effectiveness.[2]

In spite of the promise of teams, the return on organizational effort and expense deployed against them has been much less than one would hope. Yet enough extraordinary successes occur for the vision of building healthy, team-based organizations and individual high performance teams to continue to exert a powerful pull on the corporate community.

In any high-stakes endeavor, there are inevitably barriers between aspiration and achievement, between the ordinary and the extraordinary. In the sphere of human collaboration, barriers can be overcome, if we are aware of their presence and understand their nature.

A RUN FOR THE BREAKERS

My primary form of exercise is jogging and, for most of the year, it's nothing more than a miserable way to manage my weight. However, once a year I spend a week on the ocean, and my early morning runs are a highlight of the trip. Nothing beats the tranquility of running along the shore as the sun rises on the East Coast. Often I'm the only one on the beach that early in the day, and as a result I get to see baby loggerhead turtles, animals not seen by most visitors.

Every year, in spring and early summer, adult female loggerheads crawl onto shore to lay their eggs among the sand dunes and return to the ocean. Beginning in late summer and continuing through early fall, the baby turtles emerge from their nests during the night. Guided by moonlight, they make a determined, instinctual dash for the ocean.

Although hundreds of turtles are born each night, only a few make it to the water. They must overcome many obstacles between them and the water's edge. First, they dig themselves out of heavy sand piled high over the eggs by the mother turtle. Often waiting in the dune grass are raccoons and other predators looking for breakfast on the run. Once they get past the breakfast club, they must climb over logs and other flotsam washed up on the beach. Then they must still pass the sharp-eyed gulls and terns, who have been looking forward to this moment for months. If they survive these barriers and luck is with them, the tide won't be too far out and they'll have enough strength left to reach the water.

Like the journey of a newborn turtle, an aspiring team's path to exceptional results will encounter many barriers. The most elegant solution to any problem or obstacle is to avoid it, and the principles highlighted in the six characteristics of a high performance team (Chapters 4 through 9) will help you avoid the most typical team barriers. Murky missions, unclear roles, unaccepted leadership, and ineffective processes are typical pitfalls avoided by good understanding of the principles I have addressed to this point. However, there are two additional types of obstacles that can hinder team growth and progress:

- *Organizational barriers.* Teams, in many respects, are more like organisms than organizations. Like any living entity, they need healthy environments in which to become established and thrive. The organizational barriers outlined below inevitably stifle team development and, in the extreme, can spell their demise.

- *Personal barriers.* Individual team members as well as people outside the team who must interact with and support it all bring variations and vicissitudes that make up this thing we call human nature. Different self-interests, personalities, perspectives, needs, priorities, and purposes compete for attention—sometimes in healthy, constructive manners but more often not.

Organizational barriers by their very nature require solutions implemented at the enterprise level. To unpack such strategies in detail would demand a major work on how to build healthy corporate cultures, a task well outside the scope of this book. However, I can provide a brief overview of several of the major barriers as well as possible solutions.

ORGANIZATIONAL BARRIERS

Barrier: hostile or misaligned organizational culture. We must be clearly aware of the organizational soup in which the team swims. Although certain organizational cultures are more conducive to team effort than others, some aspect of every larger organization will challenge team effectiveness to one degree or another.

Organizational culture is a system of shared values and beliefs held throughout the organization that guides the behaviors and even attitudes of its members. It's reflected in their interactions, decision-making, priorities, and planning. Culture defines an organization's norms: *"How we do things around here."* Although invisible outside of an organization's statement of core values (if they have one and, more to the point, follow it), culture can be seen in what's talked about, rewarded, and celebrated by leadership, reinforced, or even reproved.

We had one client who produced several distinct categories of products for the retail trade, with each product line represented by separate district managers sharing office space in each regional headquarters. Although they were in the same office, each manager represented different products, managed different sales organizations and called on different buyers. The parent organization continually stressed that district managers should do whatever it takes to cooperate and support one another in pursuit of their goals. However, the company compensation system made it very risky for a district manager to take his or her eyes off their immediate goals to aid a colleague. One manager expressed his frustration to us by asking the questions: "What do they think we're going to do? What they tell us to do, or what they pay us to do?" The answer was obvious.

Solution: Leadership plays a significant role in creating culture. If the leadership of an organization only rewards and celebrates rugged individualism, initiative, and risk-taking rather than collaboration, the sharing of information and ideas, and team spirit, they are sending a clear signal about what is most important around there and what it would take for one to succeed. Clarity is not sufficient. There must also be congruence between the "walk and talk" behaviors and beliefs—between what the organization says is important and what they actually recognize, reward, and celebrate.

Even in organizations that, on the whole, are toxic to teams, exceptional teams can still be found. There is consistent evidence that adversity sometimes creates an esprit de corps within the team that is difficult to summon in times of prosperity. In such situations the team must pragmatically evaluate the situation and develop adaptive strategies to the furthest extent possible. The more challenging task will be to maintain a positive attitude and sense of humor about things they cannot change and yet not become cynical. In such a setting the team could easily turn inward, focusing its energy on its own needs and cutting itself off from both its mission and the mission of the larger organization.

A few years ago I saw some of these principles in practice as we worked with a subsidiary of a very large nonprofit organization that depended on charitable donations for its support. As is the case of any nonprofit, securing adequate funds is always one of the biggest challenges. This subsidiary had proven to be particularly effective at raising money. It had a dramatic story and a charismatic leader who could communicate it in a compelling manner. The subsidiary was so successful in fund development that the parent organization began to appropriate a significant portion of the reserves the subsidiary had built up.

The initial reaction of the subsidiary's management team was anger and frustration. After a prolonged period of time, team members began to lose their motivation. They were getting tired of pleading with the parent organization for money they believed was theirs—money that was truly needed to meet their goals and commitments. The parent organization, on the other hand, reminded the subsidiary that tax law considered the funds to belong to the larger organization and that it was they, the parent, to whom the donors would ultimately look for accountability.

The debate was at an impasse. Talks had broken down and compromise seemed unlikely in that both felt they had the high ground on principle. Several weeks later I arrived for a meeting with the team as we put the finishing touches on their strategic plan. I saw a significant positive difference in attitudes of the managers. They seemed to have recaptured the bounce in their step. Later, when alone for a few minutes with the CEO, I asked him what had happened.

He explained that it had become abundantly clear that the situation was not going to change. He had reminded the management team of why they had left higher-paying jobs and success in the corporate community to follow the significance they found in the mission of this organization. If the situation wasn't going to change, then they would have to change their attitudes. They were good at raising money and they must just accept the fact they would have to raise more of it. "We concluded that God loves cheerful givers," he shared with me as we returned to the planning session.

Barrier: misaligned reward systems. A significant amount of team failure can be laid at the doorstep of misaligned reward systems. Nearly 90 percent of managers surveyed by the Hay Group are satisfied with the use of teams in their companies, but only 41 percent say their method of paying teams is appropriate.[3] When you change the way people work, you must realign the supporting reward and recognition systems as well. Too often this is not done, and the results are predictable. About 30 percent of team failures are blamed on the lack of a team-based salary structure, one designed to reward the entire team when it achieves its goals. The Hay study found that "without team-based pay, the message to the team is not clear. It's telling them to work as a team, but still rewarding them for individual accomplishment."[4]

Solution: Organizational systems that inform, measure, and reward people must be realigned to support a team culture before launching such a strategy. Without alignment and reinforcement of the organizational systems, teamwork is doomed to failure. When a stoplight on a lonely country road stays red too long in spite of the lack of traffic, people soon lose respect for "the system." They look to make sure no police are around and then proceed on their way. So it is when organizational measurement systems and philosophical systems get out of alignment. And this brings us to the next barrier.

Barrier: inadequate organizational systems. An important ingredient in making teams work is their ability to communicate, manage information, and measure progress and results. Although different in concept, these needs are connected in that they all are affected by the quality of the organization's systems.

One client asked us to assist in building a team-based sales strategy that would allow the company to deploy multifunctional teams to serve its largest customers. After assessing the situation, we suggested that they delay team development until they had addressed several significant system needs. First, because of the nature of their customers, many of the teams would have geographically dispersed members. They needed a reliable communication system (voice mail, e-mail, etc.) that would facilitate communication and connection. Although the company had a basic system, it would not allow tailoring to meet specific team needs. It was so rigid we believed it would penalize the team's geographic alignment around customer needs rather than leverage it.

Second, the teams had no convenient way to access customer data regarding orders, shipments, inventory, and payments. As a result, they would find it difficult to plan, implement, and measure progress. Their customers would find little value in dedicated customer business teams that couldn't address issues without first going through company headquarters. The company wisely held off on deploying these teams for nearly a year until these system issues were adequately addressed.

Solution: We can deal with inadequate systems in several ways. If the gap is big enough, as was the case with the example I used above, one strategy is simply to wait until such systems are in place. Even though our client waited nearly a year to deploy teams, they are still ahead of where they would have been if they had forced the issue. They would not only have been building their team foundations on sand; they would also have been creating negative, skeptical attitudes among team members who would have been trying to build bricks without straw.

Sometimes waiting is not an option. The strategy then becomes to jury-rig the system while waiting for a better alternative. A manufacturing client wanted to set up a team-based system in over 20 of its plants, using the same productivity index. The dilemma was that every plant used different processes and manufactured different parts. After several months we were able to design a system that allowed plant managers and individual teams within the plants to index and compare their productivity levels. The next step was to automate the system. Here we struck out. Technology available at the time just wasn't up to the task. Even though we could see that trends were favorable, real solutions would not be available for years. Instead of waiting, the task force leading the project stitched together a system using Excel spreadsheets and manual reconciliation. It was rough, but it worked much better than the previous process. Several years later, this system, fully automated on a sophisticated database, is a source of competitive advantage for this firm worldwide.

If you believe teams really are a means to realize exceptional business results, then there must be some system or process in place that will allow the team to tie levels of team effectiveness to the results they are attempting to achieve.

Barrier: organizational boundaries. There are two organizational thinking patterns that flow from the nature of organizational structure, one horizontal (process/cross-functional) in nature, the other vertical (hierarchical). If thinking patterns become unhealthy or unbalanced, team effectiveness throughout the organization is at risk.

Functional fiefdoms. During my tour in the military, I was stationed in Berlin at the height of the Cold War and became intimately familiar with the Berlin Wall. It was an ugly, gray 26-mile structure with broken glass embedded in the top. Barbed wire gardens, dog runs, mine fields, and deep ditches to thwart escaping vehicles were supervised by a cadre of mean-spirited guards.

In more than 20 years of consulting with clients in the area of organizational and team development, I have seen a number of departmental "walls" that reminded me of my tenure in Berlin. Functions speaking different languages, going after different objectives, and using different criteria to evaluate progress, using different processes, looking at business through different perspectives of what's important, and finally being recognized with different reward systems will find it difficult to team up. All of these differences become bricks in a thick and formidable wall between departments and functions. Over the years these walls have become known as functional chimneys; and as they become taller and thicker, communication slows and the organization moves more and more slowly.

In a world in which information seems to be doubling every three to six months, specialization becomes a necessity. As technology expands our abilities to create, move, and manage data, the need for increased specialization has also grown. In many respects, where we once had *division of labor*, today we have *division of knowledge*. The organizational response to this increase of knowledge has been dramatic. Over the years, we have organized vast armies of specialists (sometimes defined as people who know more about less) to help us better cope with the complexity.

Specialization is what gives rise to the power of teams in the first place, but like so many dimensions of team, it can be either a source of synergy or strife. The dilemma is not so much the idea itself, but rather the attitudes that motivate its implementation. A functional approach to work isn't new. The Egyptians used a very sophisticated strategy of work specialization to build the pyramids, as did Solomon in constructing the first Jewish temple in 960 B.C. Adam Smith in the late 1700's and Frederick Taylor a century later brought the concept and potential power of specialization into the industrial age.

However, as we do with so many good ideas, we assume that if a little of something is good, then more would be even better. So we take the idea to extremes. In many respects, this happened with Taylor's ideas. Breaking a task down into its smallest components is a good idea if you are dealing with an uneducated, immigrant workforce, many of whom did not even speak the same language. But times have changed, and a good strategy in 1900 may not be so hot in 2000.

Peter Drucker does as good as any in summing up the dilemma. "Functional design has the great advantage of *clarity*. Everybody has a home. Everybody *understands his own task*. It is an organization of high *stability*. But the price of clarity and stability is that it is difficult for anyone, up to and including the top functional people, *to understand the task of the whole* and relate their work to it. While stable, the structure is *rigid* and resists adaptation. . . . Even as soon as it approaches even a modest degree of size or complexity, 'friction' builds up. It rapidly becomes an organization of misunderstandings, feuds, empires, and Berlin Wall building."[5]

Solution: Most organizations make extensive use of multifunctional teams, drawing team membership from any specialty needed to inform the collective IQ of the team. Whether these teams are permanent or temporary, the functional department from which individual team members come serves more like a "home room"—a place to which they can go for technical training in their specialty, performance reviews (if not done in the team), and expertise when they need help. Effective teaming requires that these team members learn how to balance the demands of dual citizenship. If their perspective is out of balance either because of their personal view or that of their functional manager (*"Don't forget on which side your bread is buttered"*), there will be tensions that bleed off energy that could better be used achieving extraordinary results. No one really wins this tug-of-war—neither the team nor the function.

Barrier: too much vertical thinking in a horizontal world. In today's business environment, organizations have become flatter, faster, and more flexible. However, regardless of how flat modern structures become, there will always be some semblance of hierarchy. Teams can and do work effectively in hierarchical structures (Figure 12-1). It's not the basic concept of the hierarchy that dampens team effectiveness but the spirit with which such hierarchies are designed and administered.

The very means of cooperation is communication. You can visualize the lines between the boxes on an organization chart as "communication lines" like telephone lines. The speed of any organization will be

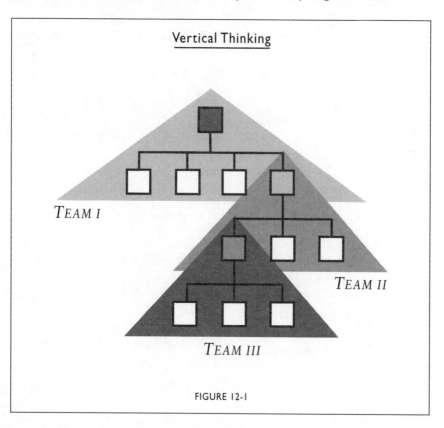

FIGURE 12-1

determined by the speed of communication among its people. The traditional paradigm of staying in the "chain of command" and following the "channels of communication" exerts tremendous vertical force on the flow of communication. In this model, communication between a specialist in one department and a specialist in another must climb up and over, following a long circuitous path (Figure 12-2). It's about as logical as using ladders to get over a wall when you could use a door!

It's not the structure that's at fault so much as the mind-set of those occupying the boxes. In the case of the traditional hierarchy, that motivation is control—managerial control over decisions, communications, and the workers themselves. As with any objective, there are trade-offs. We trade control for speed, flexibility, and creative thinking. In a world of rapid change and high, competitive intensity, we must not only shorten and straighten lines of communication; we must

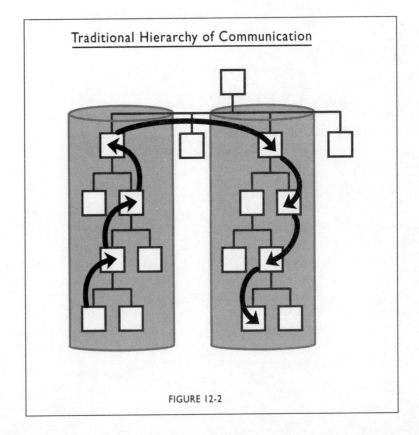

Traditional Hierarchy of Communication

FIGURE 12-2

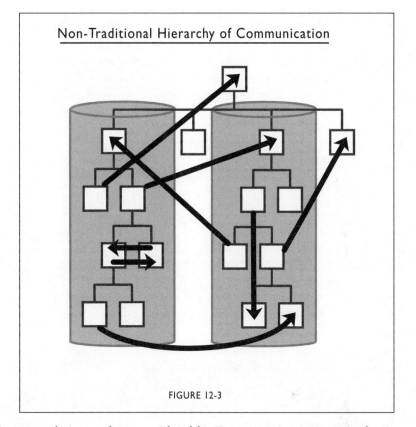

Non-Traditional Hierarchy of Communication

FIGURE 12-3

increase their number considerably. Fast organizations stress horizontal communication (Figure 12-3).

One might ask if this observation was necessary. *"Isn't all this stuff about hierarchy old thinking? Haven't we pretty well left that behind in the 1980's?"* This isn't about old organizational ideas but rather human nature. Control-oriented structures are designed and administered by control-oriented people.

Newer, team-oriented structures value horizontal communication at the expense of control. Jack Welch, the architect of GE's turnaround, said it this way: "The world is moving at such a pace that control has become a limitation. It slows you down."[6] Welch's aim is not to find better ways to control workers but rather to liberate them.[7] Welch's concept of a *boundaryless* organization is his way to liberate GE workers from the "chains" of command.

Well-designed teams weave an organization together. They integrate disparate functions, link separate departments, and hold together processes that weave their way through different parts of the formal structure. In today's world, hierarchies are how a company is organized; teams are how they work together. It's when they attempt to work or think as they are organized that companies get into trouble.

Solution: promote horizontal thinking. As we move into a new century, even the largest corporations find they can operate effectively with four to five layers top to bottom.[8] The challenge today is not to build a flatter hierarchy but a healthier one. Again, it's really more a matter of mind-set. A vertical mind-set in a horizontally focused organization is a recipe for disaster. By vertical mind-set, I mean the perspective of those who still see leadership as a "position" whose role is one of control. The dilemma is that managers who used to supervise 5 to 7 staff members in the early 1980's might have 20 to 25 direct reports today. Those who hold tightly to the concept of "span of *control*" with this number of staff will quickly become spread so thin you will be able to see light through them. We would be better served by referring to the "span of leadership" which inspires an environment in which motivated people can make a significant contribution to organizational goals.

Organizations can address this issue through several time-tested strategies:

- *Core values.* Successful organizations of the early 21st century will be value-based or principle-based rather than rules-based. Things are changing too rapidly to keep rules current. What are needed are well-designed and defined principles or values that all agree will govern relationships and decision making. These principles act as "riverbanks" that allow individual initiative to be released and productively channeled while giving the staff latitude to adjust to changing circumstances. Successful organizations of any type have a well-publicized list of corporate values, and they live by them. They are consistently and visibly reflected in the behavior and decisions of the corporate citizens.

  In this case, such values would include the commitment to servant leadership, free, multidirectional communication, the importance of individual initiative and the highest levels of collaboration. Such values would truly be "valued" by the company—that is, there must be integrity of intent that brings the stated values (that is, the behaviors that are listed on the plaque in the halls) into alignment with the real values (the behaviors that are actually rewarded).

- *Selection/promotion.* Selection criteria (that is, job and/or organization success factors) that describe the type of people who thrive in open, horizontal environments are developed and used to select, promote, reward, and train people. Such criteria might include personal initiative, a heart for collaboration, ability to maintain effectiveness in ambiguous situations, the ability to handle complexity, and the ability to build and participate in productive networks.

- *Training.* Opening up the channels of communication can greatly enhance the quality and speed of communication on one hand and create confusion, even chaos, on the other. To what extent can I, as an employee, go anywhere and communicate with anyone? How do I keep those who need to know "in the loop"? How do we ensure that people aren't communicating contradictory messages? These and other issues must be confronted. Ground rules need to be designed, agreed upon, and communicated. In the "old days" we just had one communication ground rule: *Go through your "boss"* (remember when we still had bosses?)—*don't violate the chain of command.* We haven't eliminated the need for communication ground rules, merely replaced them with some that allow faster, more flexible communication throughout the organization.

- *Reward and recognition.* Truly celebrate the behaviors that demonstrate the stated values in practice. Tell stories about people who lived out the values. Create heroes of those who demonstrated the ability to traverse organizational boundaries and bring back the information, expertise, or resources their team needed. No one corporate response will change organizational behavior faster. This where the relationship between stated values and real values becomes explicit.

- *What team leaders can do to promote horizontal thinking.* Functional and hierarchical thinking is all about boundaries. In some respects, the solution at the team level parallels that at the enterprise level. Much of the solution set falls on the shoulders of the team leaders, who must become consummate organizational networkers and boundary managers. Networks are the distilled essence of virtual organizations. As a team matures, team leaders have more time to address the diplomatic dimensions of their job. In modern organizations the ability to be productively connected to relevant networks that can provide needed information and resources is a critical leadership skill. Team leaders must reach over functional borders and help team members negotiate effective "work release" agreements with their functional leaders as well as mediate the inevitable conflicts when functional resources become scarce.

Second, team leaders can encourage team members to take the initiative to go directly to the source when they need information. In doing so it is important for the team to agree on some basic communication ground rules so that on one hand, key people aren't left out of the loop and, on the other, the team is not buried under FYI's.

When all is said and done, when it comes to organizational barriers, teams and team leaders must learn to cope—to change what can be changed and do the best they can in those situations that can't be changed. Realistic expectations, positive attitudes, and creativity at the team level can ameliorate the effects of significant organizational barriers to high performance teamwork. There are plenty of examples of the highest levels of team performance occurring in tough organizational environments.

CASE STUDY—WHEN NOTHING SEEMS TO GO RIGHT

Levi Strauss & Company provides an illustration of the consequences of these barriers to team strategies. Even though I have described them individually above, organizational barriers invariably come as a cluster, often making it difficult to determine the root cause of problems. In this case, the problem was everything—a combination of a misaligned corporate culture, inadequate systems, and lack of organizational support.

In the early 1990's, Levi Strauss & Company decided to abandon the old piecework compensation system it used in its U.S. manufacturing plants and move to a team-based system, in which groups of 10 to 35 workers would share all the tasks of making the jeans and would be paid according to the total number of trousers the entire group completed. By changing both the manufacturing process and compensation system to a team-oriented structure, the company hoped to increase worker morale, cut costs, and increase overall productivity. Instead, the result was a disaster. One year later, productivity was only 77 percent of pre-team levels, workers were at one another's throats, and labor and overhead costs surged to 110 percent.

Levi Strauss & Company had great intentions. As a company, they had a well-earned reputation for employee concern and welfare. It had often been ranked among the best companies for which to work. They were sincerely concerned about worker stress and morale prior to the change in systems. What could have caused such a great debacle? First, the compensation strategy was not aligned with the new manufacturing format. Under the previous piecework approach, the faster, more experienced workers could directly benefit in terms of pay. Now, under the new team format, the top performers were penalized because of the slower workers in the group.

Different workers handled the lower pay in different ways, none of them to Levi Strauss & Company's benefit. Some merely throttled back, resolved not to give more than they thought they were getting. Others took out their frustration on slower team members. Actions ranged from rousting non-contributing members from the bathroom to threats of bodily harm or even murder. One plant had to station an off-duty sheriff's officer at the plant entrance.

Second, Levi Strauss & Company didn't lay the proper system foundation under their team-based manufacturing strategy. Installation of new computers and handling facilities were not coordinated with the transition to manufacturing teams and, as a result, many of the possible gains in manufacturing speed were lost as loaded trucks sometimes sat for weeks at the loading dock. One operations manager summed it up this way: "We bet the farm with team manufacturing, but the whole system wasn't ready to take advantage of it."

Finally, Levi Strauss & Company implemented this strategy with less-than-adequate support, primarily in the area of training. Employee training consisted of brief team-building and problem-solving seminars. At some plants, workers were given a booklet entitled *Aftershock,*

Helping People Through Corporate Change. Many staff complained they were not given adequate training, including how to balance work flows and manage quality issues under the new process. Supervisors also received inadequate preparation. They were often left on their own to figure out the most appropriate way to implement the new system.[9]

PERSONAL BARRIERS

Additionally, several common barriers have their roots more in human nature than in the nature of organizations. However, like most human endeavors, both dysfunctional and exemplary behavior is magnified through the lens of organization, including teams.

Barrier: corrosive competition. American culture tells us that competition brings out the best in people. It taps into the roots of our heritage and releases the rugged individualism for which we are so well known. It builds character and promotes creativity. Or does it?

Teams are about posses and the Pinkertons, but the heroes of our legends are the gunslingers—tough, silent, serious, riding alone into the sunset. Some would say that competition is surely an unavoidable fact of life because it's part of "human nature." But, in reality, it's not. It's merely a cultural value that's reinforced through a lifetime of experiences. In America, we turn almost every encounter into a contest. In his book *No Contest*, Alfie Kohn quotes social psychologist Elliot Aronson: "From the Little League player who bursts into tears after his team loses, to the college students in the football stadium chanting "We're number one!" From Lyndon Johnson, whose judgment was almost certainly distorted by his oft-stated desire not to be the first American to lose a war, to the third grader who despises his classmate for a superior performance on an arithmetic test; we manifest a staggering cultural obsession with victory."[10]

In our team workshops we often start with "The 36 Square Game." In this exercise everyone is assigned to a 3-4 person group with two groups being assembled in front of flip chart sheets that had been pinned up around the room. Each sheet has a large square subdivided into 36 smaller squares (6 rows, 6 columns). Each group is given a colored marker and instructed that their mission (as an individual group) is to complete as many lines (horizontal, vertical, or diagonal) of consecutive marks as possible. Each group marks only one mark at a time and moves alternately with the other group. The group has ten seconds to make their mark or they forfeit their move.

Their instructions are carefully worded to ensure that there are no indications as to whether the two groups at each flip chart sheet are to compete or cooperate, simply that they are to complete as many rows as possible for their group. If the two groups took a few seconds to think and communicate together about the task, they would quickly see that the best strategy is cooperation.

However, seconds after we give the start command, a very interesting phenomenon begins to appear. The only sounds of communication we hear are the members of each group encouraging the individuals assigned to do the marking to "block them," "smash them," "stomp them." The competitive paradigm rules the emotion of the moment. In fact, for the majority of groups, the concept of cooperation isn't considered and rejected; it's never even considered! The purpose of this exercise is to demonstrate that in our culture, cooperation is not a "natural" instinct but rather a choice made against the gravitational force of competition.

Even though competition might be individually motivated, it is often expressed collectively. The following examples should provide sufficient evidence of its corrosive nature.

Jousting over jurisdiction. For years the Police and Fire Departments of New York City argued over jurisdiction at emergency scenes. In a number of incidences there were actual clashes at the scene itself. One such clash ended tragically. In early May 1988 a helicopter crashed in the East River. Both Police and Fire Departments arrived at the scene, but the police were first and claimed jurisdiction. They would not allow the Fire Department scuba divers to join in the search for survivors, which took nearly an hour and a half. As a result a passenger died. Mayor Koch, after witnessing the Fire Department divers standing around at the scene, wrote the Police Commissioner that such actions "defied common sense."[11] Such internal competition and jockeying for political advantage is nonsensical when the price is so high. Organizations can't expect to withstand external pressures if their energies are devoted to internal competition.

Solution: It is challenging to come up with solutions to barriers that stem from our basic beliefs. To complicate the matter, our competitive tendencies are fueled by the institutions and structures in which we operate. In the beginning our values shape the organizations we establish, but from that moment on the organizations begin to shape our values and beliefs. It is a self-reinforcing relationship, and therefore any solution must address both the individual and the institution. Creating a cooperative culture demands a persistent multifaceted approach. No one strategy element below is sufficient to turn a competitive culture into a collaborative one.

- *Awareness.* People need to be made aware that their first response in situations is often competitive. That is the insight received by the participants of the 36 square game described above. Cooperation is a choice, but people will not make that choice if they don't even know a choice must be made. In general, the default is competition.

- *Culture.* The organization must be explicit about the values that are important and what acceptable behavior informed by those values looks like. Johnson and Johnson has received much well-deserved recognition for the clear, congruent connection between their corporate belief system and behaviors. Their Credo Values outline the central tenets they believe are critical to the long-term success of J&J. Resting on top of the Credo are five standards of leadership they feel are descriptive of the type of leaders who will succeed at J&J.

J&J Standards of Leadership

- Customer/Market Focus
- Innovation
- Interdependent Partnering
- Masters Complexity
- Organizational and People Development

Within each of these standards are nestled more detailed lists of the behaviors they look for in leadership. Below I show the items supporting the Standard of Interdependent Partnering:

- Cooperates across functions, business units, and geographic boundaries.
- Leverages technology, products, and services across boundaries.

- Establishes mutually beneficial objectives; clarifies roles and accountabilities with partners.

- Fosters communication with partners.

- Communicates commitment to the success of the partnership in both words and actions.

In this list of behaviors, J&J is describing a culture that values collaboration. Organizations can't build such a culture until they can describe it. They can't recognize and reward those who live the values or chasten those who violate them unless they are communicated and understood.

- *Training.* Awareness precedes understanding; understanding precedes belief; and beliefs precede behavior. Helping people travel that path whether the destination is a new skill (for example, how to cooperate), fact, or conviction (for example, why cooperation is important) is one of the primary purposes of training.

- *Selection.* One of the best ways to change culture is to hire people who are already aligned with organizational values. When it comes to hiring, the best indicator of what a person will do is what they have done. If someone has a demonstrated track record for cooperating with others, it's likely they will continue to manifest such behavior in your organization or team.

- *Reward and recognition.* What type of behavior is rewarded and reinforced? What is celebrated? What are the stories about?

- *Discipline.* All is for naught if the organization, specifically leadership, doesn't enforce the values. It may be a subtle reminder, a rebuke, even a warning that includes clear consequences if behavior is not changed.

What does the leadership of a single team or the CEO of the larger enterprise do when individuals don't cooperate and the lack of cooperation jeopardizes the success, relationships, and values of the organization? Jack Welch of GE introduced many to his description of four types of employees based on their contribution to organizational goals and their alignment to corporate values:[12]

- Delivers on commitments/shares our values—upward and onward

- Misses commitments/shares our values—second chance
- Does not meet commitments/does not share our values—out
- Delivers on commitments/does not share our values—this call demands managerial courage and for Welch, that answer is out!

The Bible reminds us that a little leaven leavens the whole loaf of bread. If one insists on maintaining a competitive spirit in the face of the above behaviors, it may be a strong indicator of a lack of value alignment. Such individuals may need to find an organization that is more in tune with their approach to organizational life.

Barrier: too much team. Regardless of Jack Welch's desire to create a *boundaryless* organization, people need boundaries of some nature. Boundaries provide a sense of identity and help us tell who's in the group and who's not. Team spirit is a good thing. It creates a sense of membership, energy, and commitment. Without some meaningful amount of esprit de corps, there would be no team, only another group doing the job they were paid to do.

However, we can have too much of any good thing, and team spirit is no exception. Teams can sometimes draw the lines of team inclusion too tight and too thick. The team becomes an entity in itself, often losing its sense of connection to the larger organizational entity as well as to other groups within it. When this happens, our team comes first, no matter what. Even if this means that by placing our team needs or goals first, other teams or even the larger organization may fall short of their goals. Management experts call this *sub-optimization*, a group optimizing its sub goals at the expense of the goals of the larger organization.

Apple Computer in the mid 1980's provides an example of sub-optimization. Apple had successfully launched its new Macintosh computer line and was counting on it to lead the company's charge into the business computer market. In spite of a fast start, the company soon discovered that intense competition dimmed their expectations. Inventories quickly built up to the point where they had to temporarily shut down manufacturing facilities, and distributors were demanding to return unsold merchandise. To complicate the issue, all the attention given to the development and introduction of Macintosh had greatly strained its relationship with the Apple II division. Apple II had been the breadwinner for the company, and they were feeling very much like stepchildren in the shadow of the new sibling.

In his book *Odyssey*, John Scully, at this time president of Apple, observes that at this point tensions between the two groups could have cracked steel. To make matters worse, Steve Jobs, who was both chairman of Apple and operational head of the Macintosh division, "never made a secret of the fact that he had always thought the Macintosh people represented the best of Apple. Now he and his Macintosh cohorts began to openly call everyone else in the company 'bozos.'"[13] The turmoil ultimately led to Jobs's dismissal. And, although the company didn't crash, many believe Apple missed the one opportunity it had to become a major player in business computing. So much energy was expended on internal inter-team problems that little was left to capitalize on external opportunities.

Solution: Team leaders can manage this pitfall by being aware of its presence and danger and never letting the team lose sight of the fact they are part of a greater union. Boundaries are necessary, but when it comes to teams semipermeable boundaries are best. Proactively managing team boundaries by sharing resources and information and seeking the same from other groups provides an ongoing sense of connection to the larger community. The challenge of balancing the tension between team spirit and isolationism is one of the reasons team leadership is called an "art." Teams need a sense of identity and esprit de corps, but not so much that they cut themselves off from those they serve or need to accomplish their mission. That's the key: the mission. When clearly defined it should be the gravitational force that holds the team together, not merely the camaraderie. It takes a balance of both, and when team leaders sense that the team is becoming more important to team members than the task for which the team was formed, he or she must bring the needs and nature of their mission back to the forefront of team thinking.

THE BOTTOM LINE

Teams, like any organism, need healthy climates in which they can grow and thrive. Barriers to successful teams are often products of the larger organizational context in which a team must operate. The exception might be the competitive spirit that resides deep within the emotional marrow of many of us. But this too, like many of the other challenges to cooperation, is in the final judgment a product of the cultural norms in which we must operate. Some companies clearly value teamwork, while others only pay it lip service or even engender competition, believing that it is a better path to high performance.

Organizations and teams can overcome barriers to collaboration with a healthy corporate culture and astute leadership. However, the reality is that many teams must operate in somewhat hostile territory with challenges to optimal collaboration that are outside the control of the team. This doesn't mean high levels of cooperation and synergistic results can't be achieved; it merely demands that some of the creative energy of the team must be deployed to neutralize the effects of cultural challenges. Knowledge that these barriers exist is a good first step toward minimizing their impact.

MESSAGE TO TEAM LEADERS

Because many barriers are organizational in nature, team leaders as the boundary managers can play a major role in dampening their effects. In some respects team leaders can play the role of team diplomat and ambassador to other components in the organization.

As you reflect on the task of the team and the performance levels that must be achieved, ask what environmental, system, policy, and attitudinal barriers may interfere with or hinder your efforts. Talk about this with the team—what are they running into out there that, if resolved, could materially contribute to team effectiveness?

Some remedy is available for the asking. Because teams are a new strategy and structure in the corporate scheme of things, organizations have failed to understand that the underlying systems must be adapted to better support them. Executives eager to support this new initiative may be unusually receptive to ideas or suggestions for smoothing the rough edges. In other cases you might need to be an advocate for certain team members to their functional superiors, who assigned them to your respective team on a part-time basis. The key is to change what you can change and manage around the rest.

CHAPTER THIRTEEN

The Principles of Team Development

TEAM SUCCESS BEGINS IN THE CLASSROOM

Captain Al Haynes would be quick to say that regular training and formal, intentional team development were critical factors in the success of United Flight 232. He told me about two types of training that flight crews attend on a regular basis. The first is the LOFT Program (Line Oriented Flight Training), in which the cockpit crew spends several hours in a flight simulator with an instructor. The instructor enters in problems that challenge the crew's knowledge, skill, and problem-solving ability. After they "land" the simulator, they go upstairs and review a videotape of the entire exercise, discussing things that went well and identifying better ways of handling situations.

A second type of flight crew team training is called Cockpit Resource Management, which is team training for the cockpit crew. In reflecting about this training and the experience of landing Flight 232, Al Haynes said:

> On 232, we had 103 years of flying experience in the cockpit between the four crew members. Not one minute of this experience was flying an airplane the way we were flying 232. So, I had

to ask myself, why would I have any more of an idea how to do it than the other three men?

Cockpit Resource Management (CRM) taught me to go find some help. It also teaches the rest of the crew to assert themselves. To make their feelings known so that the captain and everyone else knows what they are trying to say. Finally we learn how to make a decision together, at least to make consensus input to the captain.

We had CRM teamwork in every phase of 232. It worked beautifully, and it was absolutely essential that we started working as a team in everything we did. We can't isolate ourselves. We can't have our little turf wars, where I'm going to handle things and you leave me alone. You've got to include everyone and work together or you're not going to have a successful operation, whether it's an emergency operation or just your standard business operation. It's absolutely essential you have cooperation as a group.[1]

Those attitudes and behaviors don't come naturally or easily. They certainly aren't attained spontaneously in the middle of a crisis, but rather are the product of training, practice, review, more training, and practice.

The key principle I find in Captain Hayne's remarks is that you don't form teams; you build them. In spite of the appeal such insight makes to common sense, many hold fast to several false premises that tend to stifle the idea that teams can or even need to be "built" in the first place.

FALSE PREMISE #1:
TEAMS ARE BORN, NOT MADE

Every Sunday morning I get up a little early so I can read the paper while I have my coffee. One of my favorite newspaper cartoon strips is the *Wizard of Id*. In one episode the King of Id calls his entourage together and declares, "I think of my staff as a team. You have to look, act and think like team players!" They are an alert group and quickly respond in unison, "We want more money!"

Many managers appear to believe that teams and teamwork just happen. For the uninformed, there are several typical philosophies of team development. The first, as demonstrated by the Wizard of Id, is team development by declaration. The manager calls a meeting and declares that his or her formerly dysfunctional group is now a team. He or she doesn't realize that cooperation is a choice made by individual team members. Teams are in the truest sense volunteer organizations, and volunteers do not respond well to mandate.

One author rightly observes: "Declaring people a team does not automatically make them one. . . . People bring different needs and interests into any kind of group from their location outside of it, and these can serve as the origin of politics. . . . It is a simple psychic-economic calculation: Do the gains from dropping certain interests or goals in the name of cooperation outweigh the losses?"[2] Corporate management doesn't determine whether a group of individuals will meld into a team; that's determined by the individual team members themselves.

We see similar thinking in managers who feel you can just throw a group of people together and hope that a team will form. If the right people luckily end up in the group, if the chemistry is just right, and if the situation is perfect, a team might develop.

Gary Larson in his comic strip *The Far Side*, takes everyday issues humorously to the extreme. One of my favorites shows the sheriff of an old Western town standing on the boardwalk, hands on hips, shouting in exasperation at his deputy, Matthews. The deputy is standing somewhat dejectedly in front of a jumbled, topsy-turvy pile of horses and men in the street. The sheriff shouts, "And so you just threw everything together? Matthews, a posse is something you have to organize." And so it is with teams.

Finally, some people believe good teams happen naturally. Because cooperation is a choice and not a natural inclination, the probability of a high performance team developing naturally is as unlikely as a good marriage's developing naturally. Both are products of a lot of hard work. Effective teamwork doesn't happen by declaration, drift, or default. Without some intentional development effort, the centrifugal force of individual interests or the lack of skill in how to effectively "team-up" will almost certainly guarantee that a team will never mature.

FALSE PREMISE #2:
WE DON'T HAVE TIME TO BUILD THE TEAM

In today's organizational environment, we often see building a team as one more responsibility on a plate that's already too full.

Additionally, such assignments are often found in corporate environments that provide little organizational support for such teams. Teams in these de-layered, over-scheduled climates tend to accept the fact that they have little time to get organized and develop the sense and skills of teamwork. They feel they must get right down to the task at hand. Time pressure is particularly acute for temporary task forces, which often have months, and sometimes only weeks, to accomplish their missions.

One of our clients experienced firsthand the destructive force of time pressure when four teams were chosen to redesign various aspects of a large government agency. The teams were given nine months to develop their recommendations and, in light of the scope and complexity of the task, time would be extremely tight. Given the opportunity to spend three days learning the principles of effective teamwork, three of the teams declined, feeling that time would not allow anything but focused effort on their primary mission. Only one team took the leap of faith, believing that any cooperative edge would be more of a help than a hindrance against tight time frames. In spite of time pressures, they began their effort with a three-day retreat to lay a foundation for their team, ensuring they were clear about mission, roles, milestones, and success measures. Over the course of the next several months they would periodically set aside a few hours to review how they were doing as a team and how they could become more effective.

Nine months later, each of the teams made their presentations to the cabinet secretary responsible for this agency. The recommendations of three teams were not accepted due to incomplete work or weak rationale. The suggestions of the fourth team, which had invested in team development, were accepted across the board. This team received a special commendation from the secretary, and when asked about the source of their success, they responded with one word: teamwork!

HOW AND HOW MUCH?

If teams don't happen naturally and you can't just assume a good team will develop from putting a bunch of people together, then *how* does one develop or build a team and *how much* should be invested in development? This depends on a number of factors:

- *The nature and scope of the team's mission.*
- *Whether the team is new or established.*

- *Team life-span.* Is it a temporary (for example, task force) or permanent team?

- *The degree of interdependence and integration demanded by the task.*

- *Current levels of performance.* Is the team performing well or experiencing performance problems?

Like so many interpersonal and organizational issues, these often come bundled in many different and complex configurations. From a broad perspective, here are some key considerations.

- *Nature and scope of the team's mission.* Obviously, the more important and critical the mission of the team, the more resources will be invested in its development. However, "important" is a very subjective term and is invariably defined differently, depending on one's perspective. If team members are to invest the effort to achieve exceptional results, they must see their mission as important. If the organization doesn't invest resources in the development of the team, it will be more difficult to convince the team that their task really is relevant.

  We must also remember that teams themselves have no intrinsic merit. By their very nature, teams as a structure are expensive entities. They take people and time, two of the scarcest organizational resources. Therefore, organizations need to ensure that teams are deployed against large, complex tasks that require the level of integration and the collective effort only available through teams. Once the organization is clear that the task is worthy, the investment in team development—be it time, money, or other resources—will be easier to come by.

  Just as the importance and urgency the team attaches to its task will in large measure determine the energy team members invest in pursuing it, the same must be said about team development. Acceptance and assimilation of team training will be a function of how the team perceives its mission.

  Remember that any type of team, new or established, permanent or temporary, needs to be clear about its mission and team member roles and equipped with the mission-critical skills needed to accomplish the task. Outside of these things, the nature and needs of team must determine the development strategy.

- *Established or new teams.* New teams can always benefit from a team orientation that provides them with basic terminology, principles, and an accurate set of expectations regarding team performance and what it will take to achieve it. They must be clear about their mission and their individual roles, and they must be equipped with the foundational skills needed to achieve their mission.

  Interestingly, the idea of training is front-of-mind with new teams but seldom considered with established teams unless there are performance problems. Certainly performance problems demand developmental attention, but we must look beyond that to untapped performance potential. Increasing performance levels should be the motivation for all team development. Like professionals in any arena, high performance teams always push the performance bar. Therefore, they are constantly feeling a need for increased team development. Development in established teams isn't merely about performance problems; it's about increased results the team could achieve with higher levels of performance.

  The age of the team also introduces another consideration for planned development. With new teams we must often rely heavily on principles, attempting to convey ideas and concepts they have not yet experienced. By creatively using exercises and simulations we can bridge some of the "theoretical gap," but we still do not have the power and motivation that day-to-day experience brings to the training table.

  Established teams have the benefit of experience. Development strategies can be more focused because the group is able to ask: How are we doing? What's working? What's not working? What are we learning, and how can we do things better? The answers to such questions provide a good deal of fuel for team development initiatives.

- *Temporary or permanent teams.* The development one invests in a temporary team depends on the definition of " temporary." For very short-lived teams whose life span may be measured in weeks or even a few months, it's quite likely that a brief orientation will be sufficient, but it must still include the essentials (mission, roles, and needed mission-critical skills).

Temporary teams bring a dimension to the developmental task sometimes not found in a longer-lived team. Their missions tend to be clearer and the team has a built-in sense of urgency. These factors give an added boost to their motivation to get training and expend energy in applying its lessons.

Compare the aircraft carrier catapult launch of a Navy F/A-18 Hornet and the lumbering take-off of a 747 over two miles of runway. Both planes get into the air in manners appropriate for their nature and mission. Motivated temporary teams tend to act more like the Hornet than a 747. Regardless, the developmental task is very much the same as that of a permanent team. The same principles and practices must be mastered but practically adapted to best reflect their unique circumstances and needs.

- *Degree of interdependence and needed coordination/ integration.* Some teams and tasks require higher and more intense levels of coordination than others. Common sense tells us that the more intense the level of needed coordination, the more intense the training must be. The Blue Angels, some of the Navy's best individual pilots, certainly appreciate the intense level of teamwork and coordination needed to fly 18 inches wingtip to wingtip in complex maneuvers. They invest hundreds of hours practicing close-formation maneuvers and learning how to blend their individual talents into what could only be described as exceptional levels of teamwork.

  However, the typical corporate team tends to underestimate the level of coordination they need to achieve exceptional results. The margin for error is so large in most organizational settings that we seldom see what we are leaving on the table in the way of results. The more accurately we can define expected team results and come to grips with the level of coordination that it will take to achieve them, the more energy we will invest in team development.

- *Performing well or performance problems.* Team performance problems make it easy to see the need for development. However, getting clear about what kind of development is needed is another thing altogether. Take the Order Processing Team at E-Store.com for example. The team was formed six months ago to process the orders of this new e-catalogue enterprise. They worked with a consulting firm to design the system, buy the needed hardware and software, and train the team members in how to work the process. Their objective was 24-hour turn-around on orders with a 98 percent accuracy rate, but they were averaging a 42-hour turnaround and an 86 percent accuracy rate. Turnaround was dropping because team members were engaged in fixing orders that were not filled properly the first time.

The team leader approached the Operations Manager for help, and she agreed that they would retain a consultant to help the group work through this problem. But what was the problem? Is it a process problem and if so, what kind? Do we have an ineffective design? If so, is it because it is too complex for the level of staff or because it can't handle last-minute, urgent orders? Maybe it's not a process problem, but rather a role issue. Possibly team roles as they work the process aren't clear, or maybe they are improperly assigned. Could it be a communications problem? If so, what is the root cause of that—low trust among team members? Lack of skill? An ineffective communication system?

A good diagnosis is the key to a successful development intervention. As Louis Pasteur was fond of saying, "Everything is clear if the cause is known."

What about teams who are performing well? You might think that a high performance team that is achieving exceptional results on a consistent basis might not be inclined to invest a lot of time in team training. However, we have found that high performance teams are clear that evaluation, training, and practice got them to where they are, and they aggressively continue to pursue ongoing development. In some respects they show the same characteristics as professional athletes. The better they are, the more they practice!

How much development is enough? The diagram in Figure 13-1 reminds us there are two different but closely related aspects to team life—the work part and the team part.

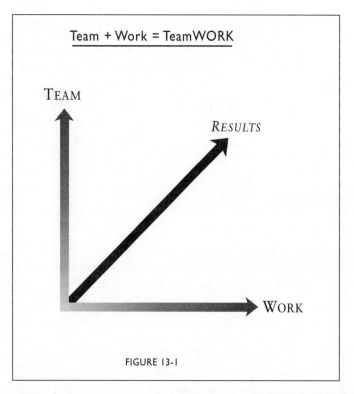

Team + Work = TeamWORK

TEAM

RESULTS

WORK

FIGURE 13-1

The vertical axis or team component in the diagram represents the need to build the team—its commitment, capacity, and competency. Here is where team training takes place, team processes are evaluated and improved, and team relationships are strengthened.

The horizontal axis is about the task of the team—what it does to accomplish its mission. Whereas the team might develop its decision making process on the vertical axis, it makes its day-to-day decisions as it goes about its work on the horizontal axis.

Teams are about tasks, and therefore the horizontal axis will always be a team's primary focus. However, the tendency is to focus entirely on the work axis at the expense of any team training. Without some proactive attention to address team development needs, it's unlikely that any team will achieve exceptional results. How much time a team spends on the vertical axis depends on its needs and stage of development and needs like those discussed previously. This chapter is about the vertical axis.

PRINCIPLES OF TEAM DEVELOPMENT

Many concepts, if effectively applied, will facilitate team development initiatives. Below are 10 principles we have found to be particularly important.

1. *Teams and team development are about results.* Teams are a means to an end. The purpose of any team is to accomplish an objective and to do so at exceptional levels of performance. Therefore, effective teams are mission-directed and measure their success against specific results. Team development must be seen in the same light. The level of team results is one of the best indicators that development is needed as well as the best indicator of how the team is developing.

2. *Know what you are trying to build.* The first step in building anything is to be clear about your objectives. What are you trying to build? No one would set out to construct a building without design criteria and plans, but when it comes to teams or any other social structure, we tend to "wing it." At best, many teams retain a facilitator and take a day or two to work through some interesting exercises and discussion about teams and team building. Although these sessions are helpful, without some type of organizing framework much of the benefit lasts only as long as the experience, and the rest dissipates under the pressure of work when the team returns to the "real world" of their office. There is a big difference between experiencing team-building exercises and the hard work and training of real team development.

   To most people, the concept of "team" is a vague, intangible idea. Some have an idea of its various pieces but are unclear about how they fit together. It's like having all the pieces of a complex jigsaw puzzle spread out on the table, but no puzzle box top showing a picture of what we're attempting to assemble. The Team Wheel (Figure 13-2) presented in detail in Chapters 4 through 9 is that box top picture, providing a memorable model or map (like a mall map telling the team, "You are here!"). It gives the team a picture of what an effective team looks like, and a picture is worth a thousand words. Such a picture brings several benefits:

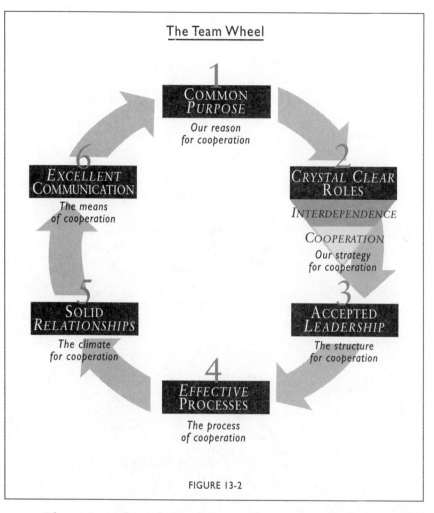

The Team Wheel

FIGURE 13-2

- *The team is clear about what an effective team looks like.* They know where they are going developmentally and if they are making progress.

- *The team can periodically take stock of how they are doing, focusing on specifics rather than vague generalities.* Team Resources has developed a short but highly effective evaluation instrument, *The Team Survey*®, which helps a team to accurately evaluate itself against each of the six characteristics of a high performance team and develop an action plan for increased effectiveness. An abbreviated version of this survey is found in Appendix B of this book.

- *It facilitates diagnosis and problem solving when things break down.*

- *It helps the team develop focused action plans for developing increased levels of team effectiveness.* In summary, the team wheel is the blueprint that not only shows the team what they are trying to build, but also provides a means for monitoring progress and diagnosing problems as they build it.

3. *Team development is process, not an event.* Increased team effectiveness is the product of a series of "ministeps" as the team works, evaluates, learns, and works better over time. Over and over and over again (Figure 13-3).

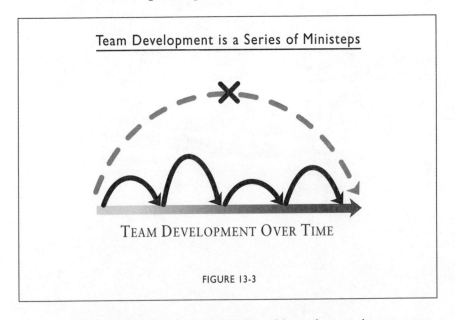

Team Development is a Series of Ministeps

TEAM DEVELOPMENT OVER TIME

FIGURE 13-3

In this hurry-up, time-challenged world, we frequently attempt to cram all the training a team might need into one get-it-over-with session, generally a long one. A dear friend of mine observes that when it comes to training, the mind can embrace no more than the seat can endure, and adult learners can't endure very much.

Spreading team training over time allows the team to master one skill or process before confronting the next.

Another reason some organizations rush through training is that they see training as a cost rather than an investment. In reality, when they violate key principles of learning, much of the effort is wasted and it really does just become a cost.

4. *Just in time is the best time for training.* Adults learn best when they see a connection between training and specific current needs. When the connection is clear there is little question of relevancy.

Recently, one of our consultants changed the long-term training schedule for a new product development task force he was facilitating. The task force was unexpectedly confronted with an urgent and complex decision. It presented a great opportunity to introduce the team to a criteria-based decision-making process, something that was on the calendar for later that year. Being able to effectively use the process taught in the morning to actually make the decision that afternoon was a big win for the team and greatly increased their appreciation not only for teams but team development as well.

5. *Development must be a felt need of the team.* If team development initiatives are not supported with a clear felt need on the part of the team, training will become a distraction and a burden rather than development. The felt need could be defined either as a problem or as a clear understanding that the team needs to perform at a higher level if it is to achieve its objectives. This is another reason why explicit team effectiveness measures are needed. Without them, the team has no clear indication if it is floundering or flourishing, and therefore no means to access development needs. If the team doesn't see tangible, profitable results flowing out of its development efforts over time, chances are it will not continue to invest the energy needed to increase team effectiveness.

One client, in discussing a training initative with us, shared that he had been attempting to get the customer teams to go through team training for years. "It has been like pulling hen's teeth," he explained. "If it wasn't one thing it would be another. No time, not of value, or the instructor doesn't know our business."

When I asked him what changed, he shared that he had lost a major customer and explained that the reason for the exit was that the team assigned to their account didn't have their act together. Calls weren't returned in a timely manner, no one on the team seemed to know what others on the team were doing, and there was a lot of rework because communications hadn't been clear. Even though the cutomer team thought they were doing well, the customer had an entirely different perspective. The shock of losing this customer created a clear felt need for increased effectiveness among the team members. Now they were very open to training. The challenge is to surface the need and value of team development so you don't lose customers in the first place.

6. *Team development demands a safe environment.* Team development is often in response to clear breakdowns in the expectations, processes, or relationships within the team. Sometimes the problem is clear ("Our project management process is terrible!"); frequently the symptoms are clear, but the causes are murky. In either case, the team's ability to communicate openly and clearly about the issues will determine its ability to effectively address the problem. High performance teams master the art of straight talk. They have learned how to confront issues and address behaviors without attacking or provoking one another. Without such skills, the team would never be able to adequately investigate the problem and invent robust solutions.

Development is about learning. To learn we must acknowledge we need to learn—that there is some skill or understanding we do not have but need to acquire. Basically we are expressing a shortcoming, and such expressions only take place in environments in which we feel safe.

7. *Use the work of the team to build the team.* If the work of the team is seen as an opportunity to grow, development quickly becomes woven into the warp and woof of day-to-day team activities rather than becoming an additional item on their to-do list that they will get to when they get time. Like an athletic team reviewing its game films, the team constantly evaluates its performance in key situations. How did we do? Where did we break

down? How can we do it better, faster, cheaper? Development is integrated into the task and not seen as a separate, unrelated activity.

8. *There are no shortcuts to team effectiveness.* I'm writing this portion of the book on the front porch of a scenic retreat in the North Carolina mountains. Outside of my calendar, the most difficult part of the effort was the drive up here. I'm terribly impatient and the six-hour drive through Georgia, South Carolina, and most of North Carolina is very trying. It takes "soooo" long that it almost seems like the whole trip is made at about 25 mph. My wife commented unjustly that I often remind her of our children who, when they were small, were constantly asking, "Are we there yet?" It's in such settings that I wish the technology of *Star Trek* were a reality: that I could "beam" from Atlanta to the mountains of North Carolina in the punch of a button.

Alas, whether it's taking a journey, constructing a building, or even the growth of a person, we must go through different stages or phases of development. Try as we might, we cannot shortcut the process. I recently read an article about artificial intelligence and robotics. In the early 1960's, one of the most advanced robots was being taught to construct a tower out of blocks, much the same exercise we attempted as small children. In this instance, the most difficult challenge of the programmers was to convince the robot to start at the bottom and work up. The robot was clear about what it was attempting to build, but couldn't seem to grasp why it couldn't start from the top and work down![3]

Likewise, every team must go through certain stages of development on their journey to high performance. We can't start at the top. We might, with energy and creativity, accelerate the development process, but we can't bypass it. Figure 13-4 reminds us of the stages of team development identified in Chapter 10. The next team development principle explains that there is a particular path through these stages that the team must follow.

9. *Willingness precedes skill.* In an earlier chapter, I noted that team development progresses first up and then to the right (see Chapter 11, Figure 11-1). Willingness must precede skill. It's the

The Collective and Individual Dimensions
of Team Development

WILLINGNESS

INDIVIDUAL DIMENSION OF TEAM DEVELOPMENT

*TEAM
DEVELOPMENT
CURVE*

SKILL

COLLECTIVE DIMENSION OF TEAM DEVELOPMENT

FIGURE 13-4

willingness (motivation and commitment to the team task) of team members that makes them open to investing the time and effort needed to develop their collaborative skills. Team development is both an individual and collective exercise. Willingness is the individual dimension of team development; the cultivation of collaborative skills is the collective dimension (Figure 13-4).

Where a team member stands as to willingness to cooperate with the other team members in pursuing the team mission is a personal decision based on the answers to two key questions:

- Is the mission of this team important to me and in my best interests? Is traveling with this team the best way to accomplish this?

- Can I rely on the other team members? Are they competent? Are they committed? Are they of good character?

The first question deals with individual alignment; the second deals with mutual trust. In very simple terms, answering the first in the affirmative removes the primary barrier to moving up from *Basic Group* to *Adolescent Team*. In its most basic terms, it's a good answer to the question: "Why should I cooperate?" Developing a good answer to the second question deals with the issue of trust and removes the biggest obstacle to moving right and becoming a *Learning Team*.

Skill development moves us to the right on our model. It also is fueled by the answers to several key questions:

* What are we here to do? What's our team task or mission?

* How shall we do it? What is our strategy? What are our roles? What do we need in the way of ground rules, systems, and processes? How will we maintain the needed level of trust and communication?

Without a clear and compelling answer to the first question, a team often drifts into apathy or bickering over irrelevant issues. A clear, positive answer, on the other hand, energizes the team and motivates them to turn their sights again to the right, seeking to find what they need to get on with the task. It is here that the team begins to experience some of the qualities and skills of a truly *High Performance Team*. They have come to grips with the importance of team skills and have begun to intentionally develop them. They have also come to appreciate the need to maintain an appropriate balance between the business and social aspects of a team as well. As we saw in Chapter 11 (See Figure 11-2), we can combine these four key questions with the stages of team development, seeing that one facet of team development is motivated by the need to wrestle with and answer several key questions.

Understanding the nature of team development and the existence of these questions allows a team to influence the speed and the quality of its development significantly. Once the members know the questions that must be answered, they can proactively move to find the answers.

10. *Team leaders need a head start.* Teams live in a complex world of individual responsibility and mutual accountability. They have both a business and social dimension and are created to discover synergies that can only be found by tapping into the collective brilliance of the group. Leading a high performance team requires a special set of skills such as coaching, facilitation, boundary management, and consensus building. In today's world, every manager must become adept at these skills, but nowhere is the need more intense than in the fragile ecosystem of a team.

For this reason, we recommend that team leaders get a head start with team training. They will need training in skill areas critical to team leadership, such as facilitation, coaching, and boundary management. They need to have a clear understanding of how to establish a clear, compelling team mission, as well as how to build and maintain alignment to that mission. They need to have a firm grasp on the principles of team dynamics and the role team leadership plays in overall team success. Our experience has shown that although a clear, common, compelling mission is the most important ingredient to team success, it is often inadequate team leadership which is the biggest contributor to team failure.

Such training gives team leaders confidence in their responsibilities and credibility in the eyes of other team members. Very often, being a member of a team is a new experience for team members. They will be asked to move into uncharted territory, exploring new ways of doing things. Because the team leader has been given an advance overview of where the team is going and how it's going to get there, he or she can model team skills, encourage others to move ahead, and take risks with more confidence.

STEPPING STONES TO TEAM DEVELOPMENT

To this point I have covered the different team situations that must be considered, as well as the principles that need to be addressed when designing team development strategies. I want to close the chapter with a summary of five components or stepping-stones in the path to team development (Figure 13-5).

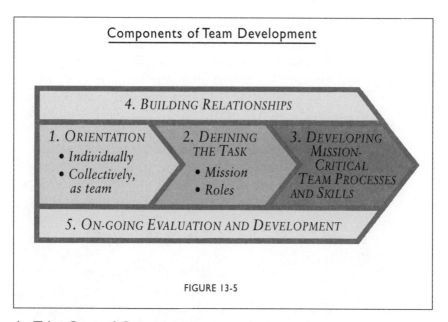

Components of Team Development

4. BUILDING RELATIONSHIPS

1. ORIENTATION
- *Individually*
- *Collectively, as team*

2. DEFINING THE TASK
- *Mission*
- *Roles*

3. DEVELOPING MISSION-CRITICAL TEAM PROCESSES AND SKILLS

5. ON-GOING EVALUATION AND DEVELOPMENT

FIGURE 13-5

1. Take Care of Orientation

Individual orientation. Team leaders must take the initiative to ensure that each team member is individually briefed on the mission of the team and why it's important to them personally as well as to the organization. Remember, alignment is an individual decision made for personal reasons. Leaders must also clarify the role of each team member: "Here's what we expect you to bring to the team, and this is why it's important." In reality, time, distance, or cost may preclude such individual attention, but a creative team leader will take the initiative to ensure the first impressions of a new team member is not at the first team meeting, even if the gap is filled with a well-written memo and phone call.

Individual orientation is even more critical for a new member who is just joining a team that has been established a while. Without such orientation it will be different for this person to develop a sense of belonging and connection to the team. The result is that they become spectators to the team's effort rather than committed, contributing "partners."

Team orientation. The team orientation will not only cover again the mission of the team but will include an introduction to the basics of teamwork as well. The initial team orientation generally takes at least a day and as many as three days, depending on the mission and nature of the team. It will address issues like: What is a team? What makes a team different from any other type of group? What are the characteristics of an effective team?

2. Define the Task

Team mission. In most corporate settings, team missions are generally established by the larger organization, often before the team is formed. As I noted above, wise team leaders work with team members individually to ensure alignment; the team should also look at, discuss, clarify, and even fine-tune the mission collectively. The message here for team facilitators is, "Don't assume we have it." In today's time-stressed, overloaded world of voice-mail, e-mail, and too many meetings about too many different things, we need to hear important things several times. To achieve the level of "ownership" needed to create volunteers, the team members need to see their fingerprints on the mission.

Team roles. During the initial orientation, the team must define and clarify roles. Even though these may have been outlined to individual team members when each one received his or her assignment, roles must be refitted to some extent in a collective setting. Each team member needs to be clear about his or her individual role as well as those of teammates.

3. Develop Mission-Critical Team Processes and Skills

For a short-lived task force, the initial orientation may be the only opportunity to equip the team with the skills they need to accomplish their mission. Depending on the mission and nature of the team, such processes or skills may be as simple as meeting management skill or as complex as an entire list of topics, including process design, project management, decision making, conflict resolution, and problem solving. Increasingly important is the need to clearly define team communication processes and ground rules. The channels of communication have become so numerous (for example, e-mail, voice mail, fax, etc.) that teams must be very intentional about how they will communicate what and to whom.

4. Build Solid Team Relationships

Solid team relationships (trust, respect, acceptance, courtesy, and mutual accountability) are the glue that holds the team together. Solid relationships don't just happen. Like any other element of team, they are a product of ongoing, intentional effort. In the very first meeting of the team, the team leader needs to facilitate the process of team members getting to know and trust one another. Too often, they leave this effort to chance, assuming it will take place naturally over time. The process can be jump-started with something as simple as introductions, a pot of coffee, and a round table.

5. Ensure Ongoing Evaluation and Development

Even if the life span of a team is measured in hours, at some point, as they progress toward their objective, the team must ask: "How are we doing? If we continue as we are, will we accomplish our task? What do we need to change in the way we are doing things to perform better?" From the very beginning, every teams needs to build the expectation that they will monitor progress and performance regularly and make midcourse corrections accordingly.

THE BOTTOM LINE

You don't form teams; you build them. The foundations of a successful team are laid in the classroom. As to the specifics of team development, they are determined by a number of interrelated variables:

- Nature and scope of the team's mission
- Established or new team
- Temporary or permanent team
- Degree of interdependence and needed coordination/integration
- Performing well or performance problems

We also identified 10 key principles of team development:

1. Teams and team development are about results.
2. Know what you are trying to build.
3. Team development is an ongoing process, not an event.
4. Just in time is the best time for training.

5. Development must be a felt need of the team.

6. Team development demands a safe environment.

7. Use the work of the team to build the team.

8. There are no short cuts to team effectiveness.

9. Willingness precedes skill.

10. Team leaders need a head start.

MESSAGE TO TEAM LEADERS

Team development doesn't just happen; it is the product of determined intentionality and hard work. Team development, like any training exercise that takes a group out of the fray, demands effective leadership—leadership that ensures not only that development is available and applied when it is needed, but that such training truly impacts the results the team is seeking. Teams are time-intensive structures, and therefore development efforts must be designed to leverage a team's time and resources rather than taxing them. Implement development initiatives that satisfy the principles discussed in this chapter, and you will most certainly move the team to increased levels of effectiveness.

CHAPTER FOURTEEN

Turning Principle into Practice: Building the Team

THE TASK FORCE

Mary Taylor has just been handed the assignment to lead the New Product Development Task Force to re-engineer the way new products are developed for North Star Enterprises. Representatives from Sales, Finance, Manufacturing, MIS, and R&D have already been assigned. In addition to being team leader, Mary will bring a marketing perspective to the team's efforts.

Although it's an exciting project, and no one disputes its need or importance, timing couldn't have been worse. The company is still digesting last year's merger, and everyone is unbelievably busy. Mary herself is already buried with a separate project involving choosing a new advertising agency. When Mary suggested to the Vice President of Marketing that he find another team leader, he merely smiled and said, "Welcome to business in the 21st century."

To complicate the matter, there are tensions between R&D and Manufacturing regarding the product development process, and Mary is confident these tensions will be imported into the dynamic of this team.

So what should she do to mold this disparate group of busy, over-worked people into a cohesive, mission-directed team? How will she convince those uncertain of their willingness to be a part of this team to go all-out and put their shoulder to the task? How will she blend a set of very different perspectives, interests, skills, and personalities so as to engender synergy rather than strife? And, finally, how will the team complete this task in 14 weeks?

Mary's team doesn't have a lot of time, but the principles and process from the previous chapter will provide a constructive framework for helping this team successfully get off the ground. Because time is so short and calendars are already full, Mary realizes she will be lucky to get everyone in the same room for a few hours, much less a few days for orientation and training. She is able to schedule two half-day sessions over the next two weeks and a full day in the third week. Any other development needs will have to take place on the fly or be pressed to accomplish its primary task. Even though this task force will exist for only 14 weeks, the qualities described in the team wheel will still determine team performance and therefore provide a good road map.

- *Common purpose*. Team members must be clear about the mission. If the team is to succeed, they must see it as compelling and be convinced that it can only be accomplished through high levels of collaboration. Like Mary, team members are under a lot of time pressure. If they don't see this task as critical, it's unlikely they will truly engage at the levels needed to achieve exceptional results.

- *Clear roles*. This team doesn't have time for any wasted motion. They need to be clear right out of the blocks about their individual roles, as well as those of other team members. They have to know not only what is expected of them as the functional representative to the team, but they must be clear about the responsibilities expected from every member, including Mary as team leader.

- *Accepted leadership*. Mary must lead in a manner that will evoke high levels of commitment from these busy volunteers. She must demonstrate the competence, character, and commitment that will gain her the needed credibility with the team. Just as importantly, she must leverage the functional leadership of each team member.

- *Effective processes*. The team must identify mission critical processes they need to accomplish their purpose and make

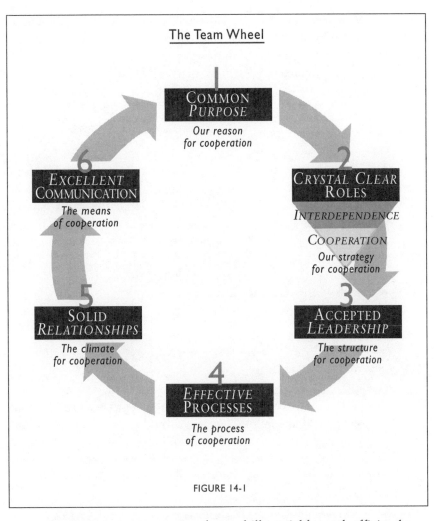

The Team Wheel

1 COMMON PURPOSE
Our reason for cooperation

2 CRYSTAL CLEAR ROLES
INTERDEPENDENCE
COOPERATION
Our strategy for cooperation

3 ACCEPTED LEADERSHIP
The structure for cooperation

4 EFFECTIVE PROCESSES
The process of cooperation

5 SOLID RELATIONSHIPS
The climate for cooperation

6 EXCELLENT COMMUNICATION
The means of cooperation

FIGURE 14-1

arrangements to acquire those skills quickly and efficiently as possible.

- *Solid relationships.* Lack of time and added pressures tend to stress any relationship. Additionally, Mary is already concerned about tensions between R&D and Manufacturing. This dimension of the team will be an important element of Mary's development strategy, even though the team won't be together very long.

- *Excellent communication.* The team must agree on its communication strategy and protocol. Who is to be copied on what? What will be the primary communication channel: face-to-face meetings, phone, voice mail, e-mail, or memo?

MARY'S DEVELOPMENT STRATEGY

In implementing her development strategy, Mary followed the principles described in Chapter 13:

- *Individual orientation.* As team leader, Mary met with three members of the Task Force individually to share with them the mission, its critical nature, and why their involvement was so important to its achievement. She also gave a brief overview of their roles and those of the other team members and answered what questions she could. The others had to be dealt with by phone, but she worked hard to communicate with every member before the first team meeting.

- *Team orientation.* Mary started the session by having members introduce themselves by giving an overview of what they did with the company, their work experience, and things like family or personal hobbies.

  For the second hour, the team, under Mary's facilitation, reviewed their mission statement, taking time to reword it so that it more clearly spelled out what it would take to succeed. They also put together a rough calendar of key milestones that helped them gain a clear perspective of the challenge before them. They agreed that this mission was very challenging, but doable if they pulled together.

  They spent the last hour carefully outlining the roles of each team member, identifying points of confusion, and answering questions raised by individual team members about their roles or those of others.

- *Second half-day session.* Mary brought in an outside facilitator to teach the team a simple, straightforward project management process. Using that process as an outline, the team identified the activities and sub-objectives they needed to accomplish, assigned responsibilities, and created a more detailed calendar.

A team member was assigned the role of team administrator and took responsibility for taking and distributing the minutes.

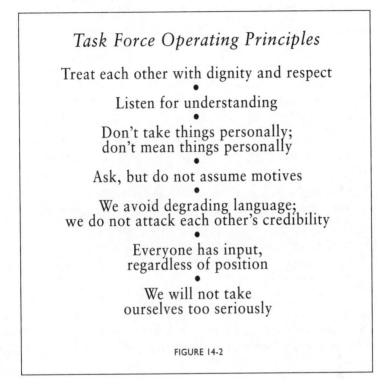

Task Force Operating Principles

Treat each other with dignity and respect

•

Listen for understanding

•

Don't take things personally;
don't mean things personally

•

Ask, but do not assume motives

•

We avoid degrading language;
we do not attack each other's credibility

•

Everyone has input,
regardless of position

•

We will not take
ourselves too seriously

FIGURE 14-2

- *Full-day session.* The team was now three weeks into the project. It spent the first half of the day reviewing progress and identifying issues that were hindering expected progress. The tensions between R&D and Manufacturing hadn't surfaced as Mary anticipated, but several team members expressed concern that the team demonstrated a tendency toward biting humor and sarcasm. During brainstorming sessions, members would kid others in a manner that would cause some to shut down. When challenged, the protagonist would respond that he or she was "just kidding." After some discussion, the team decided they would develop a list of operating principles (Figure 14-2) that would describe how they wanted to be treated in interactions with other team members. They would then hold one another accountable to follow these principles.

During the second half of the day the team discussed how to make decisions and received instruction on a criteria-based decision model that would support their process.

- *Ongoing, day-to-day development*—Throughout the project, Mary consistently started or finished working sessions with: "How are we doing and what do we need to change?" As an issue would surface, it was dealt with—adding to or rewording their operating principles, refining communication protocols, or adjusting and clarifying team member roles.

This development strategy appears so simple and straightforward that one might wonder why we would include it in the chapter. We do so for two reasons. First, to show that team development is simple. We sometimes wrap the idea of team development in mystery, thinking that we need expensive, time-consuming off-site meetings facilitated by organizational development consultants. Secondly, we include it because so many teams like Mary's start life with a business meeting and never look back. The group struggles through 14 weeks, confused about their mission and roles. The team never achieves true alignment, and therefore the team leader spends most of his or her time trying to get team members to come to meetings or briefing those who didn't. The team continually bogs down because of lacking or inadequate processes. Interpersonal relationships become strained—people start avoiding one another when what they really need is to spend more time together against the work. The group finishes the project tired, stressed, frustrated, and with a final work product that is a weak imitation of the original vision.

BUT TRAINING IN WHAT?

In addition to briefing, orientation, and team agreements about roles, goals, and operating principles, Mary introduced several specific training topics (Project Management and Decision Making). Where did she come up with these topics? Do the experts have some type of list of important team training topics and, if so, where can I get one? What kind of training does a team need? Again, it depends. The mission, nature, and needs of the team must shape its training needs. Although every team will have unique needs, we have found that there is a core inventory of skills that most long-lived teams must master at some point in their journey. Short-term teams and task forces, like Mary's team, would view such a list as a menu from which to pick the mission-critical skills the team needs to accomplish the task. We use the Team Wheel (Figure 14-3) to organize our training topics.

Not every team needs to engage every topic, nor would they approach the topics they do need in the same fashion or sequence. Certain needs demand priority such as mission and role clarity; others must be determined by the specific nature and needs of the team. Below we explore how a typical permanent team might address such a list of topics.

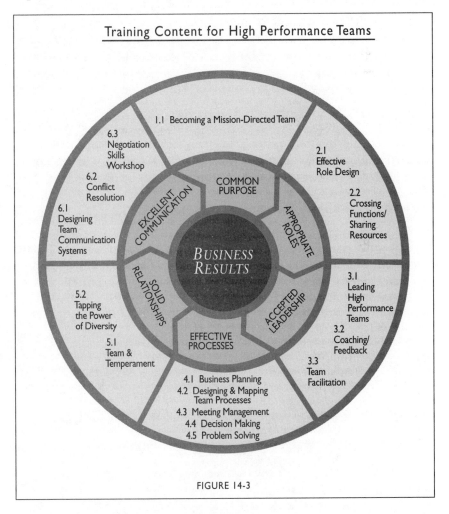

Training Content for High Performance Teams

1.1 Becoming a Mission-Directed Team

6.3 Negotiation Skills Workshop

6.2 Conflict Resolution

6.1 Designing Team Communication Systems

EXCELLENT COMMUNICATION

COMMON PURPOSE

APPROPRIATE ROLES

2.1 Effective Role Design

2.2 Crossing Functions/ Sharing Resources

BUSINESS RESULTS

SOLID RELATIONSHIPS

ACCEPTED LEADERSHIP

3.1 Leading High Performance Teams

3.2 Coaching/ Feedback

5.2 Tapping the Power of Diversity

5.1 Team & Temperament

EFFECTIVE PROCESSES

3.3 Team Facilitation

4.1 Business Planning
4.2 Designing & Mapping Team Processes
4.3 Meeting Management
4.4 Decision Making
4.5 Problem Solving

FIGURE 14-3

THE MARKETING TEAM

Tom Huber has just joined North Star Enterprises as Marketing Manager for its children's stroller division. He was hired from the outside after an extensive search and given a clear mandate to turn the division around after three years of consistent market-share decline. The previous manager had been resting on the reputation of North Star and had not seen a subtle but meaningful shift in the competitive landscape.

Tom has inherited a team of seven direct reports, four of whom have been with the company for less than a year. Although they were organized as a team, they had received little or no training and none at all for several years. They are a team in name only.

Tom spent the first 60 days getting to know the company, the division, the staff, and the overall business issues confronting them. Toward the end of that time, he had several two-day retreats during which the team began to come to grips with the business context in which they must compete and with a strategic framework that would guide their direction, priorities, and decisions over the next year. Tom was convinced that for the first time in years the group was clear about the significant challenges facing the division and the difficulty of turning it around. Then he began to turn his attention to a longer-range team development strategy for the team.

Tom retained an internal consultant through North Star's Human Resources Department who worked with him to diagnose team needs and design a tailored training strategy for the team. The consultant administered a short written survey (*The Team Profile®*) and spent several days interviewing team members, presenting a summary of their feedback regarding team needs to Tom. Based on this feedback, the counsel of the consultant, the task, and the schedule of the team, they laid out the development plan shown in Figure 14-4. There was no question that this schedule would be altered, probably many times, both by changing circumstances as well as a changing team dynamic and input, but it provided a rough road map with which to start the journey.

Because this was an intact team with some history, Tom was able to employ some diagnostics (The Team Profile® and interviews) up front so that team members could give input into specific team needs. He believed that by using an outside facilitator team members might be more forthcoming with their input. Tom was still pretty new to the

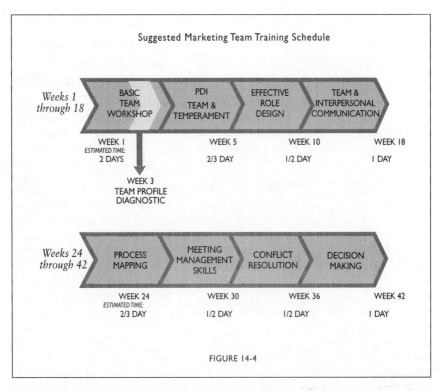

FIGURE 14-4

team, and this fact, combined with his push to introduce a serious dose of reality regarding their market position, made a few of the longer-term team members a little nervous. They were still uncertain this change was really necessary. As to the specific training modules, they are briefly described below:

- *Basic team workshop—the principles and processes of teamwork*. Topics covered include:

  * Team mission (overview by team leader and in-depth discussion with whole team during workshop).

  * Principles of effective teamwork (including the difference between a team and a group and a definition of synergy, including what synergy would look like for this team).

  * Characteristics of a high performance team, including a brief overview of team roles of team members. The team leaves with a clear idea of the Team Wheel, which becomes their road map for ongoing development.

*   Development of a list of team operating principles they want to govern their day-to-day relationships.

- *Team and temperament.* This exercise gives team members a better understanding of the work styles and personalities of both themselves and their teammates through the use of a specially designed personality inventory. *The Personal DISCernment® Inventory* (a DISC instrument) or the Myers-Briggs Type Indicator (MBTI) are both excellent resources for this purpose. Getting to know one another primes the pump for the development of trust, respect, acceptance, and valuing diversity. It also develops an understanding and appreciation for the different work styles and personalities of the other team members.

- *Defining and clarifying roles.* The team discusses and clarifies specific team roles so that everyone fully understands what they and their co-workers are expected to bring to the team, both from a technical and functional perspective (for example, sales expertise, market knowledge, financial insight) and from a team perspective (for example, team facilitator, team administrator). They also define and agree on the overall responsibilities of every team member regarding attitudes, ground rules, etc.

- *Team and interpersonal communication.* In this workshop the team discovers and discusses the principles needed to master the art of straight talk and clear communication among team members. Through a series of exercises and inventories, team members evaluate their listening skills and learn principles for strengthening them. They discuss and agree on what channels of communication should be used and how best to use them, and finally they develop a list of communication ground rules to be used in day-to-day communication.

- *Process mapping.* The team learns the skill of *transaction flow analysis* (process flowcharting), a process that helps the team to quickly and effectively map the flow of thinking and activity in their basic team processes. Such a map allows them to quickly see and address gaps and overlaps that hinder process efficiency and effectiveness.

- *Meeting management.* Meetings are the playing field of effective teams or the tar pit of ineffective ones. Most of us view meetings as an event in which we typically cram one hour of content into three hours. This waste, coupled with time pressures, makes meetings something to be avoided at all costs. But meetings are where teams make decisions, resolve conflicts, solve problems, and create solutions. I don't know where we got the idea that we could make good decisions in bad meetings, but a lot of teams are betting their success on that possibility. A session on key principles of meeting management can increase meeting effectiveness and cut meeting time dramatically.

- *Conflict resolution.* The team discovers the principles and process of managing conflict in a healthy, productive manner. In organizational settings, we tend to live on one of two ends of a continuum. We either have mismanaged agreement (conflict avoidance), or we tear the relational fabric between people to shreds. Conflict is the door to creativity, consensus, and commitment. If the team doesn't learn how to talk straight and be tough on issues without blowing one another out of the water, they will probably never experience the creative synergy needed to achieve exceptional results.

- *Decision making.* Without some well-defined process to make decisions, inevitably politics, power, and persuasion will prevail. In this workshop, the team learns a decision process that is both efficient and effective. It's an objective, criteria-based approach that makes thinking visible and facilitates teaming up on a decision.

There are numerous other training topics that are helpful, depending on the task and situation of the team. A quick review of the above list will show that not even all of the topics outlined in Figure 14-3 were used. The above list merely represents those topics we find most often needed in virtually any team situation.

The pace and schedule for training are determined by the team's level of development, the nature and importance of its mission, and its life span as a short-term, long-term, or permanent team. Additionally, there is an entire category of training needs that may be technical or industry specific. Their presence must also be taken into account when putting together a team's development strategy, schedule, and budget.

In task force situations like Mary's, we must often compress the training into one or two sessions over just a few days. Ongoing input is provided as needed, often just through the team leader. With other long-term teams like Tom's, we might start with a two-to-three-day workshop and follow with half-day workshops every four to eight weeks, during which we introduce additional topics in the sequence that makes best sense for the team. The aim is to get the team operational and in the air in a cost-effective, appropriate manner in the time available.

TIME AND PACE DO MATTER
WHEN IT COMES TO TRAINING

When my son was in his early teens he was confronted with the inevitable 7th grade science project, and it just had to be a terrarium. One evening I returned home and sensed tension in the air. Asking my wife for the cause, I was informed there was a snake in a box in the basement. "It's for the terrarium," my son responded. He was totally perplexed about why she would not let it reside in his upstairs bedroom until it left for school the next morning. Later that night, after things had calmed down, he asked, "Hey Dad, you wanna see something neat?"

"Sure, son," I responded and he led the way to the basement. There, we found the small snake snug in his box. It was filled with grass and leaves and a small pie plate filled with water. "What's the pie plate for?" I asked innocently.

"That's where you put the goldfish," he said.

"Goldfish?" I asked. "Are you sure the fish wants to live with a snake?"

"No, Dad. The snake eats the fish," he patiently explained, as though this was everyday knowledge. We both watched in fascination as the snake slowly and methodically corralled the goldfish bought for just this purpose and invited him in for dinner. The next morning as they left for school, I noticed there was a pronounced bump in the middle of the snake.

Several weeks later, it occurred to me I hadn't heard about the snake recently. As it turned out, the kids had been so captivated by the snake's eating habits that they kept sneaking into the storeroom to feed him goldfish. Now, as I understand it, God designed snakes to eat about one fish per month, but the teacher, counting the bumps as she disposed of the body, guessed that this one ate about four in the course of a week.

Too much training, too fast, makes adult learners feel a lot like that snake. Training needs to be spread out and provided, if possible in a just-in-time fashion. The best time to teach people about project management is just as they are getting a project to manage. The greater the felt need, the greater the potential for learning.

This is why Tom spread his training schedule out over a seven-month period (Figure 14-4). Many executives would not have the patience for such a pace. They would try to cram everything in as little time as possible. But, like the snake, we need the time to assimilate and apply one thing before we get too caught up in others. To understand the need for time, it might help to understand a little about how we learn.

Figures 14-5 and 14-6 provide valuable insight into learning theory. Figure 14-5 demonstrates that to get someone to know something is not very time consuming, nor is it very complex. You merely have to convey the information. Changing attitudes, however, is much more complex and time consuming. To actually get people to change behavior is a real challenge, both from a complexity and time perspective. And to

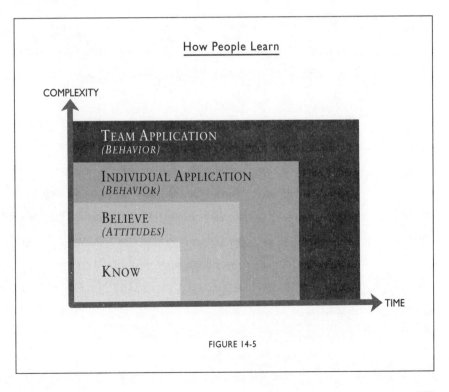

How People Learn

COMPLEXITY

TEAM APPLICATION
(BEHAVIOR)

INDIVIDUAL APPLICATION
(BEHAVIOR)

BELIEVE
(ATTITUDES)

KNOW

TIME

FIGURE 14-5

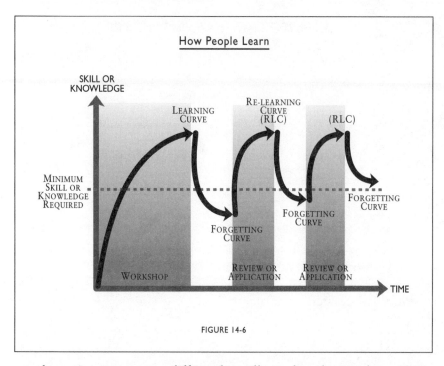

FIGURE 14-6

get the entire team to act differently really pushes the envelope. Team training is all about skill development, and that takes time.

Figure 14-6 adds another dimension to learning that must be taken into account when you are designing team development strategies. We can see that during the skill workshop our learning curve grows to meet the training objectives. But then, not long afterwards, we get on another curve, the forgetting curve. In my case, I'm on that curve within seconds after the workshop ends!

A bit later, we have a review or an opportunity to apply the skill or knowledge and we begin to climb the relearning curve. This is a steep curve because we have trail markers from passing that way before. But again, we go on to other things, and Mother Nature takes her course; we revisit the forgetting curve. Later, we review or apply and the "stuff" comes back. As the process cycles again, notice the pattern of the forgetting curve. At some point, even though we are still forgetting, we are retaining enough to be proficient. The principle is clear: REPETITION IS IMPORTANT TO LEARNING. And repetition takes time.

ONGOING DEVELOPMENT

What does a team do after it has worked through the training and things seem to be moving along pretty well? If they are to become and remain a high performing team, they keep right on training. Much development comes informally as the team regularly takes time to watch their game films and ask how they're doing and how they can do better. Such evaluation encompasses not only their basic work, but also includes team thinking and collaborative processes. Scheduling such an evaluation session is particularly helpful immediately after implementing a key initiative. For example, the best time to evaluate the decision process is just after receiving feedback on a recent team decision.

At Team Resources, we have developed several team diagnostics that help teams wrestle with the complexities of evaluating team performance. The *Team Profile®* allows a team to "position" itself developmentally (see Chapter Ten) and to visually see the difference between present and potential performance. The *Team Survey®* objectively evaluates a team against six characteristics of high performance teams and walks them through a step-by-step action planning process for increased team effectiveness (see Appendix B). As helpful sophisticated diagnostic approaches, most teams would be pleasantly surprised at the impact on team effectiveness that can be gained from a periodic cup of coffee and the question: "How are we doing?"

WHO'S ON THE TEAM?

One of the most frequently asked questions when we are invited to help an organization or team design a development strategy is, Who's on the team? Who should be included in the training? I've got nearly 45 people involved one way or another with this project. Surely not all of them are on the team, or are they? With the matrix structures so common today, this question becomes important.

One of our clients, a large pharmaceutical company, presents an excellent example of the problem. Their new product development teams might have 20 to 60 people involved in specific projects, which can span three to five years. When we started working with them, they had already determined the teams to be trained, drawing the lines of inclusion pretty broadly. It didn't take us long to realize that many of the people in the training sessions, if not apathetic, were downright angry about being there. One of my colleagues is fond of observing that any training session consists of three types of people: learners, spectators, and hostages. It appeared that we had plenty of the latter two categories in this session. After an agonizing few hours, we took a time out and had a round table session about team involvement, including roles and time commitments. The results for one team are shown in Figure 14-7.

This team had about 25 "members" attending the training. Of these, 6 spent the majority (60 to 100 percent) of their time working on team matters. Another 8 spent somewhere between 30 to 50 percent of their time on this team assignment. The rest spent less than 10 percent of their time, with several indicating their time involvement was patchy

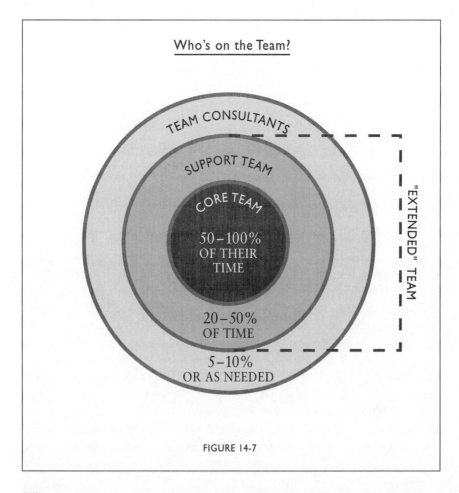

Who's on the Team?

TEAM CONSULTANTS

SUPPORT TEAM

CORE TEAM

50–100%
OF THEIR
TIME

20–50%
OF TIME

5–10%
OR AS NEEDED

"EXTENDED" TEAM

FIGURE 14-7

and never more than 5 percent. This latter group were really technical consultants whom the team could call as needed.

Figure 14-7 demonstrates that those in the center make up the Core Team. The second circle is labeled the Support Team, and these two groups make up the Extended Team. As you can imagine, our spectators and hostages were mostly from the third circle. These people were just as busy and time-challenged as everyone else, and they felt that so much training for such a limited team role was unnecessary. In this case, they were right.

We agreed that the team would be considered the Extended Team but that that the Core Team would certainly carry most of the burden and meet more frequently. We took time to discuss what training would be helpful to the groups with differing levels of team involvement and how to keep Extended Team members and team consultants in the loop from a communications perspective. The next training session was considerably smaller and the morale much higher.

Remember, it is not which circle a person stands in that determines whether or not they come to training, but rather the nature of the training. In the above example, much of the training content was relevant only to those in the inner two circles, but they were dragging everyone through it. Some training is very important to those in the outer circle, even though they have little day-to-day interaction with the Core Team.

THE NATURE OF TEAM DETERMINES THE NATURE OF TRAINING

Most large organizations in today's environment have an entire spectrum of team types. Many employees may not even operate as formal members of a specific team but still are encouraged to proactively team up whenever the opportunity presents itself. The rest might be on many teams, each structured differently, with varying degrees of interdependence.

Do organizations desiring to be team-based in spirit but having a wide variety of collaborative strategies and structures need to provide the same training to everyone? The answer is yes and no. Certain skills and collaborative processes can benefit everyone; other training content helps only in certain situations and with specific types of teams.

A clear understanding of teamwork, as well as the different types of teams, is an important ingredient in designing team training in any organization. Without such understanding, some parts of the organization may feel undertrained while others might feel smothered.

The way teams are organized or structured has implications not only for how they work together but also for how best to supply needed training. Peter Drucker creatively uses the metaphor of different types of sports teams (baseball teams, soccer teams, and tennis teams) to provide insight into the various structures teams, in any setting, can take.[1] To be productive, teams must be structured appropriately for that specific type of work.

Baseball teams are great for tasks that require each person to focus on specific, repetitive tasks. The rules are well known, and performance scores can be easily measured. Baseball players each play a specific position, covering a particular part of the field and sharing very little overlap in the accomplishment of their work.

The soccer team, on the other hand, although the players also have fixed positions, finds the players constantly moving as play shifts from one part of the field to another. These team members must work as a team, each carefully coordinating his or her part with the others. Such teams demand capable leadership as well as a well-developed playbook. Endless rehearsal ensures the "play" is accomplished flawlessly.

The doubles tennis team resembles a typical executive team. Although the players may have "preferred" positions, they are certainly not fixed, and each player must be able to cover for another. They are in constant adjustment not only to meet the changing situation in which they operate but also to adapt for the strengths and weaknesses of the other members. With all of this potential comes a very high degree of interdependence. Members must work together and practice extensively before they begin to tap into exceptional levels of output.

These teams differ in a number of ways. First as you move from the baseball team to soccer and then tennis, the degree of interdependence increases. The flow of information changes as well. Drucker explains that in the baseball-type team, a player receives information needed for his or her task independently from the information teammates are receiving. In the symphony orchestra or the soccer team, information comes largely from the conductor or coach. They are the ones who control the score or playbook. In doubles tennis, players get their information mainly from each other.

Team design must reflect both the task and the context in which the team will operate. High performance organizations not only ensure teams are used only where they can make a material difference; they also work hard to confront the task with the appropriate type of team. In large complex organizations, each type of team and probably many adapted versions are needed for different tasks.

Individual employees are constantly moving from one team to another with the highest possibility that the structure and the nature of each team is different. Although challenging, it is possible to teach individual employees to play effectively on different types of teams. It's not unusual for a member of a symphony orchestra to play as a contributing member of an ensemble or spend Saturday nights as a member of a jazz quartet.

Figure 14-8 summarizes the distinctions between one form of team and another, showing at the same time the type of training that might be considered for each form. Training needs are determined by the degree of interdependence, the complexity of the talk, and the size of the potential payoff. Typically, an organization wanting to engender a spirit of collaboration and teamwork will want everyone to be exposed to the basic, more common collaborative skills like meeting ground rules, conflict resolution, and communication. This answers a question that we are frequently asked in regards to team training—should we include administrative assistants and other support staff that work with the team but seldom sit in team meetings? Our response is yes, for training that is broadly collaborative in nature, like that shown in the left column of Figure 14-8. For all other training, if in doubt, include them or at least get their input as to the relevancy of that training to their role.

As you move right on the diagram, the training is additive. A task force whose mission is to design a new product development process will be trained in the basic collaboration processes as well as basic team training. A permanent team (for example, claims adjustment team, customer service team, or management team) might receive all of the training given to the first two categories *plus* advanced team training. Again, the training topics listed in the diagram are not an exhaustive list but are merely meant to illustrate the principle. Advanced team training should always be time-based and mission-specific.

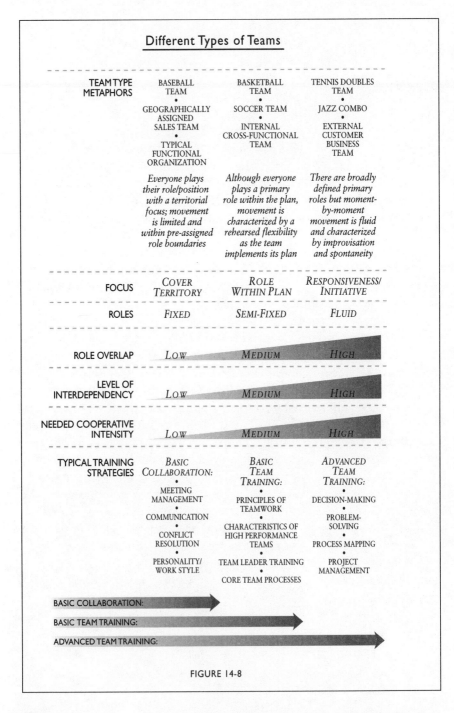

Different Types of Teams

TEAM TYPE METAPHORS	BASEBALL TEAM • GEOGRAPHICALLY ASSIGNED SALES TEAM • TYPICAL FUNCTIONAL ORGANIZATION	BASKETBALL TEAM • SOCCER TEAM • INTERNAL CROSS-FUNCTIONAL TEAM	TENNIS DOUBLES TEAM • JAZZ COMBO • EXTERNAL CUSTOMER BUSINESS TEAM
	Everyone plays their role/position with a territorial focus; movement is limited and within pre-assigned role boundaries	*Although everyone plays a primary role within the plan, movement is characterized by a rehearsed flexibility as the team implements its plan*	*There are broadly defined primary roles but moment-by-moment movement is fluid and characterized by improvisation and spontaneity*
FOCUS	*COVER TERRITORY*	*ROLE WITHIN PLAN*	*RESPONSIVENESS/ INITIATIVE*
ROLES	*FIXED*	*SEMI-FIXED*	*FLUID*
ROLE OVERLAP	LOW	MEDIUM	HIGH
LEVEL OF INTERDEPENDENCY	LOW	MEDIUM	HIGH
NEEDED COOPERATIVE INTENSITY	LOW	MEDIUM	HIGH
TYPICAL TRAINING STRATEGIES	*BASIC* COLLABORATION: • MEETING MANAGEMENT • COMMUNICATION • CONFLICT RESOLUTION • PERSONALITY/ WORK STYLE	*BASIC TEAM TRAINING:* • PRINCIPLES OF TEAMWORK • CHARACTERISTICS OF HIGH PERFORMANCE TEAMS • TEAM LEADER TRAINING • CORE TEAM PROCESSES	*ADVANCED TEAM TRAINING:* • DECISION-MAKING • PROBLEM-SOLVING • PROCESS MAPPING • PROJECT MANAGEMENT

BASIC COLLABORATION: ➤

BASIC TEAM TRAINING: ➤

ADVANCED TEAM TRAINING: ➤

FIGURE 14-8

YOU HAD TO HAVE BEEN THERE—THE CHALLENGE OF ON-BOARDING NEW MEMBERS

A specific facet of team training deserves special attention. At least several times a year, I am confronted with a team that needs some developmental attention, NOW. But the team has just lost a member and they want to wait until the team is fully staffed before they have the training experience. Of course, just about the time they find their new member, they discover another team member is being transferred. Most teams are in a constant state of turnover, further complicating the team development process.

How does a team develop if every time they seem to be gaining momentum, they lose a member? And every time they gain a new team member, the emotional, social, and skill mix of the team changes. How do we communicate a meaningful summary of team experiences to a newcomer?

A giant part of any team experience is emotional, and it is almost impossible to adequately convey to others the emotional dimension of interpersonal experiences. The frustrations, stress, conflict, exhilaration, excitement, commitment, breakthrough creativity, the feeling of winning, of lessons learned (the hard way), the highs of closing the deal, the laughs over a joke or the particular quality of a teammate, the sadness of losing one to the New York office—all seem to lose energy and color in the telling. You had to have been there. It's the sum of these experiences that provides the foundation for the team's enthusiasm, commitment, and norms—that is, the way we do things around here.

Teams probably can't prevent turnover, but you can ameliorate its effects by acknowledging it will happen and preparing for it. If you knew now that sometime within the next twelve months you would turn over a team member, what would you do? For one thing, you'd keep notes. Think about and write down what a new team member would have to know to quickly become integrated into the team and make a positive contribution.

- *Basic team orientation.* A clear, comprehensive explanation of the team mission; why it is an important task not only for the firm but for them as well; their assigned role and why it is important.

- *Team history.* Important experiences and what they fostered in terms of spirit, relationships, and lessons; team problems and conflicts and how they were resolved; and past achievements. As I noted above, conveying the emotional facet of team history is impossible, but we can at least describe it from an historical perspective. Knowing the history minimizes the possibility of revisiting old debates and resolved issues.

- *Team processes, operating principles, and ground rules.* Not only *what* they are but *why* they are.

- *Team member profiles.* Personalities and work styles, skills, backgrounds, and roles.

Communicating this material to the new team member is in itself a team effort. Much of the briefing will fall on the shoulders of the team leader, particularly the issues of mission and role. I often suggest that a team member, someone who best represents the role of team historian, be asked to review everything from history to ground rules. Finally, one-on-one meetings with each team member would be very enlightening. One top management team with whom we work uses a new member as an excuse to go out for a long lunch or dinner to reminisce and laugh over their team experiences—lessons, pitfalls, and victories. The informality conveys a lot of the emotional content that couldn't be transmitted in a "briefing," and, having been part of the bull session, the new member somehow feels a part of things.

THE BOTTOM LINE

Every team, regardless of whether its life span is defined by a two-hour meeting or a ten-year project, needs to be crystal clear about its mission and team member roles. Additionally, it must be equipped with any mission-critical skills necessary to accomplish the task at exceptional levels of performance.

Team training must reflect the unique nature and needs of the team, and it takes time. Adult learners need time to digest training, and all learners require review and repetition to master new skills. The closer training is scheduled to when an actual skill or piece of knowledge will be used, the higher the probability that learning will occur.

MESSAGE TO TEAM LEADERS

What would audiences or fans think of symphony conductors or athletic coaches who fielded untrained players, who never took the time to ensure that team members knew the score or playbook and their respective parts, or who never called a practice session or drilled the players until they could achieve the highest levels of harmony and coordination? They would be booed off the stage or fired. Yet organizational team leaders consistently attempt to win games with untrained players. Like an athletic coach or symphony conductor, team leaders are responsible for the design and implementation of the training that will allow them to perform at exceptional levels.

Figure 14-2 highlights a number of training topics important for team leaders who have the skills to build high performance teams:

- Team leadership
- Coaching/feedback
- Team facilitation

If it is not offered by your organization, seek such training from external resources, for it is unlikely you will be effective at developing others unless you have first been developed. Supplement your time and skills with outside resources. The world is filled with capable team development consultants who can help you design and implement tailored training for your team. As team leader, you're not responsible for doing it, merely for ensuring it gets done.

Finally, ensure that new team members are quickly and effectively on-boarded. Until new team members feel a part of things, and have a clear idea of the mission of the team and their role, it's unlikely they will be major contributors to the team's objectives. Left to their own devices, they may catch on in a couple of months, or they may never catch on. Either way, until they do it's like a hockey team attempting to compete with one or more members in the penalty box.

CHAPTER FIFTEEN

The Bottom Line for High Performance Teams

T he principles and techniques presented in this book are not merely theory and they weren't designed in a lab. They were developed in the caldron of day-to-day realities in real organizations striving for genuine and important goals. They have been successfully tested under fire with organizations ranging from the largest *Fortune* 500s to a single small church.

I have attempted to highlight the big ideas at the end of every chapter with a section entitled *The Bottom Line*, and it seemed appropriate to end the book with a summary of these ideas. I have listed many of them with "ballot box" bullets to allow you to check those you found to be particularly relevant to your team.

Chapter One—"What's the Standard Operating Procedure in This Situation?"

Teams and teamwork are not passing fads but rather a fundamental shift in how organizations approach work. However, unthinking implementation of teams without a clear understanding of the underlying principles, careful design, and adaptation to organizational needs can create cynical attitudes among participants and render teams useless in the pursuit of organizational objectives. We observed that:

- Business in the 21st century will be played on a new field, with new rules and formidable world-class competition.

- Competitive advantage will be determined by an organization's ability to consistently deliver quality, service, and value.

- We live and will continue to live in an era of new rules but no new playbook. The game has not only changed but is changing and will continue to do so.

- In this new game, the typical corporation must do what it does better, faster, cheaper, and with fewer resources.

- These qualities are not the product of resources only but also the result of "empowered-involvement" on the part of the work force.

- Some feel that we must not only fly the plane but rebuild it along the way. Everyone, and I mean everyone, must be involved in getting the plane to its destination and safely on the ground.

- Team-based strategies introduce a solution that spreads the stress of change, gives workers a greater sense of security, and creates a structure with speed, flexibility, and collective competence. Team-based organizations will be the survivors and winners in today's tough environment.

CHAPTER TWO — BUSINESS IN THE 21ST CENTURY IS A TEAM SPORT

- When done right, teams work. Companies have discovered and documented startling gains in productivity in the 30 to 60 percent range, increased levels of quality, reduced costs, and faster time to market.

- Although every organization should do whatever it can to foster a team spirit throughout its culture, formal teams should only be deployed against tasks that demand a team approach—big, complex, high-payoff tasks that require high levels of integration and cooperation.

- The primary distinction between a team and any other type of group is the results. Teams achieve exceptional, synergistic results on a consistent basis through synergy. Without evidence of synergy on a regular basis, you probably have a group or a team in a slump.

- Synergism is a phenomenon in which the output is greater than the sum of the inputs and occurs at the highest levels of cooperation.

- Cooperation is not an on-off concept but a matter of degree. The goal of any team is to maximize the level of cooperation of each team member.

- *Cooperation is a choice* made by each individual team member. This decision is based on their perception of whether or not cooperation is the best way to achieve a goal he or she desires. Therefore, *teams are "volunteer" organizations*.

CHAPTER THREE—THE CHARACTERISTICS OF A HIGH PERFORMANCE TEAM

Over the years, we have found consistently similar qualities and characteristics in teams that achieve exceptional results. It's a short list; in fact, it contains only six characteristics. But each characteristic plays a specific and vital role in making the team effective, and is therefore worth a closer look. If one of these six characteristics is missing or inadequate, the team is limping at best. If two or three are lacking, this group is probably not a team at all.

High performance teams have:

- Common purpose
- Crystal clear roles
- Accepted leadership
- Effective processes
- Solid relationships
- Excellent communication

CHAPTER FOUR—CLEAR, COMMON PURPOSE

We can summarize the key idea in this chapter with four words: *no task, no team.* So often, we misconstrue the concept of teams, stressing the need for good interpersonal relationships. While such relationships are an important ingredient of effective teams, it is the wrong emphasis. *The most critical component in building a high performance team is a clear, common, compelling task.* The goal of a high performance team is not merely to get *along,* but rather to get *aligned* around that purpose, and, through alignment, to get results!

The power of teamwork flows out of alignment between the interests of individual team members and the mission of the team. To achieve such alignment, team members must see the team task as:

- Clear—*I see it.* Every team member must have a crystal clear understanding of the team task. Without such understanding the needed alignment cannot be achieved. Don't assume such understanding exists. Both the team members and team leader should keep talking until the light goes on.

- Relevant—*I want it.* The degree to which the mission of the team is desirable and wanted by the members of the team will greatly influence the energy, creativity, and effort they exert to achieve it.

- Significant—*It's worth it.* Team objectives must be of sufficient magnitude to make it worth the effort.

- Urgent—*I want it, . . . now!* There is a clear time-value attached to the achievement of this mission.

- Achievable—*I believe it.* The team must really believe this task is achievable. This is where the art of goal setting resides. On one hand, the goal must be big enough to motivate the needed effort; on the other, it must be realistically achievable.

CHAPTER FIVE—CRYSTAL CLEAR ROLES

To achieve exceptional results, high performance teams creatively divide the task and then cooperate like mad. When any complex task is divided, the roles assigned to the various parts of the process must be:

- *Clear.* The different roles on an effective team are crystal clear. Team members are not only clear about their role but about the roles of their teammates as well.

- *Complete.* The roles in total cover the whole task. It is important that everyone knows where the handoffs are in every team process.

- *Compatible.* Match roles to individual skills, interests, and experiences. Look beyond merely the functional background, as some of the most leveraged contributions will come from outside a person's functional expertise.

- *Complementary.* Make sure one role is not "in the way" of another.

- *Consensual.* The team should be clear and in agreement about everyone's role.

Dividing the task introduces interdependence. With interdependent roles, both attitudes and boundaries must be carefully managed. The overarching attitude for team member roles is a thoughtful balance between individual responsibility and mutual accountability that conveys: "This is *my* part of *our* job."

High performance teams leverage the combination of team member roles. Principles for doing this include:

- Looking to the edge of expertise and encouraging input about everything from everyone.

- Reading the book on each team member and tapping into the entire pool of their experience, knowledge, and skill rather than limiting input at the boundaries of their functional expertise.

- Proactively seek input, particularly from the quieter team members who probably spent a large portion of the discussion time thinking about the issue. However, because of their nature, lack of confidence, or even the manner in which they have defined their role, they often hesitate to put forth their ideas.

- Ensuring the team has enough difference and the right kind of difference. The more different a team is, the smarter the team is— IF (and that's a big if!) it can channel that difference productively against the problems, decisions, and tasks of the team.

CHAPTER SIX—ACCEPTED LEADERSHIP

High performance teams are supported by high performance leaders—*team leaders who see their responsibility as a role rather than a position.* These leaders could be better described as facilitators, networkers, resourcers, and boundary managers. They are attuned to the needs of the team and *serve* those needs willingly, knowing that the real "boss" of their team is the task.

Leaders can't demand acceptance from followers. It must be volunteered. Team leaders who call high levels of commitment out of their followers are invariably seen by those followers to be servant leaders. Notice the order of the words: servanthood is "assumed"; leadership is "bestowed." It is their belief system that allows them to assume the role of a servant team leader:

- They appreciate the collective brilliance of a team.

- They believe in the power of diversity.

- They see team leadership as a role from which to serve, not a position to be served.

- They see leadership and power as something to be released and shared rather than something to hold and control.

- They understand that teams are all about tasks and that they must master the delicate balance needed between the task, the team, and individual team members.

CHAPTER SEVEN—EFFECTIVE TEAM PROCESSES

- A team can be no more effective than its processes and the ability of the team to execute them well. Most teams have two basic types of processes—work processes and thinking processes. Work processes are the core processes that accomplish the team's primary mission. For example, sell the product. Thinking processes are process frameworks that facilitate the thinking and discussion of the team as they resolve issues. Examples might be decision making, problem solving, and meeting management. Too often teams overlook the existence and importance of thinking processes, which need to be addressed with the same degree of deliberateness the teams invest in their work processes.

CHAPTER EIGHT—SOLID RELATIONSHIPS

- *Teammates don't have to be best friends.* In fact, the diversity and differences among the individual team members that allows the possibility of a wide spectrum of skills, knowledge, and perspectives will probably preclude close friendships. However, the relationships must be solid enough to withstand the turbulence of day-to-day interaction, misunderstandings, and an occasional bad day. Solid team relationships provide the climate needed for high levels of cooperation and are characterized by trust of both character and competence.

- *Understanding.* Understanding is a foundation for trust. Every team has a healthy amount of intimacy ("into-me-see"). We need to understand enough about team members to trust and work effectively with them.

- *Acceptance of team members' differences.* Differences among team members will lead either to synergy or strife.

- *Respect for each team member's unique contribution.*

- *Courtesy.* Often the indicator of the presence of the four previous qualities.

- *Mutual accountability.* High performance teams are characterized by both individual responsibility and mutual accountability.

To effectively cover the role assignments of the team and to ensure the needed inventory of perspectives, experience, and skills, the team must seek out, recruit, and unleash the creative aspects of diversity. Differences must be seen as value-added in a team environment.

CHAPTER NINE—EXCELLENT COMMUNICATION

George Bernard Shaw summed it up well when he observed that the biggest problem with communication is the assumption that it has taken place. Effective communication enables a team to achieve exceptional results. However, most teams find that barriers to communication are legion—barriers such as incomplete or disorganized information, too much data, poor timing, or the wrong vehicle for the message. Not surprisingly, only the most astute, pragmatic, and persistent teams overcome them, for they understand that:

- Communication is the very *means* of cooperation.

- Communication appears to be deceptively easy. As a result we often fall prey to the misconception that it has taken place when it has not.

- We tend to focus most of our energy on the sending part of communication and little on the receiving side. We would be well-served by reversing our emphasis.

- The power of a team is found in the collective IQ of the group. However, in some circumstances unhealthy group dynamics like "groupthink" can thwart effective team communication and thinking.

- Clear communication inevitably leads to conflict. In fact, conflict is one of the best indicators that the team is communicating. Teams need to master the art of conflict resolution in order to maintain high levels of straight talk.

- Teams must sit down on a regular basis and assess the quality of their communication. What's working? What's not working? How can we do better?

Chapter Ten—The Path to High Performance Teamwork

If we are to build high performance teams, then it is imperative that we are familiar with the stages of group development and the principles that help or hinder growth from one stage to the next. We can use the relationship between the team's willingness to cooperate and its skill in cooperating to define the different stages of team development.

- There are two dimensions to cooperation: *willingness* to cooperate and *skill* in cooperating.

- Interaction between these two dimensions describes different stages of team development.

- The path to high performance leads through several distinct stages of team development, each characterized by differing amounts of skill and willingness on the part of team members. There are no short cuts in the path to high levels of team effectiveness.

- Growth from one stage of development to another is not guaranteed. Seventy percent of all groups remain groups and never attain true "teamhood."

CHAPTER ELEVEN—ACHIEVING THE SUMMIT OF HIGH PERFORMANCE TEAMWORK

Team development occurs only as the team becomes more willing to cooperate and more skilled in cooperating. Skill is motivated by willingness, and willingness is motivated by some good answers to four key questions—questions that must be asked both individually and collectively:

Individually team members must address:

1. *Alignment.* Why am *I* here? Is this group going where *I* want to go? Can *I* do better with this group than *I* can alone?

   Focus: Individual team member

2. *Relationship.* Who are you? Why are *you* here? Are *you* committed? Are *you* competent? Can I trust *you*?

   Focus: Other team members

Collectively the team must address:

3. *Task. What* shall we do?

   Focus: Team task

4. *Strategy. How* shall we do it?

   Focus: Strategy

CHAPTER TWELVE—PITFALLS IN THE PATH TO HIGH PERFORMANCE

- Teams, like any organism, need healthy climates in which they can grow and thrive. Barriers to successful teams are often products of the larger organizational context in which a team must operate. The exception might be the competitive spirit that resides deep within the emotional marrow of many of us. But this too, like many of the other challenges to cooperation, is this too in the final judgment really a product of the cultural norms in which we must operate. Some companies clearly value cooperation and teamwork, while others only pay it lip service or even engender competition, believing that it is a better path to high performance.

- Barriers to collaboration can be controlled with a healthy corporate culture and astute leadership. However, the reality is that many teams must operate in somewhat hostile territory with challenges to optimal collaboration that are outside the control of the team. This doesn't mean that high levels of cooperation and synergistic results can't be achieved; it merely demands that some of the creative energy of the team must be deployed to neutralize the effects of cultural challenges. Knowledge that these barriers exist is a good first step to minimizing their impact.

CHAPTER THIRTEEN—THE PRINCIPLES OF TEAM DEVELOPMENT

This chapter could be summarized with the observation that *you don't form teams; you build them.* The foundations of a successful team are laid in the classroom. As to the specifics of team development, they are determined by a number of interrelated variables:

- Nature and scope of the team's mission
- Established or new team
- Temporary or permanent team
- Degree of interdependence and needed coordination/integration
- Performing well or performance problems

There are ten key principles of team development:

1. Teams and team development are about results.
2. Know what you are trying to build.
3. Team development is an ongoing process, not an event.
4. Just in time is the best time for training.
5. Development must be a felt need of the team.
6. Team development demands a safe environment.
7. Use the work of the team to build the team.
8. There are no short cuts to team effectiveness.

9. Willingness precedes skill.

10. Team leaders need a head start.

Chapter Fourteen—Turning Principle into Practice: Building the Team

- Every team, regardless of whether its life span is defined by a two-hour meeting or a ten-year project, needs to be crystal clear about its mission and team member roles. Additionally, it must be equipped with any mission-critical skills necessary to accomplish the task at exceptional levels of performance.

- Team training must reflect the unique nature and needs of the team, and this takes time. Adult learners need time to digest training, and all learners require review and repetition to master new skills. The closer training is scheduled to when an actual skill or piece of knowledge will be used, the higher the probability that learning will occur.

Teams will continue to be the load-bearing beams of organizational structure as we move into a new century. As we have seen throughout this book, the power of teams is compelling when used in the right setting.

High performance teams are not necessarily the product of positive and highly resourced work environments. As Captain Haynes and the crew of United Flight 232 demonstrated, that high performance teamwork often occurs in situations in which there are no resources—situations in which the only tools available are the creativity and resourcefulness of the team members. As he explains it, "There was no hero. Just a group of people doing their job." But what a job they did! They tapped into the collective IQ of a combined 103 years of flying experience and figured out how to get a plane that most considered unflyable onto the ground. It wasn't without loss, but the 184 survivors would say it was a miracle. Yes, this crew experienced luck, but they didn't luck out. They didn't just "discover" how to work as a team. They had been trained and then had reinforced that training with hour upon hour of practice.

They modeled every principle described in this book.

- Clear, common compelling purpose
- Crystal clear roles

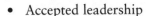

- Accepted leadership
- Effective processes
- Solid relationships
- Excellent communication

Captain Al Haynes would agree that these qualities accurately describe the team dynamic in the cockpit that fateful afternoon.

After spending many hours studying the incident of Flight 232 and several interviews with Al Haynes, I came to see the powerful influence of team leaders in the overall performance of teams. Leadership is such a critical ingredient to unleashing the power of teams that I have chosen to speak directly to you, the team leader, throughout this book.

Best wishes from the team at Team Resources as you build your team and then lead it to high performance.

Appendix A

Frequently Asked Questions

Introduction

This appendix addresses some common questions we find in our team practice. I have chosen four that relate to the principles in this book and tend not to be addressed in other team books:

- What is a self-directed team?
- How do you manage a distributed team?
- What do you do when team measurements aren't very measurable?
- What do we do when things go wrong?

What Is a Self-directed Team and Shouldn't We Be One?

One of the most frequently asked questions is what is a self-directed work team (SDT) and what does "self-directed" mean? I appreciate why there tends to be some confusion about this topic because many of the proponents of SDTs don't agree among themselves about the definition. In fact, the concept itself lives under a number of different terms—self-regulating teams, self-managing teams, autonomous work teams, empowered teams, and self-contained teams.

Going by the titles alone, the themes that come to mind are independent, self-determined, and autonomous. The term "self-managed team" quickly uncovers some important questions. What do they mean by "manage themselves"? What does this concept of self-directed or self-managed teams mean for team leadership? Where does such leadership come from if not from a designated team leader? What are the implications for the team model presented in this book, which has stressed the importance of clear, capable team leadership? How are self-managed teams connected to the larger organization—after all, isn't it the company that sets direction, goals, priorities, and policies and compensates accordingly?

The headlines tell the story: *Hang the hierarchy. Bury bureaucracy. Empower the staff. Form self-directed teams.* Ah, the heady call to freedom is in the air. After all, isn't that what teams and teamwork are all about—management finally letting go and letting us, the team, get on with the job?

Few things are more confusing about teams and teamwork than the role and style of leadership. Some counselors go so far as to advocate that high performance teams don't even need leadership. They believe that many of the traditional roles of management can be transferred to the team as it becomes "self-directed." As I review books about teams, I see titles such as *Self-Directed Work Teams, Succeeding as a Self-Directed Work Team, Creating Self-Directed Work Groups,* and *The Adventures of a Self-Managing Team.* Although most of these authors are not calling for the total abolition of leadership, many give the impression that formal leadership as we have known it in the past is passé. If they haven't abolished it in concept, they have certainly marginalized it. On the other hand, some managers and corporate leaders view such a concept with suspicion. "After all, we pay their salaries so we must have the right to tell them what to do and how we want it done!" This latter group often reveals their nature with terms such as *chain of command* and *span of control.*

I believe there's a fair amount of productive middle ground between these two positions. Even though the choice appears to be an "either-or" decision between self-led teams or leader-led teams, it is really a "both-and" situation.

So what is a self-directed team? Most authorities would agree that SDTs are small groups of people empowered to manage themselves and the work they do on a day-to-day basis.[1] Many advocates of this type of team model would explain that self-directed work teams would plan and schedule their work, solve problems, evaluate their performance, budget, and even determine who should be on the team. For the most part, supporters would qualify this list by acknowledging that the specific list of responsibilities must fit the culture of the larger organization as well as the needs, nature, and maturity of the team.

We can answer most of these questions by addressing three key issues:

- How much leadership does a team really need?
- How is leadership chosen and expressed within the team?
- What are the appropriate boundaries of team empowerment?

How much leadership does a team really need? For starters, "self-directed" is an inaccurate term, for even its strongest advocates acknowledge that every team needs some degree of leadership. The problem lies in coming to agreement about how much leadership and the most appropriate style of leadership. One author in favor of self-directed teams notes that the very term "self-direction" may conjure up images of an organization without leadership and offers the term "shared leadership" as more appropriate.[2] I agree, but want to take it even further, introducing three possible sources of leadership in any team setting.

Let's take a moment and review how leadership fits into our team model and why it is so important for high performance teamwork. Common purpose is the *reason* for cooperation. Appropriate division of labor is our *strategy*. The problem is that our strategy introduces a side effect, interdependence, for which the only remedy is cooperation. The four remaining team characteristics are all about cooperation. The first, *accepted leadership*, provides the *structure* for cooperation. As soon as we introduce the concept of interdependence, we must provide some amount of structure to coordinate our efforts. That's the role of leadership.

Every team needs leadership. The question is: how is it provided and by whom? We can represent the amount of "structure" needed by any team as a circle (Figure A-1). The entire circle represents the total amount of structure needed, and this leadership (that is, structure)

Team Leadership

FIGURE A-1

comes from three sources: team leader, team members, and the task itself (Figure A-2).

The leader can introduce structure with clear, detailed instructions, taking the initiative to provide answers to problems and decisions, ensuring close supervision and feedback on team performance. Structure can also be found in the task itself, as some tasks contain more structure than others. For example, in many manufacturing environments it is very clear what needs to be done, who needs to do what, and where one job stops and another begins. However, in many organizational settings, the task is much more fluid and ambiguous (for example, sales, marketing, management, product development, etc.).

Finally, the team itself can provide structure as the individual team members become more familiar with their roles

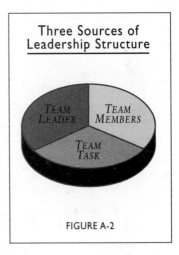

Three Sources of Leadership Structure

FIGURE A-2

and those of their teammates, and as they become skilled at basic team processes like problem solving and decision-making.

The vast majority of self-directed teams are found in manufacturing or processing environments—situations in which the tasks, roles, activities, and outputs are very clear. The task itself provides enough structure so that work is more easily coordinated, and the need for formal leadership is minimal (Figure A-3).[3] In work environments with higher levels of task ambiguity, leadership plays a critical role in team effectiveness.

In principle, team leaders should provide only the leadership or structure not provided by the team or task. In Figure A-4-A, the team is newly formed and somewhat immature. The task has only moderate amounts of clarity and definition. Therefore, the leader must provide

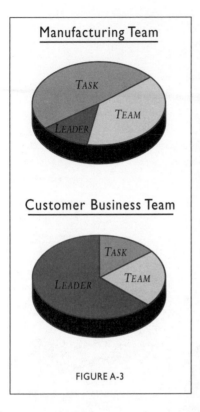

FIGURE A-3

the majority of the structure and coordination. In Figure A-4-B, although the task is no clearer, the team is maturing in its ability to work through different processes. Therefore, the leader needs to provide less of the structure. Finally, in Figure A-4-C we find an example of a mature team that has demonstrated alignment and mastered team processes. In all three situations the total amount of needed leadership direction and structure remains the same, but direction from the leader diminishes as the team matures.

How should leadership be chosen within the team? Choosing a leader represents a very important step in laying the groundwork for team success. In most instances, upper management appoints team leaders because of skill or position. Two other common methods favored by

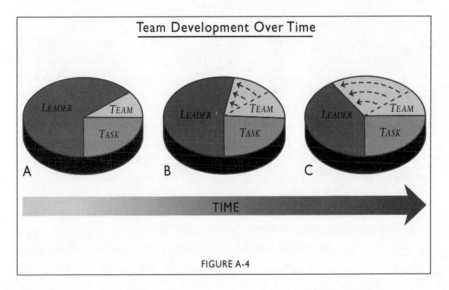

FIGURE A-4

some suggest that in self-directed teams, leaders should be elected by team members or filled by rotation. Both of these latter methods blunt the effectiveness of the team.

In addition to the role described in Chapter 6, leaders exercise other responsibilities—some formal, others informal. Invariably leaders challenge the status quo and our comfort zones as they push us into uncertain futures and higher levels of performance. They also hold us accountable, individually and as a team. People generally don't *choose* to do what leaders convince them to do. That is, they are reluctant to move out of their comfort zones, from acceptable to exceptional levels of performance. Remember, teamWORK is hard work. When given the chance, we tend to choose leaders who are a little laid back and less demanding.

Rotating the role of leader among team members could be even more problematic. In a cross-functional design team with members from Engineering, Marketing, Sales, Manufacturing, and Finance, the team wouldn't ever consider rotating the representative filling the finance position just to give everyone a crack at the job. The skills and experiences of that individual are not that transferable. In the same respect, the choice of team leader should be based on skill and experience, not just because "it's their turn."

We must choose a team leader based on a clear understanding of what is expected in the role and a clear list of criteria that describe candidates with the potential to be successful in fulfilling it.

What are the appropriate boundaries of team empowerment? Basically, teams should be given as much authority as possible within the constraints of three boundaries:

- The work context in which the team operates
- The skills of the team and team leader
- The alignment of the team to the mission and the goals and strategy of the larger organization

Context of the work. We have introduced one dimension of team context above in our discussion of the structure provided by different work environments, observing that the more structured the task, the more autonomy than can be given to the team. A second dimension of context would be time frame. Achieving the expertise, confidence, and credibility to exercise such authority takes a lot of time and training.

For example, it is unlikely that a short-lived task force would have the time to master the complexity embedded in self-direction.

Team skill levels. The better team members master the basic business and team processes, the less direction and guidance they need from the outside. As the team becomes more proficient at processes like decision-making, planning, problem-solving, and conflict resolution, the more they will be able to "figure it out on their own." Mastery of such skills will be a function of time and training.

Team alignment. The more confident management is that a team is in alignment with its team mission and to the mission, vision, values and objectives of the larger organization, the more autonomy they will be inclined to grant. Autonomy without alignment leads to anarchy.

NUMBERS 14

The Book of Numbers in the Old Testament illustrates a classic example of people's reluctance to move out of their comfort zone and into the white area of the map. God had led the Israelites out of Egypt through the wilderness of Sinai to the edge of the "Promised Land"—a land he had described as flowing with milk and honey. In preparation for their advance across the Jordan River into what would become known as Israel, Moses, God's appointed leader for this expedition, sent spies ahead to gather intelligence. The spies returned reporting that although this new territory certainly flowed with milk and honey as God had promised, it also had giants—big ones! Somehow the milk and honey got lost in the translation and the people focused on the giants.

The response to this report was fast in coming: "Then all the congregation lifted up their voices and cried, and the people wept that night. And all the sons of Israel grumbled against Moses and Aaron . . . Let us appoint a leader and return to Egypt" (Numbers 14:1-4). Given the opportunity, these people would never have voted for a leader that would take them into a land of giants.

HOW DO YOU MANAGE A DISTRIBUTED TEAM?

As we take the first few steps into a new century, our lexicon of organizational structures has changed dramatically. Unlike the mid-1990's, we don't have to explain to others what virtual, matrix, or network structures are. Not only do we know what these structures are;

many of us are actually part of one. What we are still trying to figure out is how to make one of the "newfangled" structures work! This is particularly true for teams. How do I relate to people I never see or in some cases have never even met face-to-face? How do you build and maintain trust with people you don't know? How do we maintain some sense of connection and alignment if we are spread all over the place?

The basic principles and team characteristics I have highlighted in this book provide the framework for team effectiveness in any form or setting, even one that is sprawled over five states. However, a few key ideas pertain to direction and connection:

- *Direction.* Clear purpose is a prerequisite for any team, but particularly important when the team is distributed. When team members are spread out and out of sight, it is difficult for either of them or other team members to see whether or not they are on course. Clear mission/task is what creates alignment and provides the gravitational force that holds the team together, though it's not together in the physical sense. Constant communication, discussion, and reinforcement of team mission is a prerequisite in a distributed team environment.

- *Connection.* Distributed teams not only need to be aligned, they must also be linked. There are really two issues here—communication and relationship.

  * *Communication.* Distributed teams must master the art of effective communication via the electronic media: phone, fax, e-mail, voice-mail.

    In an earlier chapter, I noted that only 10 percent of any communication was found in the words themselves, with the remainder being in the vocalics (for example, tone, inflection, pace, volume, etc.) and body language. Electronic media place a heavy emphasis on our ability to choose the right words.

    ### Medium and Message

	Words	Vocalics	Body Language
Phone/Voice Mail	35%	65%	0%
E-Mail/Fax	100%	0%	0%

    Training and discussion regarding the principles and pitfalls of these different mediums can save a lot of time and aggravation before relationships are strained. We don't tend to think as carefully when we send e-mails as we do when composing letters or memos. The political or emotional implications are seldom considered, and therefore we are generally up to our necks in hot water before we even knew we were in it.

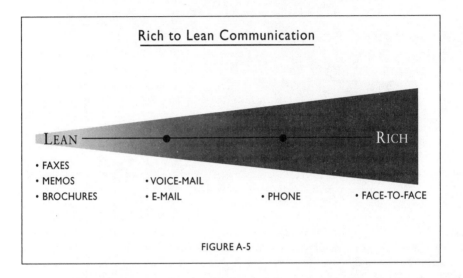

Rich to Lean Communication

LEAN ———————————————————————— RICH

• FAXES
• MEMOS   • VOICE-MAIL
• BROCHURES   • E-MAIL   • PHONE   • FACE-TO-FACE

FIGURE A-5

One team I worked with designed a team-wide protocol for e-mail communications that included ground rules like the following:

- Topic/action/urgency clearly stated in subject line.

- Don't use "hot" words, and deal with emotional issues face-to-face or on the phone.

- Don't copy others on emotionally charged e-mails without sender's permission—that is, don't spread gasoline on the fire.

- Don't use capital letters—unless their use is part of the ground rules. For example: caps mean important, or action, versus "I'm mad" (caps slow the reader by 15 percent).

- Keep them short—e-mail is for information, not for conversation.

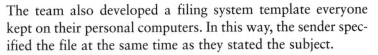

The team also developed a filing system template everyone kept on their personal computers. In this way, the sender specified the file at the same time as they stated the subject.

Dr. Beverly Langford likes to describe communication as being a spectrum ranging from lean to rich (Figure A-5).[4] She would say that faxes and memos are "lean" in that they have nothing more than the words and offer little in the way of interaction. Voice-mail and e-mail are a bit richer in that there is opportunity for some back and forth, even if it's a bit delayed. Obviously, face-to-face offers the richest possibilities for communication. In a distributed team environment the challenge is to creatively keep communication as rich as the context and constraints of your situation will allow.

It's important that the team take some time to develop communication ground rules. As with any team, but particularly those spread out geographically, effectiveness and relationships will fall victim to too little communication, too much communication, and communication that's not timely. Up until the early 1980's, the biggest complaint about team communication was that team members didn't have enough of it. With the arrival of e-mail, the bigger issue has become too much communication—that is, too much data and not enough relevant information. Indiscriminate use of FYI has turned out to be the "occupant mail" of the 21st century. The dilemma is that it comes from teammates and gives every appearance of being important until we spend unnecessary time reading it.

* *Relationship.* As we have discovered earlier in the book, the quality of relationships determines the quality of communication. The first victim of low trust is invariably communication. I won't be very transparent with someone I don't trust. I will tend to delay or distort my communication to minimize vulnerability. How do we establish and maintain trust-building relationships? Without a doubt, the answer must be communication. Lots of it.

I recently worked with a large sales team that was spread over 12 states. The entire team connected every Monday via conference call to get the results from the previous week, name goals for the coming week, and find answers to questions. The meeting was run against a tight set of ground rules (state your name when you speak, stay on the topic, don't switch topics unless you requested and received permission from facilitator, silence means agreement, etc.).

As I was researching the topic of distributed work teams, Jessica Lipnack, co-author with Jeffery Stamps of an excellent book, *Virtual Teams*, shared an interesting paradox with me.[5] On one hand, it takes lots of communication to establish trust, but on the other, if trust falters in a distributed team environment, the team can become buried in endless e-mails— "You said . . ." "I meant . . ." E-mails quickly become either ammunition or depositions.

In closing this section I want to observe that all the conference calls in the world won't be a totally adequate alternative to face-to-face meetings. Such meetings need to be built into the calendar and budget and carefully planned to ensure that the relational dimension is incorporated as well as business issues.

REFLECTIONS OF A TEAM LEADER OF A DISTRIBUTED TEAM

Richard Spoon is a Sales Vice President for the Campbell Sales Company, the sales arm of the Campbell Soup Company. For the past two years he has led a distributed cross-functional team of 35 serving one of the company's largest accounts. His team is spread out coast-to-coast. Over the course of the past several years this team has grown to exceptional levels of team effectiveness. They have become a model for the entire company. I asked him to summarize the principles he felt were particularly important in achieving those levels of effectiveness and he shared seven ideas that show creative application of the principles I described above. These insights will prove helpful for other team leaders in similar circumstances:

- *Visit people often.* Don't underestimate the power of personal presence. In a distributed situation the team leader becomes a traveling ambassador—talking, listening and constantly keeping the vision/mission of the team fresh and alive.

- *Establish clear, common values.* Values that will help the team maintain its footing in the day-to-day stress and ambiguity created from pace, change, and distance. In Chapter 8, I called these values *team operating principles.* This is the list of behaviors the team agrees must describe its relationships and interactions.

- *Create clear, simple process for communication.* The team must balance flexibility with simplicity and predictability. Standardize what you can, flex where you must. Common templates, formats, and terminology create a simplicity and predictability for the team that frees them to focus attention on the more dynamic aspects of their task.

- *Have third-grade-level processes.* In today's world of high velocity change we must do everything possible to drive complexity out of our systems and processes. This is particularly true when the role holders within the process are out of line-of-sight from one another and can't pick up immediate signals that the process is amiss. For example, how to change a priority or date and communicate the change to the rest of the team, or who makes what decisions and how they are made.

- *Meet a minimum of four times a year, even if you don't need to.* I noted earlier in the chapter that face-to-face meetings need to be built into the calendar. The seasoned team leader puts even more emphasis on this important element of team life.

- *Create team symbols and folklore.* Richard introduced his team to the "talking stick." The talking stick is an idea out of Native American Council meetings. When the Council meets, who ever has the talking stick has the "floor." In Western tradition we would call this "passing the gavel." At the end of their quarterly meetings, Richard's team would take the last hour and pass the stick. Team members would share anything from, "*I want to thank . . . ,*" to "*Here's what I'm thinking . . .*" He explained that there were few times in which a tear or two wasn't shed over one comment or another.

- *Create community.* When I asked him how his team created a sense of community, Richard provided several creative ideas. "Tell stories," he explained. "The group's identity is created and maintained by the experiences it shares and the stories it tells.

Stories create a colorful reminder of what the group is about and what it stands for." Another way to create community is to read as a group. It is an excellent strategy to foster a common language for the team.

Team members on Richard's team could also voluntarily participate in the monthly book discussion. Each month the group was assigned a best-selling book, often suggested by the team members themselves (generally a business book, but not always). On the first Monday of every month the group would again conference call and work their way through a series of discussion questions. About 80 percent of the team participated, and as they did they not only got smarter but got to know one another better as well.

One last point deserves mention. Although it would seem obvious in this age of the Internet, we find that many teams don't do a good job at leveraging technology. Video conferencing, on-line discussion and white board sessions, and DVD/video are just a few of the new technologies that are beginning to achieve both practical utility and cost-effectiveness. One large nonprofit corporation in Southern California installed video cameras on all 200 of the workstations in its new office building. The purpose was to improve the quality of communication and help maintain relationships in the large, spread out facility. Not even a *Fortune* 500 company could have afforded such a system a few years ago, but now even small organizations are wondering if they can afford *not* to have it.

But leveraging technology in itself creates the need for caution. Lipnack reminds us that success in virtual teams is about 90 percent people and 10 percent technology. "Too much of the focus is on technology," she stresses, "and not enough on the people dimension." She shares that one of her friends has observed that if we can just get rid of the carbon-based life forms things would go a lot smoother. We do need to leverage technology, but we must do so with this admonition in mind.

How Do You Evaluate Team Performance When Team Measures Aren't Very Measurable?

Occasionally team objectives are so broad, long-range, or subject to so many intervening variables that it is very difficult for the team to tie its activities and effectiveness to specific, short-term business results. The question then becomes, how do we measure team results? And how do we know if what we are doing will deliver the desired results?

In these settings we have used a process that has proven very effective in helping teams connect activities to outcomes and overall team results. In one situation we were asked to help a large consumer products firm establish sales teams to work with their five largest customers—customers like Wal-Mart, K-Mart, and Target. The dilemma was that the sales initiatives and strategies were large, complex and long-term. There didn't appear to be a way to connect day-to-day activities and priorities to these long-term goals and, similarly, it was difficult to evaluate team effectiveness against business results.

Our solution was to help the team identify the primary strategy elements necessary to achieve long-term objectives. If one is clear about the activities or attributes that drive long-term success, then these might be key indicators that provide helpful navigational guidance measurements for the team.

Working with the team, we identified a number of attributes that, if cultivated to high levels of health, could drive long-term success with their customers. We described each attribute using a continuum that moved from very negative to very positive terms. The matrix is shown in Figure A-6.

Once the matrix is developed, the team discussed and evaluated where they currently were for each attribute. Next steps included planning where they wanted to be for the next period of time and how they planned to get there. Clearly this is not an objective measure like sales, revenue, cost, or customer satisfaction, but in this setting it provides the team with a means of putting handles on a very complex, long-term objective. Team member consensus is a relatively good way to triangulate the team's position on the matrix.

This one example shows how to put some measurability into an imprecise situation. There are many others. The team is limited only by

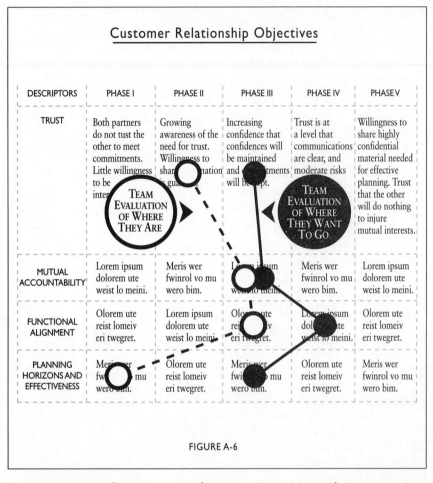

Customer Relationship Objectives

DESCRIPTORS	PHASE I	PHASE II	PHASE III	PHASE IV	PHASE V
TRUST	Both partners do not tust the other to meet commitments. Little willingness to be inter...	Growing awareness of the need for trust. Willingness to shar... ation ... gua...	Increasing confidence that confidences will be maintained and ...tments will b... pt.	Trust is at a level that communications are clear, and moderate risks	Willingness to share highly material needed for effective planning. Trust that the other will do nothing to injure mutual interests.
MUTUAL ACCOUNTABILITY	Lorem ipsum dolorem ute weist lo meini.	Meris wer fwinrol vo mu wero bim.	Lorem ipsum weist lo meini.	Meris wer fwinrol vo mu wero bim.	Lorem ipsum dolorem ute weist lo meini.
FUNCTIONAL ALIGNMENT	Olorem ute reist lomeiv eri twegret.	Lorem ipsum dolorem ute weist lo meini.	Olorem ute reist lomeiv eri twegret.	Lorem ipsum dol... te weist lo meini.	Olorem ute reist lomeiv eri twegret.
PLANNING HORIZONS AND EFFECTIVENESS	Meris wer fw... mu wero bim.	Olorem ute reist lomeiv eri twegret.	Meris wer fwi... mu wero bim.	Olorem ute reist lomeiv eri twegret.	Meris wer fwinrol vo mu wero bim.

Within the diagram: TEAM EVALUATION OF WHERE THEY ARE — TEAM EVALUATION OF WHERE THEY WANT TO GO

FIGURE A-6

creativity. But without some mechanism to "position" the team against its goals, there is no way to measure effectiveness or progress.

WHAT DO YOU DO WHEN THINGS AREN'T WORKING?

The power of the team model we have outlined in this book is that it not only helps team leaders and teams build healthy, productive teams, it also assists teams in diagnosing and addressing foundational issues when things aren't working. Typically, a dysfunctional team knows things aren't working but is uncertain as to what the specific problem is and what to do about it. They are clear that things aren't right, but they are unsure of what's wrong.

The team must first determine the differences between symptoms and causes. Symptoms are *what* hurts; causes are about *why* it hurts. We tend to focus too much on the pain and gaining relief. But until the root cause is dealt with, the pain, even if temporarily relieved, soon returns.

I grew up in Seattle in a beautiful house situated on Puget Sound. When I was about 15, my dad gave me a boat. Actually, I'm stretching the point a bit. It was an old, plank-built 16-foot boat that was lying on the property when we bought the house. It hadn't tasted water in 15 years. As I scraped the hull, preparing it for paint, I kept finding places where the wood was real soft. Being in a rush to get the boat in the bay, I quickly pulled out the bad wood and filled the hole with putty. After a few coats of marine paint, it looked practically new.

Later that summer, as I was towing my younger brother on water skis, the boat suddenly lurched forward and then began to slow and sink into the water. I quickly turned and saw that the transom (the stern of the boat that held the outboard motor) had broken away from the boat and sunk out of sight. I don't know who was more concerned: my brother, who held tightly to a 30-foot rope attached to an outboard motor sinking in 60-feet of water, or me, whose prize possession was floating half under water a mile from shore. This was a valuable lesson for me about symptoms and root causes. That soft wood was something mariners call dry rot. One must make sure one scrapes down to good wood before calking the hole. If one small bit of the bad wood is left, it would continue to spread, even under a brand new coat of paint. I had done a magnificent job dealing with the symptom, but had failed to affect the cause. Teams also tend to paint over cause issues.

Figure A-7 illustrates a concept we often use when exploring the cause of team and organizational problems. We call it the organizational onion to remind ourselves that you must keep peeling back layers until you come to the root cause.

Teams typically call for help dealing with some ill-defined issue revolving around discord and division. We probe the issues until the team feels that we have come to "good wood." Discord could be a matter of confused direction and lack of team member alignment on where the team is heading. A deeper issue would be strategy as the

Peeling the Organizational Onion

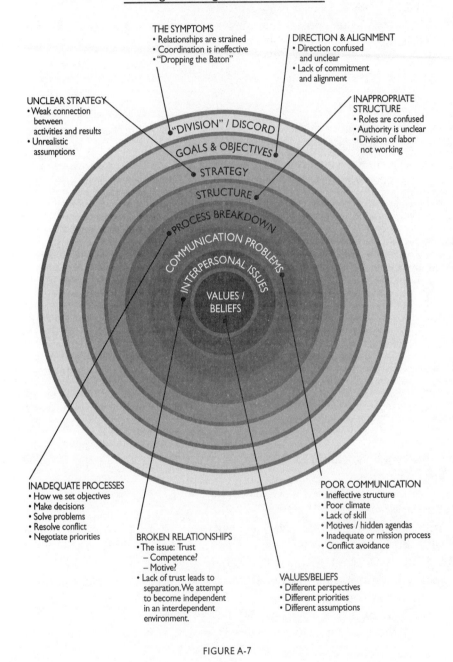

THE SYMPTOMS
- Relationships are strained
- Coordination is ineffective
- "Dropping the Baton"

DIRECTION & ALIGNMENT
- Direction confused and unclear
- Lack of commitment and alignment

UNCLEAR STRATEGY
- Weak connection between activities and results
- Unrealistic assumptions

INAPPROPRIATE STRUCTURE
- Roles are confused
- Authority is unclear
- Division of labor not working

"DIVISION" / DISCORD

GOALS & OBJECTIVES

STRATEGY

STRUCTURE

PROCESS BREAKDOWN

COMMUNICATION PROBLEMS

INTERPERSONAL ISSUES

VALUES / BELIEFS

INADEQUATE PROCESSES
- How we set objectives
- Make decisions
- Solve problems
- Resolve conflict
- Negotiate priorities

POOR COMMUNICATION
- Ineffective structure
- Poor climate
- Lack of skill
- Motives / hidden agendas
- Inadequate or mission process
- Conflict avoidance

BROKEN RELATIONSHIPS
- The issue: Trust
  – Competence?
  – Motive?
- Lack of trust leads to separation. We attempt to become independent in an interdependent environment.

VALUES/BELIEFS
- Different perspectives
- Different priorities
- Different assumptions

FIGURE A-7

team experiences frustration over wasted motion and activity that seems to have little connection to the big picture. As you can see from the diagram, one could keep peeling back layers. Even though some have a tendency to stop one or two layers short of the root cause, I don't want to communicate that every team problem is an issue of values or interpersonal tensions. Often those too are symptoms of broken processes or unclear roles.

We find that the most challenging aspect of team problems is not figuring out how to fix them but figuring out what they are in the first place. The Organizational Onion might help in that process.

ONE MORE TOOL: THE TEAM SURVEY®

Appendix B contains a diagnostic instrument, *Team Survey*®, built around the six characteristics of a high performance team. It allows the team to quickly and accurately evaluate itself against the individual characteristics. Having once determined which characteristic is weak, the survey helps the team to probe in more detail and develop an action plan for increased team effectiveness.

Team Survey

This Team Survey will enable you to evaluate your team against the six characteristics that describe high performance teams, and develop an action plan for increased team effectiveness.

> *Paper or E-version Team Surveys that allow*
> *an entire team to evaluate team effectiveness*
> *are available from Team Resources.*
> *www.teamresources.com*

INSTRUCTIONS

On the next page you will find a series of statements that describe effective teamwork. Carefully read each statement and indicate in the appropriate scoring box the degree to which you believe that statement *actually* describes your team. Use the following scoring key as a guide:

Scoring Key

   1 = Almost never

   2 = Seldom

   3 = Occasionally

4 = Fairly often

5 = Almost always

If you feel a certain statement "seldom" applies to your team, place a 2 in the scoring box next to that statement. If your team is new and/or is not consistently seeing results that could be described as exceptional or synergistic, it's unlikely that you will use a lot of 4's and 5's in your evaluation. Be candid; this exercise could be a steppingstone to team development—an opportunity for your team to identify and capitalize on its strengths and to strengthen its weaknesses.

Interpreting the Results and Developing an Action Plan

This appendix contains worksheets that will progressively narrow your focus from the broadest concept of team to one of the six individual characteristics, and then to a specific issue of interest within that characteristic. The process allows your team to attack team development needs in a confident, prioritized manner.

Team Characteristics

Below are 48 statements defining an effective team. Carefully read each statement and indicate on the score sheet (page 310) the degree to which you believe that statement *actually* describes your team.

1. As a team we are clear about our task/mission.

2. I am very clear about *my role* and expected contribution to this team.

3. Overall, I feel the team is very responsive to the leadership/direction of our team leader.

4. Our key work processes (e.g., planning, marketing, budgeting, etc.) are well defined and understood by everyone.

5. We have a written set of ground rules/operating principles that govern our relationships and interaction.

6. We have a safe team environment that encourages open, clear, honest communication.

7. I am crystal clear about our team goals, objectives, and measures.

8. I am clear about the roles and expected contribution of *my teammates*.

9. Our team leader effectively facilitates team member input in decisions, problem solving, planning, etc. As a result we consistently tap into the collective IQ of our team.

10. We have taken the time to discuss and design our processes.

11. Overall, we have a high level of trust in the character of other teammates.

12. We avoid overloading each other with low-priority e-mail and voice mail (e.g., indiscriminate use of FYI).

13. I believe that I will personally benefit by accomplishing our team goals..

14. My role matches my skills, knowledge, and experience.

15. Our team leader consistently releases the leader in everyone by supporting/encouraging individual team member leadership where his or her functional expertise is needed by the team.

16. We regularly sit down and ask how we are doing—what are we learning in order to improve our processes.

17. We appreciate the unique contribution of each team member.

18. In making decisions, solving problems, etc., there is a lot of listening and understanding.

19. Overall, team members are unified about and aligned with our team goals.

20. We consistently leverage one another's skills, experience, and knowledge.

21. Our team leader creates an environment in which initiative and creativity is encouraged.

22. Our key processes are documented (written out or mapped/flowcharted).

23. We accept the differences of each team member.

24. We productively channel conflict into creativity and commitment.

25. Our goals demand that we cooperate at high levels to achieve them.

26. Team members are quick to assist others in their role when needed.

27. Our team leader is effective in managing the boundaries between our team and other organizational entities (e.g., top management, other teams, the larger organization, different functions, etc.).

28. As a team, we take a systematic approach to meetings, decision making, problem solving, and planning.

29. We treat one another with dignity, respect, and courtesy.

30. I feel heard and understood.

31. Our team has a sense of urgency about our goals. Time is important.

32. The team is clear that although we all have individual roles and responsibilities, there is an overall mutual accountability for team results.

33. Our team leader could be described as a "servant leader."

34. We have an effective process for setting and managing priorities.

35. Overall, we trust that other team members have the competence to get their part of the job done with excellence.

36. We do our best to create "interpersonal slack" for miscommunications when they occur between team members.

37. I have work/action plans that support the achievement of our team goals.

38. Even though I have a specific role responsibility, I am expected to contribute input into other roles.

39. Team members are free to express their opinions (pro or con) on any issue relating to the team.

40. Our meetings are crisp, efficient, and characterized by effective communication.

41. Team members have a good understanding of one another (for example, aspirations, personalities, skills, etc.).

42. This team has mastered the art of "straight talk." We know how to be tough on issues and soft on people.

43. Our team routinely reviews its results versus its objectives and quickly adjusts the plan as appropriate.

44. We all understand how our roles work together around our major work processes.

45. Our team leader does an effective job at helping the team maintain clear direction, focus, and priorities.

46. We have effective systems (communications, information systems, etc.) that support the execution of our work processes.

47. We have the diversity on this team that is needed for effective decision making, problem solving, and planning.

48. All team members are routinely kept informed and connected on how we are doing against our goals.

Scoring the Team Survey

Enter your evaluation (1 to 5) for each of the 48 statements on the previous pages into the appropriate scoring boxes below.

Scoring Key

  1 = Almost never
  2 = Seldom
  3 = Occasionally
  4 = Fairly often
  5 = Almost always

Scoring Instructions:

1. Total the score for each of the columns below. The maximum possible score for a single column is 40.

2. Add the total columns for each team characteristic to determine the overall team score, entering this total in the box to the far right.

Question
Numbers

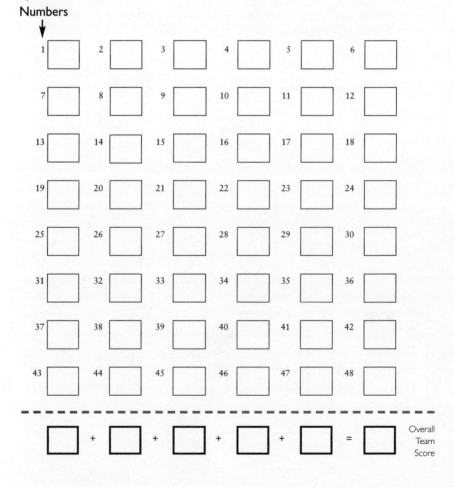

Identifying the Strengths and Weaknesses of Your Team

The score sheet on the previous page contains six columns. Title each column as shown.

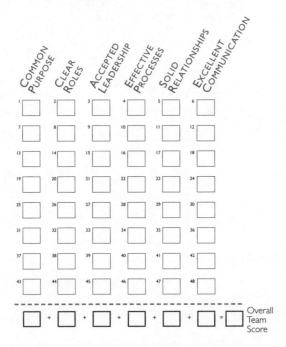

Reviewing the totals for each column, answer the following questions:

1. Overall, which characteristic was scored highest?_____

2. Weakest? _____

3. Relatively speaking, do these scores present a reasonable assessment of the strengths and weaknesses of our team? ☐Yes ☐No ☐Unsure
   If not, why not? _____

4. Were there any surprises in these scores for you? That is, lower or higher than you would have guessed? ☐Yes ☐No ☐Unsure
   If yes, for which characteristics, and why do you think there is a difference?_____

   _____

   _____

   _____

5. As you reflect on the current performance of your team and the scores above, what one characteristic, if strengthened, could most improve the effectiveness of your team?
   ☐ Purpose ☐ Roles ☐ Leadership
   ☐ Processes ☐ Relationships ☐ Communication

6. Now, as a first step in increasing your team effectiveness, you will identify a *specific issue within that characteristic* that you want to improve.

Each of the six characteristics in the Team Survey is addressed by eight questions, each focusing on an important issue for that particular characteristic. We have listed these primary issues on the following pages under each of the six team characteristics.

A. For each characteristic you have chosen to strengthen, enter scores for each question.

B. Choose the specific issue that you want to develop (possibly the one with the lowest score or average). This issue becomes your action-point on which you will develop a plan for improvement on the *Action Plan Worksheets*.

LIKE PROFESSIONALS IN ANY ARENA,
HIGH PERFORMANCE TEAMS ALWAYS
PUSH THE PERFORMANCE BAR.
THEY CONSTANTLY FEEL THE NEED FOR
INCREASED TEAM DEVELOPMENT.

COMMON PURPOSE

This is the cornerstone of a team. Purpose asks the question: "Why are we in existence?" Teamwork is not an end in itself, but rather a means to an end. By definition there must be unity of purpose; otherwise, the various elements will pull in different directions. The purpose of a team is to accomplish an objective—an objective bigger than we can accomplish individually. Therefore, we believe an effective team is purpose/mission-directed. It will be judged against its results.

Survey Questions   Score

1. Team has a clear task/mission _____
7. I am clear about team goals, objectives, and measures _____
13. I will benefit by accomplishing goals _____
19. Team members are unified and aligned about goals _____
25. Our goals demand high levels of cooperation _____
31. Team has a sense of urgency _____
37. I have work/action plans that support goals _____
43. We routinely review results versus objectives _____

Developing an Action Plan

1. Circle the specific issue within this characteristic that you believe most needs improvement.

2. Describe **current** situation (feelings, results or impact, symptoms)

   _____

   _____

   _____

3. Identify probable causes (attitudes, lack of skill or knowledge, etc.)

   _____

   _____

   _____

4. What specific action steps are needed to improve this issue?

   Action Steps   Responsibility   Date

   _____   _____   _____

   _____   _____   _____

   _____   _____   _____

   _____   _____   _____

   _____   _____   _____

CLEAR ROLES

Dividing the task is breaking it down and matching its various elements to corresponding strengths and skills of the various individual team members. This process becomes the key to tapping the synergistic potential of the team.

Division of labor brings leverage into the equation, introducing the possibility of synergism. But with it comes interdependence—that is, every member's contribution is needed, and without that contribution the purpose cannot be achieved.

Survey Questions   Score

2. I am very clear about *my* role   _____
8. I am clear about goals of *teammates*   _____
14. My role matches my skills, knowledge, experience   _____
20. We leverage each other's skills, knowledge, experience   _____
26. Team members are quick to assist others   _____
32. Mutual accountability for team results   _____
38. Everyone is expected to contribute input into other roles   _____
44. We understand how our roles work together   _____

Developing an Action Plan

1. Circle the specific issue within this characteristic that you believe most needs improvement.

2. Describe current situation (feelings, results or impact, symptoms)

   _____

   _____

   _____

3. Identify probable causes (attitudes, lack of skill or knowledge, etc.)

   _____

   _____

   _____

4. What specific action steps are needed to improve this issue?

   Action Steps   Responsibility   Date

   _____   _____   _____

   _____   _____   _____

   _____   _____   _____

   _____   _____   _____

ACCEPTED LEADERSHIP

Effective teams are characterized by clear, formal, strong leadership. However, although formal leadership is clearly present at all times, an effective leader in a team environment knows that it is often best for moment-by-moment leadership to be task-driven, with significant contribution by the team member whose skills, strengths, or experience best match the demands of the current situation.

Survey Questions   Score

3. The team is responsive to leadership   _____
9. We consistently tap into the collective IQ   _____
15. Team leader releases the leader in everyone   _____
21. Team leader creates environment for initiative and creativity _____
27. Team leader effectively manages boundaries   _____
33. Team leader is a "servant leader"   _____
39. Team members can express their opinion   _____
45. Team leader helps team maintain clear direction   _____

Developing an Action Plan

1. Circle the specific issue within this characteristic that you believe most needs improvement.

2. Describe **current** situation (feelings, results or impact, symptoms)

   _____

   _____

   _____

3. Identify probable causes (attitudes, lack of skill or knowledge, etc.)

   _____

   _____

   _____

4. What specific action steps are needed to improve this issue?

Action Steps	Responsibility	Date
_____	_____	_____
_____	_____	_____
_____	_____	_____
_____	_____	_____
_____	_____	_____

EFFECTIVE PROCESSES

Purpose deals with *what* and *why*. Here we focus on *how*. How do we accomplish the task? What are the basic processes of the team? How do we make decisions, solve problems, resolve conflict?

Survey Questions   Score

4. Key work processes are well defined   _____
10. We have discussed and designed our processes   _____
16. We regularly ask how we are doing and
    what we are learning   _____
22. Our key processes are documented   _____
28. We have a systematic approach to meetings,
    decision making, problem solving, and planning   _____
34. We have effective processes for setting and
    managing priorities   _____
40. Meetings are crisp and efficient   _____
46. Effective systems support our work processes   _____

Developing an Action Plan

1. Circle the specific issue within this characteristic that you believe most needs improvement.

2. Describe **current** situation (feelings, results or impact, symptoms)

    _____

    _____

    _____

3. Identify probable causes (attitudes, lack of skill or knowledge, etc.)

    _____

    _____

    _____

4. What specific action steps are needed to improve this issue?
    Action Steps   Responsibility   Date

    _____   _____   _____

    _____   _____   _____

    _____   _____   _____

    _____   _____   _____

    _____   _____   _____

SOLID RELATIONSHIPS

Interpersonal conflicts on a team are like friction in a machine. Solid relationships are the lubricant among the human beings who make up a high performance team. The objective is not to become best friends, but to learn how to work together. The quality "solid" implies that the relationship can withstand the blows of occasional misunderstandings, conflicts, and "bad days." It is also important that individual team members feel a relationship with "the team" as well, as expressed by a sense of belonging and camaraderie or *esprit de corps*.

Survey Questions   Score

  5. We have written ground rules that govern our relationships   _____

11. We have a high level of trust   _____

17. We appreciate the unique contribution of team members   _____

23. We accept differences   _____

29. We treat one another with dignity and respect   _____

35. We trust that team members have needed competence   _____

41. We have a good understanding of each other   _____

47. We have the diversity needed for effective decisions   _____

Developing an Action Plan

1. Circle the specific issue within this characteristic that you believe most needs improvement.

2. Describe **current** situation (feelings, results or impact, symptoms)

   _____

   _____

   _____

3. Identify probable causes (attitudes, lack of skill or knowledge, etc.)

   _____

   _____

   _____

4. What specific action steps are needed to improve this issue?

Action Steps	Responsibility	Date
_____	_____	_____
_____	_____	_____
_____	_____	_____
_____	_____	_____
_____		

EXCELLENT COMMUNICATION

This one element permeates every other characteristic of an effective team. Communication provides the means of cooperation–the glue that holds the team together. Through excellent communication, we coordinate our team by assigning roles, providing feedback, clarifying details, and resolving conflicts.

Survey Questions   Score

6. We have a safe environment that promotes communication   _____
12. We avoid overloading one another with
    low-priority communications   _____
18. There is a lot of listening when we make decisions   _____
24. We productively channel conflict into creativity   _____
30. I feel heard and understood   _____
36. We create "interpersonal slack" for miscommunication   _____
42. We have mastered the art of "straight talk"   _____
48. Members are kept informed about team goals   _____

Developing an Action Plan

1. Circle the specific issue within this characteristic that you believe most needs improvement.

2. Describe **current** situation (feelings, results or impact, symptoms)

_____

_____

_____

3. Identify probable causes (attitudes, lack of skill or knowledge, etc.)

_____

_____

_____

4. What specific action steps are needed to improve this issue?

Action Steps	Responsibility	Date
_____	_____	_____
_____	_____	_____
_____	_____	_____
_____	_____	_____
_____	_____	_____

Windemere Farm
Alype Carbonell

231-499-7973
4.5¢ Relove Pence
$30 ° English

Coming Home for
Christmas
Dec 11 12 13 +14 -53¢
P
Bayou Wesleyan
$30
947-3792

TOM'S FOOD MARKETS-REFUND/RETURN SLIP

DEPT	ITEM	REASON	AMT

Was item bought with Food Stamps? ☐Y ☐N

Was items bought with WIC Coupons? ☐Y ☐N

Had receipt? ☐Y ☐N   Had Item? ☐Y ☐N

Name: _____

Address: _____

Phone: _____

Signature: _____

Cashier: _____

Supervisor: _____

Date: _____

Appendix C

Personality Inventories

Knowing how people will react and relate to tasks, other people, and circumstances is of immeasurable value as we attempt to work with, serve, and communicate with others.

Behavior is influenced by a number of complex factors in our basic personality or temperament, our current emotional and physical state, our skills, experiences, IQ, and motivational needs. These and many other factors play both direct and indirect roles in shaping our responses.

Many of us have discovered that the more we know about ourselves and others, the better we can anticipate behavior in certain situations and, therefore, better serve and relate. Both of the personality inventories presented below (DISC and MBTI) allow people to gain good insight into their personalities as well as those of others. Both instruments are educational in purpose and not, in themselves, suitable for making placement decisions. However, when coupled with other test instruments, they add a valuable dimension to assessing potential job fit.

DISC

The DISC system was originally developed by Dr. William M. Martson, a Columbia University psychologist in the 1920's and 1930's. He focused his research on the emotions and behavior of normal people and developed a theoretical model that provided the foundation for future test instruments.

Today, I estimate there are 25 to 35 different versions of DISC instruments. The newest is the *Personal DISCernment® Inventory* (PDI) published by Team Resources, Inc.

A number of features make the PDI unique:

- The PDI is self-contained, providing all necessary explanatory and interpretive information in the instrument itself.

- The PDI confronts the issue of strengths and weaknesses in a clear, positive, straightforward manner.

- The PDI shows the implications and dynamics of behavioral styles in different settings.

- The PDI incorporates a series of application modules to assist individuals in applying insights regarding their personality to situations and subjects such as team, time, task, and sales.

All DISC instruments provide insight on four key elements that influence behavioral styles:

Dominance: The drive to overcome and achieve. The basic intent is to conquer.

Influence: The drive to influence, to express and be heard. The basic intent is to persuade.

Steadiness: The drive to be steady and systematic. The basic intent is to support.

Competent: The drive to be right, sure, and safe. The basic intent is to avoid trouble.

Although all of us have threads of all four elements woven into our basic temperament to one degree or another, most of us find that one or two of these elements express themselves more strongly in our behavioral system.

An excellent book on personalities based on the DISC concepts is *People Smart* by Tony Alessandra, Ph.D., and Michael J. O'Connor,

Ph.D., with Janice Alessandra (La Jolla, Calif.: Keynote Publishing Company, 1990).

For more information on the DISC concept in general and the *Personal DISCernment® Inventory* contact:

Team Resources, Inc.
2100 RiverEdge Parkway
Ste 800
Atlanta, GA 30328
770-956-0985
www.teamresources.com

MBTI

The purpose of the Myers-Briggs Type Indicator (MBTI) is to make the theory of psychological types, as first described by Carl G. Jung (1921-1971), understandable and useful in people's lives. The manual used for the MBTI, *A Guide to the Development and Use of the Myers-Briggs Type Indicator* by Isabel Briggs Myers and Mary H. McCaulley, notes:

> The essence of the theory is that much seemingly random variation in behavior is actually quite orderly and consistent, being due to the basic differences in the way individuals prefer to use their perception and judgment.
>
> Perception involves all of the ways of becoming aware of things, people, happenings, or ideas. Judgment involves all the ways of coming to conclusions about what has been perceived. If people differ systematically in what they perceive and in how they reach conclusions, then it is only reasonable for them to differ correspondingly in their reactions, interest, values, motivations, skills and interest.
>
> The MBTI is based on Jung's idea about perception and judgment, and the attitudes in which these are used in different types of people. The aim of the MBTI is to identify, from self report of easily recognized reactions, the basic preferences of people in regard to perception and judgment.[1]

Use of the MBTI requires a trained, certified facilitator. It has proven to be a popular, very creditable instrument in teaching people about themselves and others.

Several excellent books describe the people types identified in the MBTI and explore the implications on how we relate to the people in the world around us.

- Briggs Myers, Isabel. *Gifts Differing*. Palo Alto, Calif.: Consulting Psychologist Press, 1980.

- Kroeger, Otto, and Thuesen, Janet M. *Type Talk*. New York; Delacorte Press, 1988

- Lawrence, Gordon. *People Types and Tiger Stripes, A Practical Guide to Learning Styles*, second edition. Gainesville, Fla.: Center for Application of Psychological Type, 1979.

For more information about the MBTI contact:

Center for Applications of Psychological Type
2720 Northwest 6th Street
Gainesville, FL 32609
800-777-CAPT

Notes

Chapter 1, "What's the Standard Operating Procedure in This Situation?"

1. Thomas S. Kuhn, *The Structure of Scientific Revolutions* (Chicago: University of Chicago Press, 1970), 97.

2. Richard Tanner Pascale, *Managing on the Edge* (New York: Simon & Schuster, 1990), 13.

3. Kuhn, *Scientific Revolutions,* 64.

4. John Kotter, *The Leadership Factor* (New York: Free Press, 1988), 6.

5. Carol Loomis, "Dinosaurs?" *Fortune,* May 3, 1993, 39.

6. Pascale, *Managing on the Edge,* 11.

7. "The Bankruptcy DataSource," *USA Today,* February 3, 1992.

8. Noel M. Tichy and Stratford Sherman, *Control Your Destiny or Someone Else Will* (New York: Doubleday Currency, 1993), 14.

9. Charles Garfield, *Second to None* (New York: Avon, 1992), 15.

10. Robert A. Irwin and Edward G. Michaels III, *McKinsey Quarterly,* summer 1989, 149.

11. Peter F. Drucker, "The Coming of the New Organization," *Harvard Business Review,* January 1988, 45.

12. Lloyd Dobyns and Clare Crawford-Mason, *Quality or Else* (Boston: Houghton Mifflin, 1991), 41.

13. Tom Peters, *Liberation Management* (New York: Knopf, 1992), 714-15. Peters quotes from Richard C. Whitely, *The Customer Driven Company: Moving from Talk to Action* (Reading, Mass.: Addison-Wesley, 1991), 9–10.

14. Tichy and Sherman, *Control Your Destiny,* 241-42.

15. Lloyd Dobyns and Clare Crawford-Mason, *Quality or Else* (Boston: Houghton Mifflin, 1991), 28.

Chapter 2, "Business in the 21st Century Is a Team Sport"

1. Aircraft Accident Report, United Airlines Report, United Airlines Flight 232 (July 19, 1989), National Transportation Safety Board, Report number NTSB/AAR-90/06 (November 1, 1990), 73.

2. John Quinlan, staff writer, *Sioux City* (Iowa) *Journal,* July 26, 1989.

3. James H. Shonk, *Team-Based Organizations* (Homewood, Ill.: Business One Irwin, 1992), 5.

4. Ibid.

5. Ibid., 54.

6. Shonk, *Team-Based Organizations*, 6.

7. Ibid.

8. Brian Dumaine, "Who Needs a Boss?" *Fortune*, May 7, 1990, 52.

9. Del Jones, "Teamwork Speeds Boeing Along," *USA Today*, November 18, 1998, 5b.

10. Robert M. Fulmer, *The New Management* (New York: Macmillan, 1974), 132.

11. "Lessons from Geese," from a speech given by Angeles Arrien at the 1991 Organizational Development Network and based on the work of Milton Olsen. A transcription of this speech was circulated to Outward Bound staff throughout the United States.

12. Exodus 18:13–27.

13. Robert N. Bellah, Richard Madsen, William M. Sullivan, Ann Swindler, and Steven M. Tipton, *Habits of the Heart—Individualism and Commitment in American Life* (New York: Harper and Row, Publishers, 1985), 142, 145.

Chapter 3, "The Characteristics of a High Performance Team"

1. National Transportation Safety Board, Aircraft Accident Report, United Airlines Flight 232 (PB90-910406, NSTB/AAR-90/06), 1.17.10.2 Flight Simulator Studies, 72–73.

2. "Capt. Al Haynes," *People*, December 25, 1989, 102.

Chapter 4, "Clear Common Purpose"

1. If this were a book about strategic planning, I would make careful delineation between the terms *mission* and *task*. But for the purposes of this book, allow me to treat *mission, purpose,* and *task* as synonymous. For many teams the mission is stated so clearly and specifically that it could easy be called a task or goal. In other instances, teams (particularly permanent ones) are given mission statements that outline broad direction and are not measurable. In these instances the team must break that mission down into performance goals that lend themselves to greater specificity and measurement.

2. Peter Senge, *The Fifth Discipline* (New York: Doubleday Currency, 1990), 235.

3. Jon R. Katzenbach, Douglas K. Smith, *The Wisdom of Teams* (Boston: Harvard Business School Press, 1993), 12.

4. John Kotter, *A Force for Change* (New York: Free Press, 1990), 5.

Chapter 5, "Crystal Clear Roles"

1. The full title is an *Inquiry into the Nature and Causes of the Wealth of Nations*.

2. Adam Smith, *An Inquiry into the Nature and Causes of the Wealth of Nations* (1776; Modern Library reprint. New York: Random House, 1937), 734–35.

3. Steven R. Rainier, *Recreating the Workplace* (Essay Junction, Vt: Olive Write, 1993), 24.

4. Ibid, 22.

5. Michael Hammer and James Champey, *Reengineering the Corporation* (New York: Harper Business, 1993), 65.

6. Bill I. Russell, *Second Wind Memoirs of an Opinionated Man* (New York: Random House, 1979), 126–27.

7. George H. Reavis, *The Animal School* (Peterborough, NH: Crystal Springs Brooks, 1999).

8. Tom Peters and Robert Waterman, *In Search of Excellence* (New York: Harper & Row, 1982), xxiii.

Chapter 6, "Accepted Leadership"

1. Nova, *Why Planes Crash*, 1987, WGBH Educational Foundation. Used with permission.
2. This training was pioneered by United Airlines in the early 1980s. It has since been renamed Cockpit Resource Management, but Haynes prefers its former designation. United wasn't the only airline to initiate this training. Now it would be considered standard fare for almost any air carrier.
3. Rosabeth Moss Kanter, *The Change Masters* (New York: Simon & Schuster, 1983), 248. Italics are mine. The last sentence comes from an article (origin unknown) that presents a similar text based on the research for *The Change Masters*.
4. Robert K. Greenleaf, *Servant Leadership* (New York: Paulist Press, 1977).
5. Matthew 20:25–28 NIV.
6. James O'Toole, *Leading Change* (San Francisco: Jossey-Bass, 1995), 84–85; Robert R. Blake and Jane S. Monton, *Effective Crisis Management* (The New Management Times, 1985), 3(1), p. 14.
7. Ibid.
8. Rosabeth Moss Kanter, "The New Managerial Work," *Harvard Business Review*, November 1989, 89.
9. Tom Peters and Nancy Austin, *A Passion for Excellence* (New York: Random House, 1985), 325–26. Chapter 19, on coaching, is well worth reading.
10. Many ideas in this section were adapted from Larry Hirschhorn, *Managing in the New Team Environment* (Reading, Mass.: Addison Wesley, 1991), 14–19. This is an excellent resource for team leaders.
11. James M Kouzes and Barry Z. Posner, *The Leadership Challenge* (San Francisco, Jossey-Bass, 1987), 16–21.

Chapter 7, "Effective Team Processes"

1. Much of this description was adapted from a speech by Captain Haynes and my interview with him.
2. Ibid.
3. Roger K. Mosvick and Robert B. Nelson, *We've Got to Start Meeting Like This!* (Indianapolis: Park Avenue Productions, 1996), 4.
4. Team Resources provides self-facilitated Team Meeting Discussion Workbooks that help a team to evaluate meeting effectiveness, using this survey and others, to identify the foundational principles of effective meetings, and to develop the ground rules to implement them. See www.teamresources.com for details.

Chapter 8, "Solid Relationships"

1. Laura Fisher, "The Latest Word on Teamwork? 'Mush,'" *New York Times*, January 12, 1992, 23.
2. There are many excellent books on diversity in the workplace. See, for example, R. Roosevelt Thomas Jr., *Beyond Race and Gender* (AMACOM), *Differences Do Make a Difference* (source of the subhead for this section of the chapter), and *Redefining Diversity* (New York: AMCOM, 1996). Charles Garfield has an excellent chapter on diversity in *Second to None* (New York: Avon, 1992). He does a great job documenting the connection of effective diversity management to innovation. Lee Gardenwartz and Anita Rowe, *Diverse Teams at Work* (Irwin, Professional Publishing) is a superb book on how to capitalize on diversity; it presents strong conceptual models and has a wealth of helpful exercises.
3. Thomas., *Redefining Diversity*, 80.

4. Garfield, *Second to None,* 269.

5. Thomas, *Beyond Race and Gender,* 20.

6. Ibid., 279.

7. Ibid., 28.

8. Jack R. Gibbs, *Trust, The Guild of Tutors Press* (Los Angeles: International College, 1978), 14.

9. Douglas McGregor, *The Professional Manager* (New York: McGraw-Hill, 1978), 165. The italicized words are mine.

10. See Appendix C for a brief overview of the DISC instruments.

11. See Appendix C for a brief overview of the MBTI instruments.

Chapter 9, "Excellent Communication"

1. Jerry A. Dibble and Beverly Y. Langford, *Communication Skills and Strategies* (Atlanta: Dibble and Langford, 1990), 14.

2. Irving L. Janis, *Groupthink,* 2d ed. (Boston: Houghton Mifflin, 1982), 174–75, 262–70.

3. David R. Hampton, Charles E. Summer, and Ross A. Webber, *Organizational Behavior and the Practice of Management,* 3d ed. (San Francisco: Scott Foresman, 1978), 284.

4. Pauline Graham and Mary Parker Follet, *Prophet of Management,* (Boston, Harvard Business School Press, 1995), 67–68.

5. Ibid., 72.

6. Ibid., 71.

7. Genesis 19:1–9.

8. Janis, *Groupthink,* 246.

Chapter 10, "The Path of High Performance Teamwork"

1. Studies of group development began in earnest in the early 1960's. Because group development is subjective, much of the research comes from observations and interviews over the life of a group. Thus, these studies are called anecdotal and inductive rather than hard science. Most observers of group development have noticed that groups, over time, tend to move through four or five predictable stages of development. Researchers have been fairly consistent as to the characteristics of groups in various stages of growth. B. W. Tuckerman, a pioneer of group research, concluded that most groups grow through five stages of development. He coined some memorable and useful terms for each stage: forming, storming, norming, performing, and adjourning (B. W. Tuckerman, *Psychological Bulletin* [1965]: 384–99. Reviewed in depth in *The Life Cycle in Groups,* by Roy Lacoursiere [New York: Human Sciences Press], 27–41.).

2. *The Team Profile®* is an excellent team diagnostic and discussion instrument that helps teams "position" themselves developmentally and, based on this insight, design a strategy for increased team effectiveness. It is distributed through Team Resources, Inc., Atlanta, GA 1–800 214–3917 or www.teamresources.com.

3. See www.relianceinsurance.com/history.htm.

Chapter 11, "Achieving the Summit of High Performance Teamwork"

1. W. Russell and T. Branch, *Second Wind: Memoirs of an Opinionated Man* (New York: Random House, 1979), 155.

2. Peter Senge, *The Fifth Discipline* (New York: Doubleday Currency, 1990), 235.

3. One of the first people to see the significance of these issues for team development was Jack R. Gibb. Building on his work, Drexler, Sibbet, and Forrester developed their own model of team development, a portion of which I've adapted in this chapter. Adapted with permission from NTL Institute. "The Team Performance Model" by Allen B. Drexler, David Sibbert, and Russell H. Forrester, pp. 45–61, Team Building: Blueprints for Productivity and Satisfaction, edited by W. Brendan Reddy with Kaleel Jamison, copyright, 1988. NTL Institute for Applied Behavioral Science, 300 N. Lee Street, Suite 300, Alexandria, VA 22314. (703) 548–8840.

4. Jack R. Gibb, *T-Group Theory and Laboratory Method* (New York: Wiley, 1964), 279–309. The focus of Gibb's interest was trust. He continued to develop his ideas, providing a further refinement in a later book, *Trust: A New View of Personal and Organizational Development* published in 1968.

5. Ibid., 54.

6. Mark D. Youngblood, *Eating The Chocolate Elephant* (Richardson, Tex.: Micrografx, 1994) is an excellent resource for learning how to quickly and easily flowchart team processes and activities.

Chapter 12, "Pitfalls in the Path of High Performance"

1. Ellen Neuborne, "Why Teams Fail," *USA Today*, February 25, 1997, Money Section.

2. As quoted by Steven Gross of the Hay Group, Ellen Neuborne, "Why Teams Fail," *USA Today*, February 25, 1997, Money Section.

3. Neuborne, "Why Teams Fail."

4. Ibid.

5. Peter F Drucker, *Management* (New York: Harper & Row, 1973), 559–60.

6. Noel M. Tichy and Stratford Sherman, *Control Your Destiny or Someone Else Will* (New York: Currency Doubleday, 1993), 21.

7. Ibid.

8. Peters and Waterman observe that one of the biggest contrasts between Japanese and American corporations is the number of middle-management levels. In the early 1980's Toyota had 5 levels of management between the chairman and the first-line supervisor in contrast to over 15 at Ford. (Thomas J. Peters and Robert H. Waterman Jr., *In Search of Excellence* [New York: Warner Books, 1982], 313.) Over the past 15 to 20 years there has been significant progress in creating healthier hierarchies. DuPont has reduced the levels of management in many of their plants from 7 to 4; the Brunswick Corporation, a Fortune 500 Company with over 22,000 employees, cut management levels to 4; Federal Express with over 70,000 employees has only 5 levels between the CEO and operational levels (D. Keith Denton, *Horizontal Management* [New York: Lexington Books, 1991], 22, 32, 36). Under Jack Welch's leadership, GE has trimmed management layers from 10 to an average of 4 to 5 (Tichy and Stratford, *Control Your Destiny*, 235).

9. This entire example was excerpted from Ralph T. King Jr., "Jeans Therapy, Levi's Factory Workers Are Assigned to Teams and Morale Takes a Hit," *Wall Street Journal*, May 20, 1998.

10. Elliot Aronson, *The Social Animal*, 153–54, as quoted by Alfie Kohn, *No Contest: The Case Against Competition* (Boston: Houghton Mifflin, 1986), 2.

11. Richard Levine, "At City Hall, More Than the Usual Ill Will," *New York Times*, May 8, 1988, sec. E1, p. 6.

12. Tichy "Why Teams Fail," 230.

13. John Scully, *Odyssey* (New York: Harper & Row, 1987), 241.

Chapter 13, "The Principles of Team Development"

1. Conversation between the author and Captain Haynes.
2. Rosabeth Moss Kanter, *The Change Masters* (New York: Simon & Schuster, 1983), 260.
3. Eileen C. Shapiro, *Fad Surfing in the Board Room* (Reading, Mass.: Addison Wesley, 1995), 94.

Chapter 14, "Turning Principle into Practice: Building the Team"

1. Peter F. Drucker, *Post-Capitalist Society* (New York: Harper Business Books, 1994), 86–89.

Appendix A, "Frequently Asked Questions"

1. John R. Schermerhorn, James D. Hunt, Richard N. Osborn, *Managing Organizational Behavior* (New York: Wiley, 1994), 343.
2. Richard S. Wellins, William C. Byham, Jeanne M. Wilson, *Empowered Teams* (San Francisco: Jossey-Bass, 1991), 34–35. This is an excellent book on self-managed teams based on a survey of 272 companies, 95 percent of which were in manufacturing.
3. Wellins, Byham, and Wilson would agree and do a superb job of outlining the process to true self-direction.
4. Beverly Langford, CEO of Language Management Associates, Atlanta. Langford is a well-known speaker, consultant, and teacher on communication.
5. Jessica and her partner-husband are co-CEOs of NetAge (see www.netage.com). They have written five books that frame the principles of network structures and processes. I highly recommend Jessica Lipnack and Jeffery Stamps, *Virtual Teams: Reaching Across Space, Time, and Organizations with Technology,* 2d ed. (New York: Wiley, 2000). This is a must-read for teams attempting to "work together apart."

Appendix C, Personality Inventories

1. Isabel Briggs and Mary H. McCaulley, *A Guide to the Development and Use of the Myers Briggs Type Indicator* (Palo Alto, Calif.: Consulting Psychologists Press, 1985, p. 1.

Index